ARAB AND REGIONAL POLITICS IN THE MIDDLE EAST

Arab and Regional Politics in the Middle East

P. J. Vatikiotis

CROOM HELM
London & Sydney

ST. MARTIN'S PRESS
New York

© 1984 P.J. Vatikiotis
Croom Helm Ltd, Provident House, Burrell Row,
Beckenham, Kent BR3 1AT
Croom Helm Australia Pty Ltd, First Floor,
139 King Street, Sydney, NSW 2001

British Library Cataloguing in Publication Data
Vatikiotis, P.J.
   Arab and regional politics in the Middle East.
   1. Near East—Politics and government
   I. Title
   320.956   JQ1758.A1

ISBN 0-7099-2609-X

All rights reserved. For information, write:
St. Martin's Press, Inc., 175 Fifth Avenue, New York, NY 10010
First published in the United States of America in 1984

Library of Congress Card Catalog Number: 84-40051

ISBN 0-312-04692-8

35040

ꗃ ꝡ

Printed and bound in Great Britain

CONTENTS

Preface

Part One: Islam and Politics

Part Two: Inter-Arab and Regional Politics

Part Three: History and Politics of Modern Egypt

PREFACE

This book comprises a selection of articles, essays and reviews on the history and politics of the Middle East which were written or published over the last twenty-five years. It does not include specialised studies of medieval Islamic political history and theory, or essays written in Arabic and Greek, or shorter pieces written for weekly magazines and review periodicals. The studies included are concerned with three main topics. The first is the problem of religion and politics, or religion and state, as the major and long-standing preoccupation of Muslims themselves. The second is that of inter-Arab and regional politics, approached mainly from a local-regional rather than an international perspective. The third is Egypt.

Most Westerners have become aware of the complex relation between religion and politics in the Middle East only recently, mainly as a result of events in Iran since 1978. Two of the essays dealing with this matter were written and first published in 1956-8. If these are compared with those included in Part One, 'Islam and Politics', it will become clear that the fundamental difficulty of the relationship between religion and politics remains unresolved. In fact, these studies were originally intended to form part of a larger work on tradition and politics in the Middle East, which the pressure of other work prevented me from completing.[1]

Throughout the 1950s I was, as a result of my earlier study of the Ismaili revolution in the tenth century culminating in the establishment of the Fatimid Caliphate in Cairo,[2] still concerned with the question of the relation between Islam and politics. The study of the Fatimids moreover led me to focus my work for several years on Egypt, with the result that I was able to complete two studies of the post-1952 regimes, and a general history of modern Egypt.[3] The studies on modern Egypt included in this volume therefore are a by-product of this long-term concern after 1958. It was not until the 1970s when I was struck by the contrasting concern of Westerners for order and rationality in political life, and the multi-dimensional and near-disorderly dynamic of Arab politics, that I was drawn to the study of inter-Arab and regional politics,[4] only to return now, in the 1980s, to a reconsideration of more far-reaching developments and protean questions against the broad historical experience of the region.

Completed studies, published or unpublished, which are concerned mainly with cultural and literary themes are not included.

Notes

1. A study of *Islam and the Nation-State*, based on the Patten Foundation Lectures I delivered at Indiana University, USA, in 1982, is to be published soon.

2. *The Fatimid Theory of the State* (1957).

3. *The Egyptian Army in Politics* (1961, 1975); *The Modern History of Egypt* (1969, 1972, 1976), 2nd edn *Egypt from Muhammad Ali to Sadat* (1980, 1983); *Nasser and his Generation* (1978).

4. *Conflict in the Middle East* (1971).

PART ONE: ISLAM AND POLITICS

1 MUHAMMAD 'ABDUH AND THE QUEST FOR A MUSLIM HUMANISM

The question of Muslim response to Western influence has often been put to the Muslim intellectual. The beginnings of reform in Islam and the Near East in general first found expression in men like Sayyid Ahmad Khan, Muhammad 'Abduh, Ameer 'Ali, and Muhammad Iqbal. Western civilisation, its science, and its material benefits, were known to these intellectuals, enabling them to establish rapport with the West. One must be cautious, however, not to identify educational contact with the inner life of the two peoples — the Muslim world and the West. For, traditionally, they have run apart. The contact between East and West on a mass level has been preconditioned and marred by political considerations, the intellectual crosscurrents notwithstanding. Such contact has been further complicated by the unreadiness of the Muslim to rationalise, since his religion has never constituted for him an abstract intellectual system. Islam, on the contrary, is regarded by him as an active existential religion that discourages isolation and quietude.

Nevertheless, the gradual awareness of the masses today of their heritage and national destiny has diffused the responsibility of response to the present challenges into a wider spectrum of society. The intellectual, therefore, cannot merely superimpose a modification of traditional values, in the light of his Western training. He must be aware of the vacuum that may be created and provide a solid replacement of indigenous origin and character, albeit a synthetic one.

Can there be a so-called 'Protestant' revolt within Islam today? The Protestant Reformation in Europe paved the way for the relatively free development of modern science, philosophy, and historical criticism. Conversely, while Europe lay dormant in its darkest hours of inquisitorial ignorance, Muslim thinkers were probing nature and philosophy. But the contentment of imperial power, extending too far to be adequately controlled, allowed for degeneration from within, until destruction from without became inevitable. Ultimately, prolonged occupation, together with rigid emulation in matters of religion and thought, engendered an atmosphere of inertia and social stagnation.[1]

Response by the Muslim intellectuals of the last seventy-five years

Source: *Arabica* (Paris), vol. IV (January 1957), pp. 57-72.

to the challenge presented by Western penetration has been in the main apologetic. It romantically attempted to recast Islam as a super-philosophy containing all the elements that were operative in the phenomenal rise of the West. The Muslim apologist, in contrasting the lack of authoritarianism in Islamic politics to European political history, for example, is only offering superficial resistance to Western influence.[2] So far, the mere claim that the religion, properly interpreted and understood, allows for all exigencies of change, has proven insufficient stimulation for improvement at the mass level. For it is necessary to get people thinking in terms of this viability as a matter of course. On the contrary, the old pre-Islamic resignation to inscrutable *dahr* or blind fate, was transformed socially to the just as rigid and immobilising Islamic *qadar* or predestination, without the benefit of a dynamic concept of destiny.

Apologies are neither useful nor adequate today, for they tend to petrify the Islamic community before a fast shrinking, yet shaking, world community. Twenty years ago the attempts at rational revolt against the rigidity of the past by men like Taha Husain and 'Ali 'Abd al-Raziq outlined the fundamental question before the Muslim Near East; which question also carried with it the seeds of possible salvation. These two men were asking their people, in effect, the extent to which they were willing to apply the rules of modern historical and rational criticism to their scriptures and tradition. They were both gravely concerned with the proper evaluation of the authority of tradition. Can reform cope with the power of tradition in Islam today? Can a rationalist adaptation come about, to mould a new tradition similar in development, if not content, to that distinguishing the modern Western tradition from its medieval predecessor.[3]

Excluding the superficial and limited impact from the West, one cannot overlook the few but creditable efforts along these lines within the Muslim community itself. For it is the indigenous forces alone that can effect lasting changes in the Islamic world. Thus, it is relatively uncommon knowledge among Westerners that the expression of abstract thought and the vivid satirisation of social, political, and economic problems has been developed to highly articulate standards by Near Eastern contemporary writers. Fiction, drama, and periodical literature have become vital and integral aspects of the lives of the increasing literate masses. Like any new literature, it does not purport to serve art for art's sake, but tends to be didactic, and is often loaded with social and political messages. Let not the New Critic, however, persuade us to overlook its value as literature, for today it is the most readily available reflection of the ideological currents and struggles agitating the Islamic mind and world.[4]

In the light of these remarks, it is felt that a systematic analysis of the Islamic reform movement is appropriate, beginning with the early attempts at a modern Muslim 'humanism'.[5] This paper will confine itself to the expression of Muhammad 'Abduh in *al-'Urwa'l-wuthqa*, who, the writer begs to submit, was one of the first 'humanists' in modern Islam.[6] The discussion will consider only the leading articles by 'Abduh that appeared in the newspaper *al-'Urwa'l-wuthqa* from 13 March 1884 to 16 October 1884.[7] It does not consider, however, the articles or news editorials published in the paper on specific questions such as Egypt, the Sudan, British policy in the East, etc.[8]

'Abduh's movement for religious reform is 'humanistic' because he was primarily interested in giving an ethical focus to the religion of Islam, in short, a new native system of values not at variance with modern scientific society. As a brand of 'humanism' it is still more interesting because it does not blindly subscribe to the romantic confusion of many other Muslim modernists and apologists, but tends to base its strength on a reformulation of systematic theology and doctrine with the gradual reintroduction of historical criticism into the study of tradition. This 'humanistic' trend is important today not for the Muslim intellectual alone but even more for the mass of Muslim believers. Professor W.C. Smith of McGill University discusses the need for 'a synthesis ... of the Islamic religious tradition with an intellectualist perspicacity of modernity — a synthesis which, with due regard to Point IV, seems the area's most fundamental need'.[9] The transformation of isolated individual conceptions of reform into a system of social thought and action remains the foremost requirement in the modern Muslim communities. Recent developments in Egypt, for example, indicate that such a public philosophy and system of values are absolutely necessary for the development of a strong nation.[10]

The need for an ethical system, guided by rational criticism and insight, has never been greater in the Muslim world than it is today. Old regimes have been overthrown, but old systems and habits of thought and action have not been totally discarded. In order to retain their leadership, present rulers must transform political revolution into social and political patterns of thought acceptable to the Muslim masses. The claim, for instance, by Egypt's present rulers to a new 'national philosophy', 'elan', and vitality must prove empty unless related to an emergent tradition.

There can never be a completely secular attitude in Islam. Neither can traditional attitudes be legislated out of existence.[11] It is important, therefore, to realise at the outset, that any new cultural personality that is to develop in the Muslim East must of necessity be a synthetic one, drawing from the Islamic and pre-Islamic ethnology of the area and its people, as well as from its inevitable intercourse with non-Muslim ideas and institutions.

A rigidly-cast socio-religious philosophy is presently unable to perpetuate the old value system. The latter has been seriously challenged to the extent of external economic and political control. Only a 'humanised' version of the religion can institute a personal and collective system of ethics — ergo a theory of action — dependent to a large extent on the principles of rational and historical criticism and introspective evaluation.

The ethical appeal of Islam and its introspective admonitions were first examined and advocated in modern Islam by Muhammad 'Abduh (1849-1905).[12] In basing this discussion on 'Abduh's writings in *al-'Urwa'l-wuthqa*, an attempt is being made to throw light upon the issue; should the Muslim East develop into a modern cultural force on the basis of Islamic unity, or on the basis of independent and inter-dependent cultural groups, most of whose ethnic personalities are already predetermined and crystallised by pre-Islamic factors? In other words, can Islam, the faith, *per se* adequately replace the Pakistani cultural and ethnic personality and complexion, the Turkish, the Egyptian, the Syrian, Iraqi or Persian?[13]

When Jamal al Afghani and Muhammad 'Abduh founded the secret society of *al-'Urwa'l-wuthqa*, the Muslim countries were in a state of political and social retrogression and frustration. Egypt, a vassal of the Ottoman Porte, had been occupied by British forces in 1882, putting an end to the 'Orabi revolt.[14] Persia was being exposed to more direct foreign influence as a result of Russian and British interests in the country.[15] The Ottoman Porte itself had just gone through a brief and abortive attempt at constitutional reform in 1876-8 under the leadership of Midhat Pasha, reverting to the despotic lethargy of the new Sultan 'Abdul Hamid. Inevitably, the 'indissoluble bond' established by these two men was primarily devoted to the resuscitation of the Islamic spirit and faith, as bonds of unity against divisive outside influences. In this respect the editorials of 'Abduh in the journal, *al-'Urwa*, may be viewed as apologetic exhortations to Muslim action against foreign infiltration. Such exhortation is neither complete nor at its polemical best, however, unless considered in conjunction with his *al-Islam wa'r-radd 'ala muntaqidihi*.[16]

Jamal's hope, at least, was to propagandise the specific political aims of a Muslim League on the basis of the brotherhood of all Muslims. This League, we must assume, envisaged a political union of the Muslim East under one ruler, preferably a *khalifa*. Realising the remoteness of this aspiration, however, he sought to publicise more immediate struggles for Muslim freedom such as the Egyptian question, the Sudan, and Persia.[17]

Publication, then, was meant to serve as a polemic mouthpiece for Jamal in his interpretation of the Islamic cause against Britain. Fortunately, it acquired a twin character, also serving as a literary vehicle for the expression of 'Abduh's ideas of reform. The claim, therefore, in the *Encyclopedia of Islam* that *al-'Urwa'l-wuthqa* expressed entirely the views of Jamal is not justified, as we shall attempt to show in the succeeding pages. Although 'Abduh may have voiced, in part, Jamal's ideas, he was already disillusioned with programmes such as political Pan-Islam, realising the many prerequisites necessary for genuine reform. It would even be difficult to accept without reservation Zaidan's conclusion that if both men agreed on aims, they disagreed on the means of achieving them. 'Abduh's basically pacifist-Sufi temperament permitted him to prefer the wiser, albeit slower, process of education over political eruption.[18] And herein lies the difference: to Jamal, Pan-Islam was primarily a political concept. 'Abduh, on the other hand, recognised its limitations in a Muslim world already directed and preconditioned by political and geographical considerations.

Instead of bringing about a strong Muslim union under a *khalifa* Jamal's Pan-Islamic agitation resulted in no unity at all. Instead the individual development of Muslim nation-states in the past thirty-five years has become the trend of political evolution in the Muslim world. This is neither a derogation nor a nullification of Jamal's efforts or effect upon the awakening Muslim mind. But this particular Muslim development was destined to give a more lasting character to 'Abduh's concept of religious and social reform. For the expectation that Jamal's 'Urwa' would effect a revolution in the East never materialised. Neither was the combined Pan-Islamic policy of Jamal and Sultan 'Abdul Hamid received warmly by the Muslim subjects of the Ottoman empire in 1909, or 1914, under the Young Turks of Enver Pasha. On the contrary, these subjects sought their national salvation *outside* the caliphial authority.[19]

By editing the journal, 'Abduh was laying the theoretical foundations of a neo-religious *esprit de corps*. In pleading for the observance of an ethical system favourable to progress and strongly influenced by rational processes, 'Abduh underlined the essence of a Muslim 'humanism'. Considering disbelief (*ilhad*) a 'social disease', he introduced the novel concept of social responsibility for the first time. Its basis was the verse, 'Verily, God will not change the state of a people until they change their own state.'[20]

The starting point of Abduh's 'humanist' approach to Islam and an Islamic 'feeling of unity' is his idea that Islam is a 'social religion', which has combined in its message the welfare of man in this world and in the hereafter. Therefore, if disbelief be a 'social disease' causing Islam's impotence, it becomes necessary (a) to free thought from the shackles of *taqlid*, or blind emulation of patristic tradition, and depend on the authority of 'historical proof', and (b) to consider religion as being compatible with ('friend of') scientific knowledge (*'ilm*). In view of these basic assumptions, 'Abduh inevitably confined his main interest in religious reform as the basis for all other reform in the Muslim East. His philosophy of reform and 'religious humanism' extended into his concept of political independence and maturity. Insisting upon internal reform, first through the spread of education and the elevation of public character to a standard of social responsibility, he gave political and social maturity precedence over political independence without them.[21]

Before proceeding to formulate 'Abduh's 'humanist' approach to Islamic reform, one must assess briefly the obstacles in Islam to 'humanism' of any kind. 'Modernism', says Professor Gibb, 'is primarily a function of Western liberalism. It is only to be expected, in consequence, that the general tendency of modernists would be to interpret Islam in terms of liberal humanitarian ideas and values. In the first stage they contended that Islam was not opposed to these ideas; but they soon went on to claim that Islam was the embodiment of them in their highest and most perfect form.'[22] This overall criticism can be fairly directed at the non-theologian liberal reformers and modernists who, in their hasty enthusiasm, assumed that the adoption of Western political and legal institutions would *ipso facto* produce political and social institutions of a liberal and democratic nature.[23] It cannot be equally directed at a trained theologian like 'Abduh, who came closer to a reformulation of the fundamental position of Islam.[24]

Nevertheless, 'Abduh, in attempting a rational-humanist reformulation of Muslim doctrine had to contend with three major solidly anti-liberal forces in the Islamic socio-religious organism. First was Tradition and the sanctity it receives from Sacred Law, or *Shari'a*, codified as it was some thousand years ago into a *corpus juris* of lasting value, defying change. This strongest bulwark of the Islamic socio-religious structure has resisted change as well as Muhammad 'Abduh's attack upon it in the guise of his *antitaqlid* campaign. Second was the highly transcendental

Quranic concept of Allah, which has contributed to the regimentation of the processes of organic change, especially on the lower strata of Muslim society. The slightest attempt at its immenantisation could mean apostasy.[25] Third is the ever-present anti-rational disposition of orthodoxy as well as the average Muslim's.[26] The masses, for example, continue in their intuitive adherence to the Qur'an, in addition to the multitude of cultish accretions that make up the sum total of their daily religious experience and worship.

Cognisant of this dilemma, 'Abduh stood between the outright secularist on the one hand, and the romantic modernist on the other, by insisting upon the systematic reformulation of dogma without its divorce from the religious experience of the masses, in fact, the only possibility open to organic change in present-day Muslim communities. His hope for a more dynamic concept of God's relationship to the believer was intended to render personal religious experience an existentially strong stimulus for action towards the best possible life. Muhammad 'Abduh was well aware of the difficulty inherent in a strongly monotheistic religion that assigns to man an eternal destiny (popularly referred to as 'fate') and retribution in the hereafter. It is, perhaps, this fundamental problem which led Professor Louis Gardet to conclude that what is required in Islam today is a 'creative humanism', because, so far, 'Islamic humanism' has sought refuge in the glorification of the past, glossing over traditional works, and maintaining traditional life.[27]

From the beginning, 'Abduh grasped the obstacles inherent in a religion ossified by tradition and complicated by a concept of nationalism. Consequently, any humanist reform on his part, had to presuppose a 'humanism with God' (that is, one which would never question the notion of a supreme being). He came closest to a humanism that called for the highest life possible, without unnecessary limitations on man's virtuous achievements. It had to be a religious-oriented humanism, in contrast with the secular-nationalist variety, if it were truly to benefit the masses. It had to be one in which secular values would become part of popular endeavour and social philosophy, through an invigorated religious doctrine. It is this sensitive understanding on 'Abduh's part of the importance of religious reinterpretation in any cultural development — a point discarded, misunderstood, or glossed over by the majority of Muslim modernists — which led Professor Gibb to emphasise boldly that 'He ('Abduh), more than any other man, gave Egyptian thought a centre of gravity and created, in place of a mass of disconnected writings, a literature inspired by definite ideals of progress within an Islamic framework.'[28]

The difficulty, however, in Muslim religious reform derives from the closeness between the spiritual and temporal, and even more, the political. Thus, 'Abduh's so-called 'liberalism' of religious interpretation must be limited by this factor.[29] In analysing his call for religious reform as the only possible means to a better society, one detects certain contradictions. In his article, 'Nationality and the Religion of Islam', 'Abduh rejects the idea of 'nationalism'.[30] He refutes it as a 'natural state of being or nature' and recognises it as a mere acquired feeling. Thus, Islam transcends it, for 'he who belongs to the Muslim faith, once his belief is firmly entrenched, is diverted from his nationalism and racialism. Rather he turns from the *special* bond to the *general* one – that of the believer.'[31] Because Islam is not merely an admonition for the good and the true, it is also a just legislator who does not discriminate between one nationality and another. He invokes the example of the Orthodox Caliphs to emphasise the lack of nationalist fanaticism in Islam, saying that 'nothing elevated [the caliph] to a position of rulership other than his reverence and obedience for the law, and his care in observing it'.[32] The Orthodox Caliphs were, however, the leaders of the strongest political party at the time, an Arab one, leading the newly unified tribes into vast conquests under the banner of Islam. Neither does Islamic history bear out the assertion that divinely inspired behaviour through the proper observance of the scriptures has always replaced, in Islam, 'racial' and 'national' bonds. During the Abbasid hegemony, for instance, Persians, Turks, and Afghans had a crystallised pre-Islamic ethnic character and personality which Arab-dominated early Islam was never able to break down or replace. This very insistence by Muhammad 'Abduh on the return to the true religion as the only source of power seems to indicate clearly the dilemma of reform in Islam. First, the precept has not been followed in the recent economic and political development of the modern Muslim nation-states such as Turkey, Egypt, and Iraq. These national entities seem to have rejected the idea that the source of Islamic prowess at one time was the true religion; all-inclusive both for human needs and the building of a prosperous society. Recognising the beginnings of this dual, but mutually contradictory, political development, Muhammad 'Abduh was faced with the problem of retaining the ethical content and precepts of Islam, while trying to render more flexible the legislative aspects of the religion in the light of modern requirements.[33]

Although 'Abduh begins by rejecting the idea of nationalism, as a counteraction to individual national units in Islam, his own attempt at a 'religious patriotism' leads him to a befuddled concept of religious 'nationalism'. He considers national fanaticism (*ta'assub*) in contrast to a religious feeling of solidarity. One must be careful with 'Abduh's discussion of nationalism for it is full of contradictions and erroneous presuppositions.

First, he appears to use *ta'assub* synonymously with *'asabiyya*, or *esprit de corps*. The latter he calls a characteristic of the human soul and personality, causing it to defend its own. The ensuing self-pride leads to members of a community uniting in the promotion of good society. He goes so far as to assert that this strong feeling for one's own moulds a nation's virtues.[34] Apparently, 'Abduh is trying to establish a 'religious patriotism' that would counteract individual national ones. Consequently, he criticises secularists who wish for an anti- or non-religious modernism by reminding them that religion is the 'foremost sustainer of a virtuous secular life', thus emphasising the humanist aspect of Islam.

Religion is the first teacher . . . and best guided leader for the human souls in their pursuit of knowledge . . . the greatest educator . . . training the souls in the good values and virtuous character, inculcating them with justice, urging them to mercy and magnanimity, and especially Islam, which elevated a nation from the deepest savagery . . . to the highest wisdom and civilisation in the shortest time . . .[35]

'Religious patriotism' ('Abduh's concept of *ta'assub*), then, is more sacred and pure, implying broader benefit than national fanaticism.

Pursuing his warning to the secularists, 'Abduh asserts further that 'nationalism' (*al-wataniyya*) among Muslims is a limiting factor, often causing disunity. Thus, he deplores those who discard Islam without understanding the true nature of Western-imported nationalism. It should be noted that, under the circumstances, 'Abduh was reacting to the conditions of the Muslim world towards the end of the nineteenth century. But his contention that there is no *nationality* (*jinsiyya*) for Muslims other than their religion is an exaggeration, its Quranic and prophetic assertions notwithstanding.[36]

It was indicated earlier that the dictum, 'the faithful are brothers' was not able to prevent the development of nationality-conscious groups within Islam, as well as among the Christian world community. The early nationalisation of Islam into an Arab-dominated movement proved an obstacle to any acculturation in a multi-cultural environment through the religion. Historical events were to show that Islam was not free from the political ascendancy of national groups within it. The Turks and the Ottoman Empire are a case in point. Thus 'Abduh's article 'Islamic

Unity' is perhaps at best an oratorical appeal to unity. It is glaringly anachronistic in its historical development and facts. And yet, together with his 'Nationality and the Religion of Islam', it shows a deep understanding on his part for the necessity of developing a native system of values for the Islamic community at large.[37]

Throughout his articles in *al-'Urwa*, Muhammad 'Abduh is trying to establish three major requirements for a religious reform that would constitute the beginnings of a 'humanist' tradition in reformed Islam. First is what I term a system of virtues, to be developed and spread by the strength of a reformed religious teaching. Such development of virtue on a religious basis would instigate an inclination for introspection that would encourage internal reform, constituting the second requirement. The third consideration would be that of a public philosophy for the Muslim community, evolved within the context of the problems and needs of a modern society.

Beginning with 'Virtues and Vices',[38] 'Abduh indulges in sermons on virtue in an effort to establish a 'social didache'. The essence of his effort in this series, to revitalise a living religious humanism among the Muslim masses, may be summarised in the new focus he gives to the social duty and responsibility of the faithful. 'The sum total of virtue is justice (*al-'adl*) in all actions.'[39] The principle of justice would eventually lead to a situation wherein 'every citizen will respect the right of all; not willingly choosing an aim contrary to that of the whole; not seeking aims sharply contradictory to those of the group until the whole presents a solid structure'.[40]

This didactic call to virtue is based on a *dynamic* belief in God, dynamic in the sense that it is a *moving* concept to action. 'Abduh here is deliberately trying to activate the expectation of a future life in the beyond into earthly improvement. For he urges that 'hope [eschatological or otherwise] is a feeling that [should] produce(s) action, carrying the soul [self] against evil . . . towards strife and hard work'.[41] The belief in God, therefore, should produce action, because 'none despair from the spirit of God except the non-believers'. 'Abduh's view of God, moreover, is one of a Supreme Being who demands the attainment of a virtuous and just life through a developing effort for knowledge as a positive good. Despair, then, as a result of collective resignation, is a definite sign of sickness and disbelief.[42]

In order to further activate the belief in God into social action, 'Abduh offers a bold admonition: 'Weeping does not raise the dead, neither does pity bring back the past, nor sorrow prevent catastrophe. Action [work] is the key to success.'[43] He considers this God's test of the faithful, for true belief leads to fruitful activity.

Reference was made earlier to 'Abduh's 'humanism with God'. It is important, therefore, to bear in mind that moderation in character and the acquisition of virtue are to be attained within the religious framework, with the new difference that the religion is to be bolstered up by the deliberate and conscious attempts — striving — of man. This is what 'Abduh means when he reminds his readers that 'Allah shall not change the condition of a folk until they change what is in them', and when he introduces rational choice over against *taqlid*. For these virtues established by the Divine Law as definite realities are accepted and lived only after they have been defined by man's reason.[44] Thus God has revealed His way forever. It is up to man to look into himself with a critical eye, for he cannot blame other than himself for his shortcomings. And, in the final analysis, 'change' in people must come about through reason and perception.[45]

'God promised those who believe and do good that He shall make them inherit the earth as those before them.' It becomes imperative, therefore, that justice is the rule upon which men shall act for the attainment of the good. This presupposes the corollary rule that public interest is the basis for the perpetuation of the state, demanding human cooperation. And, as oppression causes destruction, justice becomes the only progenitor of a happy life. 'God has rendered the agreement on the public welfare, and cooperation in the attainment of the general good, sources of power . . . and comfort in this life, enabling man to arrive at eternal happiness in the hereafter.'[46]

But any discussion of 'change through action' in Islam is inevitably confronted by the traditional question of 'free will and predestination'. The treatment of this delicate subject by Muslims has been frequent, and a source of great controversy. It is, indeed, characterised by polemic and much confusion. Basically, it concerns the Muslim idea of a transcendental God, and the destiny of the believer, who must carry on with an earthly existence. Today, the problem facing the modern Muslim consists primarily of his ability to gauge this wide gap between an omnipotent God and His weak subject, man, who must, of necessity, grapple with the bitter adversities of daily living. Those, of course, who hold to the utter helplessness of man and his subjection to the predetermined will of God regardless of his deeds do not recognise the existence of the problem at all. Those, however, who are puzzled by the fact (a) that man has certain potentialities that he, on his own, can develop maximally and, perhaps, actualise on earth, and (b) that there are certain living examples in the world today of groups and communities that have

accomplished a more materially comfortable and better organised existence, feel that the problem is a pressing one for the revitalisation of the
Muslim community. Their task is difficult, for it is not simply a matter
of accepting or rejecting freedom on the one hand and predestination
on the other. It is more complex in that, if Muhammad 'Abduh is taken
as an example, the question must be approached within its religious
ramifications.

'Abduh views the problem of freedom as choice *with obligation demanded by the Shari'a*, or Sacred Law.[47] This view is not too different
from our Western concept of freedom under or within the wide scope
of a higher law. He realises, however, that the famous question of *al-
qada' wa'l-qadar* has pre-Islamic origins extending far into the Muslim
tradition, because of the natural proclivity of cultural ethos to perpetuate itself through generations. Consequently, 'Abduh's task was to give
this whole question a modern interpretation — even character — that
would differentiate it from its antecedents. This he tries to do by mani-
pulating *al-qada' wa'l-qadar* into a concept of *destiny* in which man has
an important role to play. One might call this 'Abduh's 'activisation of
the popular belief in fate' for possible action in the pursuit of a better
life, instead of popular inactive resignation.[48] For 'Abduh realised that
the concept of destiny in Islam after the early Muslim conquests was
nothing like the *force civilisatrice* of the West.

There are also dangers inherent in Muhammad 'Abduh's efforts to
gauge the power (*qadar*) or will of God and the helplessness of the
believer and his freedom of choice. In later writings, for example, he
accuses the Persians of allowing heretical accretions to Islam.[49] One
might well ask if 'Abduh assumes that only 'Arab Islam' is true Islam. In
other instances he refers to the pollution of Islam by foreign elements,
as in the case of the Abbasids. The further question might be asked as
to whether Islam should have remained Arabic. Is 'Abduh calling for
an Arab Islamic unity?[50] Needless to say, this would be a most deter-
ministic position. It may be quite possible, however, that Muhammad
'Abduh is seeking a base from which to attack traditionalism. For he
holds that it is not really what is in the Qur'an regarding free will and
predestination that presents a problem. It is rather the rigidity superimposed by *taqlid* which seeps into the social order, creating apathy in
soul movement, or soul atrophy.[51] And he seems to accept the theory
that the work of man has much to do with the growth of his soul. It is
in essence 'Abduh's attempt to render the relationship between man
and his Creator a closer and more viable one, reflected in man's relentless struggle for a better life in an earthly human society.

There is frequent reference today to 'rapid change' in the Muslim countries. The term is especially favoured among Westerners genuinely or superficially concerned with events in the Islamic world since the end of the Second World War. It is a term current in the press as well as in civic and women's clubs. The questions 'what change?' 'in what direction?' and 'how?' are rarely examined with any persistence. Some hold, for example, that 'dictatorship' will be the means of change; others console themselves with technical assistance as the vehicle of future economic and social change, reaching from these foundations, in good time, to the political structure. Whatever the differing opinions, all are agreed that there *is* change.

I may be accused of choosing a poor springboard in discussing change in the Islamic world, especially the Arab Muslim countries, in Muhammad 'Abduh. It may be argued that after all he died over fifty years ago; that there are today governments in the Muslim world operating from relatively modern bases; that talking of a Muslim 'humanist tradition' is irrelevant, because a man would much rather drink healthy milk made accessible to him by the kind services of technical assistance than continue with religious practices of dubious value and benefit. May I submit, then, as justification for seeing in Muhammad 'Abduh a basis for a more flexible Islam, the proposition that material change by no means implies change in individual and social modes of thought, habits of feeling, and action at the mass level? Such fundamental change in the few who control the reins of government is not adequate proof of comparable change in the community at large.

Inter-war, as well as present experience in the Islamic countries, points to the inability so far of the Muslim 'intellectual' and political leader to undergird whatever 'rapid change' has occurred with a viable social philosophy acceptable to the masses. Outright secularists, demanding the relegation of religion to the sphere of individual conscience without bearing on social and political legislation and action, are very few.[52] There is, on the other hand, a plethora of 'educated' Muslims who have romantically accepted the theory that the adoption of certain political forms will of itself produce change. But they fail to realise that mere form, however ideal, can produce only what the social context permits. The adoption of Western political institutions, supremely embodied in a written constitution, is a case in point. Intellectuals have failed to grasp the reality that a constitution setting out the political, social and economic purposes of a society can survive and produce the desired results only in so far as a community is willing to allow. This willingness is contingent upon the understanding not merely of a very few, but on the consensus of the whole. Thus a constitution alone does not guarantee desired change. It must receive its life from the social context. If it envisages change and development as a goal of the body politic, it is imperative that the individual members of the society accept the maxim that there is no *final* quality in their present existence, which is liable to change with circumstances. Flux rather than a predetermined order becomes the rule and guiding principle. It is easy for the Muslim intellectual to rationalise such principles against traditional teaching. But it is more important that the mass accept it *emotionally*.

It is this confusion on the part of Western-educated Muslims that deprives them of influence. Thought, though 'liberal', fails to provide the intellectual conditions for the healthy and steady development of Muslim society. Those who reject religion as useless find themselves lacking any contact with the masses. Those clinging to religious orthodoxy refuse to re-examine their position in the light of a changing world, thus gradually alienating all those inclined to creative thought.

Muhammad 'Abduh set out to revitalise society by bridging the gap between the perplexed educated Muslim and the orthodox believer. He recognised the dangers in the dichotomy of separate systems of value for the few and the many. He saw the necessity of an indigenous value system in which all could participate. His preoccupation with religious reform was based on the assumption that religion reflects the cultural personality — the soul, if you wish — of the Muslim. For generations religion had moulded the Muslim's view of man and the universe. Muhammad 'Abduh recognised the need for a satisfying psychological experience to accompany the Muslim's re-examination of his position involving the hitherto forbidden 'unknown'. He felt that the new intellectual experiences resulting from such examination would provide a dynamic element in a society that had long resisted change.

Professor Charles Adams, in characterising the contents of the organ of *al-'Urwa' l-wuthqa*, summarised the basic ideas expressed in it as (1) the unity of all Muslims without racial distinction, (2) the necessity of returning to the rules of religion, and (3) the warding off of foreign influences.[53] These ideas accorded with the professed, albeit secret, aims of the society. It should be emphasised, however, that throughout his active teaching and writing, Muhammad 'Abduh actually came very close to introducing into Islamic thought an evolutionary concept of historical development. Hence his attack upon *taqlid* by (a) the purification of the mind from superstition, (b) the striving for human perfection through independent reason, virtue, and reasonable conviction, and (c) education, since human knowledge is acquired not by dispensation but through investigation.

'Abduh felt uneasy about Jamal al-Din's nationalist interpretation of Islam. The 'religious patriotism' he tried to substitute for it was a necessary prerequisite to a religious basis for reform. He understood well that the nationalism of the West was confined among Muslims to a few intellectuals, but was unintelligible to the masses. His humanism, therefore, was never wholly utilitarian but rather bridged the gap between a transcendental God and a dynamic society, seeking, and badly needing, organic change through the application of honest individual introspection and historical criticism. For liberalism to impress the average Muslim, it must first break down theological petrifaction. 'Abduh took the first steps in this direction by reformulating doctrine. He sought to revitalise Islamic religion through systematic revision and new expression.

The Romantics in modern Islam meanwhile retreated into dubious mysticism. The conservative apologists, by virtue of their defensive position, presented ridiculous interpretations of historical fact and dogma. Finally, the secularists alienated themselves completely from the mass of citizens. Muhammad 'Abduh's position differs from that of all these in so far as he tried to bridge the gap between a transcendent God and His *active* subjects — what was referred to earlier as the basic dilemma of Muslim reform — by introducing the idea of personal virtue and social ethic, making possible the belief in a transcendent God reflected in man's active life of endeavour towards higher goals.

What disturbed Muhammad 'Abduh was the disconnection between social action and religious belief. Bringing about a viable relation between the two was one of his primary concerns. His choice of *education* as the fundamental means to that end is significant. For 'Abduh, contrary to many superficial modernists, was aware of the necessity of a vigorous value system within the community. This would afford a distinction between change genuinely accepted by the masses and that formally embodied in superimposed institutions from non-indigenous sources without public understanding. Thus, 'Abduh preached a liberal and humanistic Islam, free of rigid traditional formulations and invigorated by rational and historical methods of criticism. He advocated belief in Man as part of the greater belief in God, on the assumption that human values are largely formulated by earthly experience.

Notes

1. One cannot fairly claim mental sterility in view of developments like the

Puritan Wahhabi movement in the eighteenth century, the Pan-islamism of the nineteenth century, and more recently the Salafiyya and Muslim Brotherhood movements, and the secularist tendencies of Taha Husain, 'Ali 'Abd al-Raziq, and Khalid Muhammad Khalid of the present century.

2. See M. 'Abduh, *al Islam wa'r r-radd 'ala muntaqidihi* (Cairo, 1928). More recent works are those of Muhammad al Ghazzali, *The Beginning of Wisdom* (NETP, American Council of Learned Societies, Washington, DC, 1953), and Sayyid Qutb, *al-'adala' l-ijtima'iyya fi' l-Islam* (Cairo, npd).

3. See Taha Husain, *Fi'l adabi' l-jahili*; 'Ali 'Abd al-Raziq, *al Islam wa usulu' l-hukm*. Dr Taha Husain is calling for the simplification of the written Arabic language as the only means of combating illiteracy on a mass scale. He proposes mainly phonetic orthography: a radical deviation from classical orthographic rules of grammar and syntax. See *Al-risala* (literary monthly published in Cairo), *al-ahram* and *al-gumhuriyya* of June-August, both dailies published in Cairo, for a debate on this subject between the Taha Husain literary forces and those who support the classicist Mahmud 'Abbas al 'Aqqad. Earlier, Taha, in an effort to urge Egypt and the Arabs towards modernisation, has taken the extreme and rather dubious position of claiming that the native Egyptian mind is totally Hellenic and ergo Western in its orientation. See his *Mustaqbalu'th-thaqafa fi Misr* (Cairo, 1939). Granted that ancient Egyptian civilization may be considered Mediterranean, the Hellenisation of the Egyptians cannot be assumed without argument at any period of history, especially under Alexander's diadochic empire of the Ptolemies. The present writer, on the basis of available researches in that period of history, is inclined to the view that the Hellenisation of the Egyptian population and community never really occurred, the Alexandrian School notwithstanding. The tendency among the Macedonian-Greeks was to live apart and distinct from the subject peoples as a ruling aristocracy. What is more, the indigenous population led by their powerful priests tended to actively or passively oppose the foreign rulers. As it turned out, the Greek Ptolemies eventually adopted more of the native Egyptian culture. See I.G. Bell, *Egypt* (Oxford, 1948), and Mahaffy, *Progress of Hellenism in Alexander's Empire* (Chicago, 1905).

4. For example, the dramatists Nagib ar-Rihani (d. 1948) and Tawfiq al-Hakim. See excellent studies by H.A.R. Gibb, 'Studies in Contemporary Arabic Literature' I, II, III, *Bulletin of School of Oriental Studies*, vols. IV and V. The desire for reform and characterisation of the Muslim dilemma is to be found expressed at its very best in Ahmad Amin's autobiography, *Hayati* (Cairo, 1952).

5. The fact should not be overlooked that an Arab-Muslim humanism of letters, science and philosophy developed during the Abbasid period. See discussion in Louis Gardet, *La Cité Musulmane* (Paris, 1952), pp. 273-322.

6. Muhammad Iqbal and Ameer 'Ali of India and Pakistan may perhaps be considered as the humanists *par excellence* in modern Islam. However, they belong chronologically to another generation, that of the present century. See Iqbal, *Reconstruction of Religious Thought* (1938), and Ameer 'Ali, *The Spirit of Islam* (1902).

7. Text used is that of *al-matba'a'l-ahliyya*, Beirut, 3rd edn. (1933). Another text of these articles is reproduced in Sheikh Rashid Rida, *tarikh al-ustadh al-imam al-shaykh Muhammad 'Abduh*, 3 vols., vol. 1, pp. 290ff (Cairo, 1931).

8. These summary news items and editorials can be found in Part II of the Beirut edition under the title 'an-nutaf wa-'lakhbar', pp. 270-525.

9. See his 'The Intellectuals in the Modern Development of the Islamic World' in *Social Forces in the Middle East*, Sydney N. Fisher, ed. (New York, 1955), p. 200.

10. See the English translation of the new Egyptian Constitution promulgated in January 1956, and adopted June 1956, in *Middle Eastern Affairs* (February,

1956), regarding the emphasis placed on social democracy, justice, people's rights and duties. See also the speeches of President Abd-el-Nasser in *al-Ahram* and *al-Gumhuriyya* for the months of June and July 1956.

11. Even in Turkey the official severance of the religion from the state had its repercussions among the Turkish public. On this subject, see Bernard Lewis, 'Islamic Revival in Turkey', *International Affairs*, XXVIII (January 1952), pp. 38-48.

12. The Mu'tazila school in medieval Islam as well as Imam al-Ghazzali (d. 1111) may be considered among the foremost advocates of a viable system of Muslim ethics.

13. For a brilliantly incisive analysis of this question, see E.A. Speiser, 'Cultural Factors in Social Dynamics in the Near East' in Fisher, *Social Forces in the Middle East*, pp. 1-22.

14. See 'Abdur-Rahman ar-Rafi'i, *ath-thawaratu 'l-'urabiyya* (2nd edn, Cairo, 1949), and W.S. Blunt, *Secret History of England in Egypt* (London, 1907), for a sympathetic account of this revolt.

15. For a history of the conditions in Persia during the latter part of the nineteenth century, see, E.G. Browne, *The Persian Revolution*, and Sir Percy Sykes, *Persia*.

16. (Cairo, al-matba'a'r-rahmaniyya, 1928.) This work is actually a collection of essays refuting certain contrasting views of Christianity and Islam, by Gabriel Haneteaux.

17. See Muhd. Rashid Rida, *Tarikh*, vol. 1, 306ff., who talks of immediate and distant aims of *al-'Urwa*.

18. See *Mashahiru' sh-sharq*, I (3rd edn, Cairo, 1922), pp. 305-7. Proof of 'Abduh's painstaking approach to the problem of Muslim reform is in his efforts at improving the Azhar curriculum, his fatwas, and public education policies. See *Tarikh*, vols. II and III. For Jamal's political personality and programme, see *Encyclopedia of Islam*, I, pp. 1008-10, Browne, *The Persian Revolution*, pp. 2-30; Zaidan, II, p. 61; Adams, *Islam and Modernism in Egypt* (Oxford, 1933), p. 13ff; *Tarikh*, I, Introduction, p. 73ff, pp. 1-20.

19. Thus Rashid Rida's remark that *'al-'Urwa* began to inflame the fires of rebellion in the East', is too far-fetched and projectory. See *Tarikh*, I, p. 304.

20. H.Q. xiii, II. It is interesting to note that 'Abduh invokes this verse repeatedly in *al-'Urwa*, but in an incomplete manner. Other translations render the same verse, 'Lo Allah changeth not the condition of a folk until they [first] change that which is in their hearts; and if Allah willeth misfortune for a folk there is none that can repel it; nor have they a defender beside Him.' (Pickthall, *The Glorious Qur'an*, 1954.) The deletion must have been deliberate on the part of 'Abduh, for this second part of the verse renders almost meaningless the freedom of action suggested in the first.

21. This position was characterised by the late Ahmad Amin in his autobiography, as 'Abduh's 'rational nationalism', in contrast to Mustafa Kamil's 'emotional nationalism'. See, *Hayati* (Cairo, 1952), p. 82.

22. See his *Modern Trends in Islam* (Chicago, 1952), pp. 69-70.

23. Cf. Ameer 'Ali, *Spirit of Islam* and Sayyid Qutb, *al-'adala'l-ijtima'iyya fi'l-Islam* (Cairo, 1946).

24. See his *Risalatu't-tawhid* (Cairo, 1943).

25. The constant struggle in Muslim history between orthodoxy and the Sufi mystics is the paramount instance of the struggle between those who desire a more immanent – therefore, nearer – God, and the overpoweringly transcendent one of the Qur'an.

26. This is even seen among many of the modernists themselves, whose apology for Islam is more an emotional and romantic presentation of a perfect system – a dishonest intellectual attitude at best.

27. See his *Cité Musulmane*, pp. 273-322.

18   *Muhammad 'Abduh and the Quest for a Muslim Humanism*

28. 'Studies in Contemporary Arabic Literature', *BSOAS*, vol. IV, part iv, pp. 757-8.
29. *Tarikh*, I, pp. 307-8.
30. *Al-'Urwa*, pp. 47-54.
31. Ibid., p. 49.
32. *Tarikh*, p. 51.
33. See especially his articles 'The Decline of the Muslims' and 'Christianity and Islam', *Al-'Urwa*, pp. 72-95.
34. *Al-'Urwa*, p. 99. Professor Charles Adams in his *Islam and Modernism in Egypt*, p. 58ff., renders *jinsiyya* as race.
35. *Al-'Urwa*, p. 103.
36. Ibid., pp. 107, 150.
37. *Al-'Urwa*, pp. 47-53, 146-57.
38. 'Al-fada'il wa'r-radha'il', *al-'Urwa*, pp. 131-45.
39. *Al-'Urwa*, p. 132.
40. Ibid., p. 134.
41. Article entitled 'al-'amal', ibid., pp. 177-8.
42. Ibid., p. 145.
43. *Al-'Urwa*, p. 156.
44. Ibid., pp. 203-12.
45. Ibid., p. 242. 'Min nuri'l-'aql wa sihhati'l-fikr wa ishraqi'l-basira.'
46. *Al-'Urwa*, p. 230.
47. Article entitled 'al-qada wa'l'qadar', *al-'Urwa*, pp. 114-30.
48. Ibid., pp. 128-30.
49. See his *al-Islam wa'r-radd 'cla muntaqidihi* (Cairo, 1928), pp. 37-40, where he refers to al-jabariyya, an Aryan heresy imported into Islam by Persians from India.
50. *Al-'Urwa*, pp. 191-94.
51. *Al-Islam wa'r-radd 'ala muntaqidihi*, p. 38.
52. An interesting, although weak, example is Khalid Muhammad Khalid, author of *Min huna nabda'* (Cairo, 1949), with his attack upon 'clericalism' and orthodox conservatism in Islam. His other two works, *Citizens not Subjects* (*Muwatinun la ra'aya*) and *Democracy Forever or Absolutely* (*Ad-dimoqratiyya abadan*) (Cairo, 1950), are a pursuit of his attack upon orthodoxy and a call for the complete separation of politics and religion. *Min huna nabda'* has been translated into English by the American Council of Learned Societies, Washington, DC (1953). See also a review of this book by PJV in the UNESCO PEN Bulletin, October–December 1952.
53. Adams, pp. 58-64.

2 RECENT TRENDS IN ISLAM

It would be presumptuous to attempt a total assessment of recent developments in Islam, for it is not possible to encompass all that pertains to the millions of Moslems living in Asia and Africa. One's knowledge is, at best, limited, and could, if used to pronounce broad generalisations on Islam today, be dangerously misleading. Islam, to borrow Professor Franz Rosenthal's phrase, 'is an eminently historical religion'. It is still making history, and to analyse history in the making is difficult. One may construct theories about the past, but the present impinges on the future, and the theorist, unaware, turns prophet. One may venture merely the formulation of hypotheses regarding current trends in Islam on the basis of recent developments.

Such hypotheses as I shall offer will be limited to the Arab countries, Turkey, and Pakistan, with only passing comment on Iran and North, West, and East Africa. I will focus attention on those recent developments in Islam that tend to increase or lessen tension in the Middle East.

Scientific technology and its pragmatic outlook have seriously challenged the traditional unity of Islam, resulting in a pervasive uncertainty, extending to law, literature, politics, and education. One has only to recall the encroachment on the sacred law of positive legislation adopted by almost all the Islamic countries to meet pressing social and economic problems.[1] The sacred law, as the perfect embodiment of the social-religious-political ethic and ideal, is thus being compromised. What does this signify? Is the Moslem actually convinced that earthly existence can be improved by man-made laws?

Furthermore, in the recent past we have witnessed in Syria and Egypt the abolition of confessional jurisdiction and the discontinuance of religious bequests (*waqfs*) for private use, both measures being designed to expand the jurisdiction of civil authority.[2] There is novel experimentation in literature, expressed in the battle between classicists and innovators.[3] One observes a radical deviation from traditional Islamic forms. The metrical but unrhyming verse is gaining legitimacy. The short story — in its Western form — is increasing in popularity. The art of

Source: P.W. Thayer (ed.), *Tensions in the Middle East* (The Johns Hopkins University Press, Baltimore, Maryland, 1958).

representation in painting, sculpture, freehand and woodprint is steadily developing.

All this would seem to indicate that Islamic society, having defined its aims, has deliberately chosen to move along a certain path. Why, then, the gnawing uncertainty? I submit as my first hypothesis that, the changes mentioned notwithstanding, the Islamic societies of today,, even though reluctant to admit it, are caught on the horns of a great dilemma: on the one hand a steadily growing desire to adopt the techniques of modern civilisation for their advantages in terms of welfare and national strength, and on the other hand a marked reluctance to abandon traditional ways of life and values. Deep attachment to traditional Islam manifests itself in varying degrees of intensity among the different Muslim countries. Though anxious to fit Western technology into an Islamic context, these countries have only partially succeeded, inasmuch as their desire to borrow from the West is mixed with resentment towards it.[4] Moslems, from North Africa to Pakistan, are calling for economic and social reform, insisting, however, that such reform should be undertaken in harmony with the principles of Islam. How this harmonious adjustment is to be achieved is not clear.[5] Does modern legislation derive from the principles of the *sharia* as such or from the general spirit of Islam? The most recent constitutions of Syria and Pakistan require, ambiguously, legislation derived from the principles of the *sharia*. Similar ambiguity is reflected in the new Egyptian constitution, which declares Egypt a 'democratic socialist Republic' with Islam as the religion of the state. Thus, in the most recent rationalisations of social and political organisation, Islam still asserts itself.

Let us take the still older case of Turkey. It is common-place to refer to Turkey today as a modern state in the midst of the patriarchal, dictatorial, and fake parliamentary regimes of the Middle East. Such a characterisation, I am afraid, is rather hasty, reflecting not the fact but the seeming success of Atatürk's ruthlessness. Prudence would withhold the final word on Turkey.

Under the Ottoman regime, Turkey achieved a highly elaborate Muslim judicial system and religious hierarchy. The Islamic institutional structure was indeed a feat of Ottoman statecraft. Yet so serious were the maladjustments in the twentieth century, and so violent the resentment against it, that Atatürk undertook to legislate it out of existence. Then, suddenly, at the end of the Second World War, a counter-reaction appeared, which, from 1950, constituted a veritable 'revival of Islam'.[6] So far, the repercussions of this revival have not been such as to challenge seriously Kemalist principles, especially that of laicism. Yet the revival is genuine enough for us to question the durability of the revolutionary ideology underlying the Kemalist order – especially as the basis for a national myth totally acceptable to the masses.

Agitation for religious education has been the foremost manifestation of the resurgence of Islam in Turkey. The issue was first discussed in the Grand National Assembly in December 1946. The timing of the issue raises many interesting questions. Was it a spontaneous reaction to the monolithic regime of the Peoples Republican Party, with its thought-control aimed at the generation of a secular-republican climate of opinion? Or, again, was it a sincere Islamic antagonism to an imported philosophy and way of life?

These questions cannot be fully answered here, but it appears that the authorities were unable to continue ignoring the basically Islamic ethic of the people. Positivist doctrine, apparently, was unable to displace the Islamic value-system, strengthened as it is in Turkey by other cultural and folk elements. The government established the Faculty of Theology at Ankara in October 1949. Working closely with the Government Religious Agency (Diyanet Isleri Resligi), it serves as a centre for Islamic studies and trains religious teachers for state schools. It has been editing and translating Islamic classics while a committee of the Faculty of Literature at Istanbul is preparing a Turkish edition of the *Encyclopedia of Islam*. By the end of 1955, the government announced that religious instruction would be available in middle (*orta*) schools for those who wished it.[7]

The textbooks adopted for purposes of religious instruction are interesting. One by A. Hamdi Akseki, entitled *Islam Dini*, gives a modern ethical content to Islam and tries to reconcile Islamic tenets with a republican-humanistic philosophy. Another, *Ilkokul Kitaplari-Dini Dorslori II*, prepared by the government in 1954 for use as a primary school text, goes further, by imparting a utilitarian aspect to faith, emphasising the ability, worth, and active life of the individual Moslem. 'My faith in God,' one passage asserts, 'brings me security and makes easy for me even the most difficult tasks. I never fall into hopelessness.' Could this be a precautionary antidote to a possible relapse into traditional lethargy? Furthermore, it asserts the brotherhood of man rather than that of Moslems alone. 'All people are brothers whatever religion they have.'[8]

Here is a calculated policy by which the government seeks to guard the Kemalist gains in the social, economic, and political spheres. The government is loath to permit the reappearance of religious groups with political, or even social, influence. Having recognised the necessity of minimum concessions to religious sentiment, it is anxious to direct that sentiment to ends acceptable to it.

The Turkish public has been showing great interest in Islam, as indicated by the proliferation of periodicals, magazines, pamphlets, and books devoted to Islamic subjects. Some of these publications reflect a reformist view, an attempt to give to Islam an orientation consonant with scientific thought. This is not a novel attempt by Moslems, as we shall see presently in the case of Pakistan. More novel is the attempt paradoxically to utilise the revived interest in Islam as a means for bolstering the brief secular-republican tradition begun by Atatürk. Ismail Hakki Baltacioglou, editor of *Din Yalu* (*Religious Road*), is probably the most active exponent of this object.

It would appear, at least on the surface, that the religious challenge is being adequately met by the Turkish government. One might further assume that the revivalist movement in Turkey is, under official guidance, taking on the character of a spiritual, personalised religion, compatible with the secular requirements of the state. Indeed, the Turkish ruling elite has rationalised its support for religious education by viewing it as the basis of character-building and national solidarity. In a speech delivered at Konya in December 1955, Prime Minister Adnan Menderes, though reiterating the basic principles of Kemalist secularism, emphasised the fact that 'Turkey was and would always remain Moslem'. It is also quite probable that the Democratic party of Celal Bayar was able to command wider popular support in both the 1950 and 1954 elections through its religious concessions.

We have seen how the Sharia with its intricate institutional structure in Turkey was abolished overnight. Its formal absence, however, does not seem to have minimised the traditional attachment to Islam of the Turkish people. Then is formal reinstatement of the *sharia* necessary for Islamic revival and reform? If not, can Islam be a religion of the 'spirit'? Can it be an ethical outlook? These are some of the questions that Muslim Turks must answer if they propose the integration of Islam as a religion into the social and political philosophy of the Kemalist Revolution.

It is unlikely that the Turkish rulers will countenance any new formula short of separation between religion and state. Their sober realisation that continued support from the masses meant partial identification with the popular myth, Islam, is bolstered by realism. The government's realistic attitude is reflected in its quick action against the fanatic Nation or Millet party of Fevzi Cakmak, when that group was using Islam for political agitation. At the same time, as a result of its religious compromise, the government lost some of its adherents. The Freedom party, for example, is a splinter group consisting of those members in the Democratic party who felt republicanism was being compromised. Semi-official organisations, like the Divic Ocagi (Society for Preservation of the Ideals of Revolution), also sprang up to lobby against the government's religious policy.

Whether the Turkish authorities will succeed in reintroducing into Turkey an Islam influenced by the borrowed ideas of the Western liberal-humanist tradition remains to be seen. Realising that Islam as an emotional force is still a determinant of political life, the elite has used it to broaden the base of its popular support. What is more curious, however, is its fanatic use by the mob. It would not be an exaggeration to say that even the Turkish government itself was shocked and surprised by the September 1955 Black Friday in Istanbul.

Some have gone so far as to interpret Turkey's partnership with Iran, Pakistan, and Iraq as a Muslim alliance, through which Turkey is vying for Islamic leadership. Admittedly, Nasser of Egypt is not very popular with the Turkish press and government. Yet it would be a mistake to interpret the alliance as related to anything but the political, military, and strategic interests of Turkey.

In its recent development Turkey has been the most consistent among the Islamic countries. Now she has officially agreed to reconsider Islam as the religious force strengthening her national existence. It remains to be seen how this reconsideration will be accomplished and how it will affect the future development of Turkey. That task alone carries the uncertainty of reconciling two opposite social ideals — a positivist one and a religious one.

The emergence of Pakistan is possibly the most significant event in contemporary Islam. Its establishment as an independent nation-state is the fulfilment of the aspirations of the pre-1947 Moslem League of India. The fact that Pakistan is predominantly Moslem is not of particular significance, for so are Egypt, Syria and Iraq. What is singularly interesting, however, is that Pakistan has declared itself an Islamic state, an Islamic republic, and claims to have adopted an Islamic constitution, which has succeeded in reconciling the parliamentary concept of limited government with the universal sovereignty of God. Constitutional debates lasted some seven years, from March 1949, well into 1956, the basic issue being the formulation of the concept of an Islamic state. A corollary consideration, depending on the successful resolution of the basic issue, was the accommodation of this Islamic state to a twentieth-century environment.

By an Islamic state the Pakistanis mean a political community governed by the precepts of Islam as revealed in the Koran and recorded in the Tradition. God, to whom universal sovereignty belongs, rules by delegating authority to the state of Pakistan, exercised through its people according to His limits. Because it is an Islamic state, the Pakistanis argue that it embraces the principles of democracy, freedom, equality, tolerance and social justice.

The first problem that arises is how to distinguish between the sovereignty of God and that of the people. A related problem is how to establish a legal framework for the distribution of sovereign power, a problem especially complicated in the case of a federal state like Pakistan. In Pakistan that is done by a written constitution. Is this constitution supreme law in Pakistan? If it is, what happens to the higher law of God? If that law is reflected in the constitution by a strict observance of the Koran and Tradition in legislation, who determines discrepancies between the two? Indeed, what interpretation of Tradition and which school of law is to be followed?

Legislation in accordance with the sacred law presents serious problems of jurisdiction. It cannot have uniform applicability because non-Moslems cannot be subjected to the *sharia*. Indeed, within the *sharia* itself the diversity of sects precludes uniformity.[9] At the one extreme, secular opinions point to the basic incompatibility between an Islamic state and a democratic parliamentary system. At the other, fanatic supporters of the idea of the Islamic state have claimed that Islam is not one among many religions, but the one final, universal religion. It is very difficult to conceive of an open, free system that permits such dry finality. One of the basic conditions of a free parliamentary system is the entertainment of alternative solutions, a flexibility that permits change with circumstance. A system based on doctrine preconceived by nature cannot tolerate radical deviation.

Because of these and other problems, there is today in Pakistan great confusion over what constitutes an Islamic state. To meet this problem some are taking a new look at the Tradition with a view to giving it a modern and uniform interpretation. In February 1955, a special issue of *Islamic Literature*, published in Lahore, was devoted to the question of the 'Islamic State'. In 1956 the same journal concentrated on 'Islamic versus Western Civilization'. The latter inquiry reflects desire on the part of Pakistanis, who suffer from dangerous romanticism, to show perfect harmony between Islam and scientific philosophy. But it is an apology at best; it does not tackle the real problem of Islamic doctrine. It is one thing to liberalise a religious message; it is another matter to make it work. In spite of these efforts there is still no clear definition of what an Islamic state is. Those subscribing to the idea do so because of emotional attachment to an ideal, not because they are reasonably convinced of its practicability.

Apart from the romantic modernists just cited, there are also in Pakistan those who call for a pure theocracy, arguing that Islam is nothing less than God's direct rule on earth. Self-government is to them heretic, because it implies man's ability to regulate his social and political existence. Abu'l-Ala-al-Maududi, the foremost exponent of the theocratic doctrine, has formed the Islamic Society (Jama'at-i-Islami) of Pakistan, representing this conservative ideal. Fortunately or unfortunately, it also acts as a political party of the opposition.

The question of an Islamic state of Pakistan is actually unresolved, marked still by uncertainty and contradiction. Emotional attachment to the traditional view of man ruled by the sacred law is complicated by the desire, through modern legislation, to provide for the economic and social well-being of Pakistan. Thus tension is inevitable when, as in Pakistan, there is an attempt to use a Western-conceived and organised state structure for the implementation of traditional Islamic values. What is more, the tension will increase as the rulers of Pakistan try to foster and identify a homogeneous national object of loyalty, namely, the Republic of Pakistan. That cannot be achieved by retaining a dual framework of government, one for Moslems, the other for non-Moslem minorities. It looks more to us as if the Pakistanis have established a republic inspired by 'Islamic nationalism' (really nationalism idealised through Islam) rather than an Islamic state that is a republic.

In the Arab countries developments have been more complicated. All we can hope to do here is mention a few of these developments on the basis of which we may hypothesise on the general trend. The past five years have seen the steady revival of the concept of an Islamic community (*umma*), especially in Egypt. Influenced by the ideas of modern nationalism, this is not merely a community of faith, but a political community as well. Writing in a special issue of *al-Hilal* (January 1957), on 'Our Arab Nation', Nasser asserts that Arabs are the only people with a *qibla* (direction for prayer), a potential source of national strength and international leadership. In the same issue, Ahmad Zaki emphasises the sharpened cultural-religious antagonism between the Arabs and the West. Ahmad Hasan al-Baquri, Minister of Waqfs, writing in 1956, underlines the religious basis of the Arab social and political renascence.[10] Besides these specific instances, there is the usual but accelerated idealisation of Islamic historic personalities in popular magazines.

Recent measures by the Egyptian government in the field of education are significant. A law that became effective in December 1956,
makes obligatory the teaching of Islam to Muslim pupils in Christian
schools operated by foreigners. Noncompliance with this law renders
a school liable to seizure by the state. The Republic of Egypt was proclaimed in May 1953, in the name of Allah and the Qur'an, while Naguib,
in accepting the oath of allegiance (*bay'a*) from the ulema first and the
people later repeated the words of the first caliph, Abu Bakr.[11] Could
this be a reiteration of Islam as the foundation of all legitimate political
power? The results of the June 1956 plebiscite for the adoption of the
new constitution were publicly expressed in the form of the *bay'a*. In
both Jordan and Saudi Arabia one reads about the frequent denunciation
of Western culture as a degenerating influence upon Moslem society.[12]
In 1955 the Egyptian Ministry of Waqfs established an office to supervise and encourage the role of the mosque and the imam in community
life, to promote the kind of preaching that would extend Islamic education. (A 1955 royal decree in Arabia prohibits students from attending
primary and secondary schools abroad.)

Here we might venture a hypothesis: For the Arab countries, during
the interwar period, nationalism was a formula of national salvation
derived from and based on Western ideas. The tendency today is to
reject the Western origin of nationalism and to base it on Islam. Western
nationalism, embodied in the imported concepts of liberal constitutionalism and representative institutions, failed to work in the Arab
countries. This failure was due partly to the resistance of a traditional
society unacquainted with Western concepts. Consequently, even revolutionary regimes in the Middle East today must integrate this traditional
element into their political programme. Islam seems to offer the common ground for this accommodation. They also feel that Islam can ultimately free them from intellectual dependence on the West.

If this is a fair estimate of the present trend, we must look closely at
any recent attempts by Arab Moslems to establish an Islamic basis for
their national existence. Interwar experience showed that the Moslem
intellectual and political leaders were unable to undergird any change
with a social philosophy acceptable to the masses. Educated Moslems
had romantically embraced the idea that adoption of certain forms
would of itself produce change. They failed to realise that mere form,
however ideal, can produce only what the social context permits. It was
this confusion of the Western-educated Moslem that deprived him of
influence. His thought, though liberal, failed to provide the conditions
necessary for the healthy development of Arab Moslem society. Those,

on the other hand, who rejected religion, found themselves lacking any contact with the masses. And those clinging to conservative religious orthodoxy refused to re-examine their position in the light of a changing world, thus gradually alienating all those inclined to creative thought. The debate that raged between 1949 and 1951 between Khalid Muhammad Khalid (calling for a complete separation between state and Islam, and the socialisation of national programmes) and Muhammad al-Ghazzali (asserting that ideal social justice was found in Islam) is almost a thing of the past. Neither did this debate seem to have greatly affected the traditional observation of ritual by the masses.[13] Indeed, a more serious attempt to restate the position of Islam began in 1955 in India through a fresh examination of Tradition.[14] In the Arab countries, mass Islamic movements, which purport action on all fronts — social, economic, educational and political — thus avoiding the creation of an intellectual gap between them and the public, have had greater success in the recent past. The Moslem Brotherhood is a good example. Although officially suppressed in January 1954, at its Egyptian home base, the brotherhood is still a formidable religious-political force in the Arab world. Its suppression in Egypt required the establishment of an Islamic congress to promote the Islamic quality of Arab nationalism in the face of alien challenges and penetration — a recognition of the brotherhood's success.

A pressing problem facing Arab Islam is the construction of a formula for unity. The political fragmentation of the Arab countries, themselves a product of nationalism, would indicate that the nation-state as an object of loyalty must be fostered. But, individually, these countries do not show the homogeneity necessary for a uniform national myth. We may, therefore, assume that a nationalist Islam may prove an alternative. It can have greater appeal because it is a traditional concept it is indigenous. We saw how previous adoption of a liberal ideology by the intellectuals deepened the chasm between them and the masses. It produced a two-level society without contact, sympathy, or understanding between them. The social-political consciousness of the few was unable to produce a new order, because it was counteracted by the traditional conservatism and inertia of the many. The masses, with their devotion to the past, were beyond the reach of the intellectuals. It is not strange, therefore, that Islamic nationalism can have a greater appeal; it asserts the sentiment of religious-communal solidarity — a vague, yet emotionally acceptable, concept.

Parallel to the emergence of this new brand of Islamic nationalism, there is a general decline in liberal thought, a general discrediting of the intellectual. This is reflected in the decay and collapse of parliamentary government in many of the Arab countries and the growth of strong monolithic regimes. These are characterised by vociferous reaction to, and rejection of, Western ideas and principles, accompanied by a conscious utilisation of state power for the identification of national aspirations with the principles of Islam.

Before we can inquire whether resuscitated Islam can serve as the basis for renewed spiritual strength and a means to achieving homogeneity and solidarity among the Arab Islamic countries, we should note any forces that militate against it. First, there is no consensus among Arab Moslems regarding the validity or desirability of this trend. Political considerations at this time preclude general agreement. The Islamic orientation of Saudi Arabia, for example, does not prevent the political estrangement from Egypt or Syria. The same divergence of opinion is found among intellectuals.[15] In North Africa, Habib Bourguiba of Tunisia contends that 'constructive nationalism' is preferable to the Islamic variety.[16] Consequently, there is today a division of the Arab world marked by a struggle for power. This is aggravated by the vacuum that the retreat and disappearance of foreign control has produced.

The problems of Arab Islamic society are also complicated by external shocks. The psychological trauma resulting from the establishment of Israel has yet to be assessed. More irritating has been the Anglo-French invasion of Egypt in the fall of 1956. Have these two encroachments upon the Arab world sharpened Islamic antagonism to the extent of rejecting Western norms, while at the same time causing greater political fragmentation in the area?

Other developments in the Arab countries tend to undermine the identification of national aspirations with a revived and active Islam. Everywhere, in Iraq, Egypt, Arabia, Syria, and North Africa, governments are concerned with the economic and social development of their respective countries. As their programmes for reform acquire shape and meaning there is a gradual emergence of a proletariat and a middle class. As education becomes widespread, as services are extended to a larger portion of the population, these and other classes will demand greater participation and representation in the social-political process. As the gap between the few who have traditionally held power and the masses is narrowed down, new centres of power will arise, demanding a role in political life. The possible transformation of the social structure from its traditional form may totally change the role played by the various groups in Arab society and politics. At present, these emerging groups are not finally committed in their allegiance. They are rather uprooted and confused. Will Islam be able to command their allegiance in the future?

On the basis of recent developments, it is improbable that resuscitated Islam will serve as a basis for Arab solidarity and integration. Political considerations causing differences among the Arab countries still predominate. Although appealing, Islamic nationalism has not, so far, broken through individual national barriers. Neither has it seriously accommodated the techniques required for the administration of a modern state in its total interpretation of existence. The question of the compatibility between Islam and modern nationalism is unresolved. Instead, the dualism consisting of a desire among a few for modernisation, on the one hand, and a mass attachment to a traditional view of society, on the other, paralyses national development and minimises the chances for greater unity.

Reformulating our hypothesis, we may conclude that there is today an attempt at a Muslim renascence throughout the Islamic countries. This revival, however, is marked by struggle, tension, and uncertainty regarding the future. External forces such as the political-economic-strategic interests of the West and Communism are actual factors in this struggle. In seeking national strength, some of these countries are rejecting Western-inspired principles of national existence in favour of a new Islamic base. Unfortunately, this new Islamic base is still vague and not formulated in clear terms. It is more of an emotional stimulant than a formula of positive action. The dualism of values between sections of the public — one set of values primarily learned from the West, the other native — is still an obstacle to the creation of a homogeneous society. This dichotomy is widened by the increased use of non-Islamic techniques for the promotion of national welfare. Political and economic considerations continue to direct policy in a world quite divided in its loyalties.

The recent Islamic revival is still negative in character. The attempt among Moslems to gain intellectual as well as political freedom from the West has not been accompanied by a parallel introduction of a native value system, one that is not only rationalised by the intellectuals, but is also emotionally accepted and followed by the mass. Thus, the positive aspects of this revival are still vague and confused. Whether Islam, in rejecting influence from abroad, will succeed in generating its own formula for social and political salvation, is the most exciting unknown factor of the future. Now that Islam has revived its political aspirations, this task becomes critical. Similarly, it is always dangerous to telescope changes that require centuries into a short span of years. It is doubly dangerous when there is no agreement on what changes, and in which direction.

Notes

1. In Saudi Arabia one still finds strong opposition to modern legislation. A 1950 royal decree providing for the payment of income tax (*daribat ad-dakhl*) instead of the religious *zakat* (alms) was strongly opposed and quickly suppressed.

2. May 1949, in Syria, and December 1952, in Egypt. See G. Busson de Janssen 'Les Waqfs dans l'Islam Contemporain', *Revue des Etudes Islamiques* (Paris, 1953), pp. 43-76.

3. See the 'language debate' between Taha Husayn and Abbas M. al-'Aqqad in *al-Ahram*, LXXXII, and *al-Gumhuriyya*, III, of June-August 1956. See also discussions on literary trends in *al-risala'l-gadida* (Cairo, 1956-7).

4. On this problem, see the excellent discussion in G. von Grunebaum (ed.), *Unity and Variety in Muslim Civilization* (Chicago, 1955), especially pp. 357ff.

5. See especially the *Islamic Review* (Woking, Surrey), XLI (August 1955), pp. 6-13, and the *Islamic Literature* (Lahore, Pakistan), special issue, 'Islamic Civilization versus Western Civilization', VIII (May-June 1956), nos. 5 and 6.

6. B. Lewis, 'Recent Developments in Turkey', *International Affairs*, XXVII (July 1951), pp. 320-31. Also his 'Islamic Revival in Turkey', *International Affairs*, XXVIII (1952), pp. 38-48.

7. See Howard A. Reed, 'Revival of Islam in Secular Turkey', *Middle East Journal*, XIII (Summer 1954), pp. 267-82.

8. See the translation by Helen L. Morgan, 'A Turkish Textbook in Islam', *The Muslim World*, XLVI, no. 1 (January 1956), pp. 13-23.

9. It should be noted that the recommendation for a nominated Board of Mullahs (doctors of religious law) to review and pass on the constitutionality of legislation has met with great opposition. See Grace J. Calder, 'Constitutional Debates of Pakistan', I, II, III, *The Muslim World*, XLVI (January, April, July, 1956), pp. 40-60, 114-56, 253-71.

10. See *al-Hilal*, LXV (January 1957), Special Issue, 'Our Arab Nation', pp. 6-7, 41-4, and *al-Ithnein*, no. 1170 (12 November 1956), p. 17.

11. 'O people, I have been designated to be your chief even though I may not be the best among you. If you judge my conduct as satisfactory retain me. If you find me in error correct me.'

12. This trend may be especially noted in the Saudi Arabian daily, *al-bilad as-su'udiyya* (August 1956). A new Jordan monthly, *hadi 'l'islam*, contends that the danger of 'imperialism' to Muslim society is to be found lurking even in the Western-run schools and hospitals, as well as in Western literature.

13. See the well-known work *From Here We Start* by Khalid M. Khalid (Cairo, 1949), and its refutation by Muhammad al-Ghazzali in *The Beginning of Wisdom* (Cairo, 1951), translations by the American Council of Learned Societies, Near East Translation Program, Washington, DC, 1953.

14. See excerpts of the call in 1955 by the Hyderabad Academy of Islamic Studies for the re-examination of Tradition in *The Muslim World*, XLV (July 1955), pp. 299-300.

15. Cf. Abd ar-Rahman al-Bazzaz, 'Islam and Arab Nationalism', *Die Welt des Islams* (1954), Parts 3-4, pp. 210-18, where he asserts that 'Arab nationalism

devoid of the spirit of Islam is like a body without a soul', and Sati al-Husri, *al-'uruba awwalan* (Beirut, 1955).

16. See his article 'Nationalism: Antidote to Communism', *Foreign Affairs*, XXXV (July 1957), pp. 646-53.

3 ISLAM AND THE FOREIGN POLICY OF EGYPT

Although President Nasir appears to be trying to replace the Islamic basis of Arab identity for Egypt with an indigenous revolutionary socialism,[1] Egypt's historical position in the Islamic world remains culturally and politically crucial for any consideration of the role of Islam in Egyptian foreign and domestic policy. Today, a revived but sharpened sense of identity with the Islamic ethos, civilisation and culture permits the rulers of Egypt to promote a politically useful Arab consciousness among the masses.

Since the end of the eleventh century, Egypt has been directly involved in the sharpest and most direct confrontations between Christian Europe and the Islamic Arab lands. After a few centuries during which the Arabs were relatively isolated from Europe — although there never was a total break — the confrontation between Europeans and Arabs was renewed in 1798 with far-reaching impact through Egypt. Since that time, a new dimension has been given to the socio-economic and political evolution of the Arab world, a dimension which until now has been considered by most students to be directly contradictory, if not in opposition, to the Islamic nature of Arab societies.

It is not possible or practical, within the limits of one chapter, to trace all the Egyptian reactions and responses to this modern outside force over the past 150 years.[2] I will therefore limit myself to a discussion of certain phenomena relevant to the relationship between Islam and Egypt's policy toward other Arab countries.[3] Further, I assume that the use of Islam as an instrument of Egyptian foreign policy cannot be concretely documented by a chronological listing of official acts or public policy statements. A content analysis of the Egyptian press and radio is deliberately avoided, because such an analysis would be exposed to the inevitable contradictions of official and unofficial public statements about Islam and Islamic unity. Thus, in an interview with American newsmen on 3 March 1960, President Nasir, commenting on the Baghdad Pact, said:

I do not believe in mixing religion and politics . . . What would the

Source: J. Harris Proctor (ed.), *Islam and International Relations* (Praeger, New York, 1965).

world be like if we had an Islamic Pact, a Jewish Pact, a Buddhist Pact? I do not think that such pacts would make the world wonderful. Peoples of different creeds would not thereby be able to live together. Although Pakistan is an Islamic country, and the UAR is an Islamic country, I cannot find anything in this to justify the conclusion of a military pact between the two countries.[4]

Yet the following month, in Lahore, he devoted his entire speech before the Anjuman Himayat-i-Islam society to the value of Islamic teachings and to the community of spirit that exists between Pakistan and the UAR.[5] In his press conference at Lahore on 14 April 1960, when asked whether he favoured the creation of a Muslim bloc, Nasir replied that 'an association of nations on the basis of religion would give one to fanaticism and would not aid world peace. Minorities, moreover, would suffer as a result.'[6] But two days later, at the end of his visit to Pakistan, Nasir emphasised, in a joint communiqué with Ayub Khan, that the friendship and co-operation between the two countries was inspired by the Islamic bonds of brotherhood which united the two nations.[7] Later in the same year, in a speech welcoming Ayub Khan to Egypt, Nasir explained Pakistan's non-recognition of Israel as having been determined by the 'urge of Islamic comradeship felt by Pakistan'.[8]

No clear role for Islam in Egyptian foreign policy can be elicited from such statements. Thus, in February-April 1959, the Egyptian press and radio ascribed Egypt's differences with Iraq to Islamic values — Islam versus atheistic Communism, and Islamic solidarity versus the sectarian fragmentation of the *ummah*, or community of the faithful. And since May 1962, a distinction between the true Islam, 'the religion of justice and equality', and the deviationist Islam of 'corruption, reaction, exploitation, and tyranny' has been promoted and publicised by all Egyptian mass media, as well as by President Nasir himself. This distinction was made in order to exclude the so-called reactionary regimes of Saudi Arabia, the Yemen of the Imams Ahmad and Badr, and the Hashimite Kingdom of Jordan, from the pale of the 'religion of Islam' — a religion synonymous with a 'revolution which first laid down the socialist principles of justice and equality'.[9] The results of this deliberate differentiation of Islam, between Egypt, representing radical nationalism and 'Arab socialism' on the one hand, and Saudi Arabia and Jordan, together with the Yemen until September 1962, representing backward anti-Islamic autocracy and tribalism on the other — is too well known to outline in detail here.

Although the role of Islam in Egyptian foreign policy cannot emerge clearly from an examination of public pronouncements by state officials and other political leaders, it would be hasty and injudicious to conclude that Islam has no place in Egyptian policy orientation and policy formation. In fact, a further premise of this essay is that there is a significant and fundamental relationship between Egyptian policy and Islam, especially in the complex area of ideology -- in the formulation and reformulation of social and political goals and values for modern Egypt, and in the Nasir regime's conception of Arab nationalism and the unity of the Arab countries. The subtle involvement of Islam will be found in recent Egyptian ideological considerations of Arab socialism and the requisites of revolution. In the course of the chapter that follows, this kind of relationship between Islam and Egyptian policy, especially in the period since July 1961, is examined briefly and placed in historical perspective. Such an examination enables us to assess the use of Islam as an instrument of Egyptian policy, particularly the role of the religious institutions,[10] represented by the Azhar Mosque and University, in the mobilisation and effective utilisation of a religion-sanctioned political programme that can serve a so-called 'revolutionary Arab socialist policy' of liberation, industrialisation, and modernisation.

In this connection, it is suggested that all three variants of Islamic consciousness — solidarity, religious reform and socio-political activities — are involved in Egypt's recent bid, at least as expressed since May 1962, in Nasir's National Charter, to pre-empt the leadership of an emerging modern and socialist 'Arab nation'. Implicit, also, in this discussion, is the view that the revolutionary ideology and policy of radical reform in Egypt, as well as Egypt's policy against reactionary conservative regimes in some of the Arab states, are not really at variance with Islamic religious practices. To this extent, an intense preoccupation with the alleged conflict between religion and policy (or politics) would be unjustified and futile. At the same time, the incompatibility between Islam and nationalism assumed by students in the past becomes an academic myth (although theoretically tenable). For one may agree that the religious institution, which, according to Sir Hamilton Gibb, was characteristically separate from the political institution,[11] has lost the kind of independent influence it used to exert, say, in Mamluk or Ottoman Egypt, and has now come under the more direct and total control of the ruling establishment. Thus, it is now mobilised, or called upon, both to intellectualise and popularise the revolutionary nature of Islam, its socialist principles, and its modernising force. To be sure, it continues to check many proclivities on the part of the political institution to further secularise Arab society, or to recast its socio-political values on the basis of an ideology free of Islam, its tenets, or virtues. To this extent, religious leaders may exert a certain amount of influence over the rulers. But the objective of the state's policy is not hindered by such influence; on the contrary, in the pursuit of its political goals, the state tends to orient in its favour the men and institutions of religion by allocating new tasks to them. The state has thus been able to win the support of religious leaders and organisations, which, in turn, have recently tried to present the Egyptian revolutionary regime to the rest of the Muslim Arabs as the model of regenerated Islam and the harbinger of another Islamic Golden Age.[12]

More controversial, perhaps, is the suggestion that the belief and national-myth infrastructure of the political community, which Egyptian policy seeks to establish both in Egypt and in the other Arab countries, necessarily antedates secular nationalism. Realising the mistake of earlier liberal nationalists who attempted to undermine and displace the pre-nationalist Islamic ethos with a purely secular conception of nationalism, the present Egyptian regime is careful to avoid committing the same error in its search for a formula and basis of solidarity. The principles of its revolutionary Arab socialism are carefully linked to those of pre-nationalist ideological structures. Thus, Islam-sanctioned revolutionary nationalism — even socialism — serves to assimilate politically individuals and groups who for a long time have identified themselves with groups lesser than the state or nation, let alone an Arab nation. Thus, Islam-based revolutionary nationalism and socialism can more readily achieve the equation of the nation with the state and supersede all other group loyalties. The totalitarian nature of nationalism's demand for allegiance is more easily achieved when such nationalism derives from, or is inspired by, the value system of a religion which for over 1,300 years has regulated the social, political and cultural relations of individuals and states. One might even suggest, first, that there can be no purely secular Arab nationalism in Egypt, and, second, that secular nationalism is not really necessary for the attainment of modernity, a concept and condition until now essentially Western-inspired.[13] In this case, however, modernity does not presuppose or prescribe a democratic polity.

Besides the historical and legal background of Islam's inevitable involvement in Arab politics, and, in this case, in contemporary Egyptian policy, the Arabs' own preoccupation with their identity with Islam, both as a religion and a civilisation, renders it a major source, if not *the* source, of their national consciousness. It centres upon the Prophet Muhammad and the Holy Qur'an. One may well ask, 'What about pre-Islamic Arab consciousness?' The question is irrelevant, because modern

Arabs think in terms of a political consciousness that is directly identified with the political, military and imperial success of Islam, and, more
simply, the relation of this success to the spread of the Islamic message.
Thus, although the first political success of the Arabs on a mass scale
was achieved under the banner of Islam, Egyptians and other modern
Arabs began their national regeneration by questioning the strength
of the Islamic community *vis-à-vis* outside forces, before they could
awaken any feeling for an Arab nation. The theory holds for Egyptian
policy today. It was developed so that the political or national decline
of the Arabs was inexorably connected with the decline of Islamic
power. In this sense, Islam came to form the core of Arab national
ideology, a point of view accepted by apologists for Islam, particularly
the fundamentalists and conservatives among them. Their argument,
briefly, was that Islam minutely defined the relations between man and
God, man and the state, man and man; that it set up a system of values
and virtues whose attainment and maintenance constituted the Islamic
ideal state and society. Arab national strength declined with the deviation and unwillingness, or inability, of Muslims to strive for the attainment of this Islamic ideal. Instead, they strove for the attainment of an
ideal imported from Europe. This, according to Islamic nationalists, was
a mistake.

The Egyptian regime accepts these premises, but without the apology
or the fundamentalism. It merely starts with the assertion of a special
and privileged position for the Arab in the Islamic nexus. In such a
position, the Arab is duty-bound to effect the modernisation of Islam,
this in turn being measured by socio-economic and political advancement.

The first political feelings of solidarity along modern nationalist lines
were mixed with an Islamic aversion to control by infidels. Somewhat
later, there was an attempt to exclude the Islamic element from the
level of political organisation, administration, legislation, and economic
activity, in order to produce the machinery required for a viable modern
state. This practical exclusion of religion from state functions has not
only been accepted by many Arabs but continues unimpeded. What the
Egyptian regime has revived is the earlier conception of Arab Islamic
solidarity in order to activate the desire for independence, revolution,
and modernisation. In doing so, it has also found it necessary to re-
interpret the role of the Arabs in Islam, as well as the socio-economic
and political meaning of Islam itself. This reinterpretation of the role of
Islam in the so-called new Egyptian (or Arab socialist) society, which is
allegedly desired by all Arab revolutionaries and progressives, becomes

the arena of conflict with those who are opposed to such a society.[14]

An outline of the phases of Islamic reform in Egypt since 1870 will serve to illustrate these trends. Jamal al-Din al-Afghani brought to Egypt the call for Islamic solidarity, strength and unity with a view to opposing the encroachments of Europe. His legacy was one of active agitation for a stronger and united Islamic world. His disciple Muhammad 'Abduh settled for a quiet evolutionary and rationalist reform of Islam (i.e. one within the strict rules of theological discipline), in an attempt, first, to reconcile faith (or revelation) with reason as the basis for reform and modernisation, and, second, to educate the members of the Islamic community in such a way as to provide them with a responsible ethic or theory of action. 'Abduh's disciple, Rashid Rida, and his *Salafiyah* movement, with its theologically more systematic, albeit apologetic and therefore less positive, endeavour, represented a return to the practices of the orthodox religious doctors and a possible reinstitution of the caliphate. The ideas put forward by 'Abduh — that evolutionary reforms in theology, the educational institutions of al-Azhar, and the *Shari'ah* judiciary would gradually educate the Muslims and liberate their society from its backwardness and difficulties — were by the 1930s rejected in favour of more activist, authoritarian, and less theoretical Islamic nationalist tendencies[15] — a sort of a return to Afghani's activism, but with a serious difference. The activism now would apply specifically to Arabs, as the 'best' (*al-afdal*) in Islam, and would not seek a fundamentalist puritan return to the past, as did, for instance, the Wahhabi movement. This trend can perhaps explain the recent concentrated interest of Egyptian and other Arab authors in the Syrian 'Abd al-Rahman al-Kawakibi. The latter was very conscious of the weakness of the political community, which to him was synonymous with the *ummah*, or the religious community. But he was not disturbed by the weakness of the Ottoman state, only by the weakness of the Arabs, for they had the first role in Islam.[16] He was seeking to establish Islamic leadership for the Arabs to the exclusion of all other Muslims. This was also a goal of later Islamic nationalists, including the Muslim Brethren in Egypt, of theorists of Islamic nationalism such as 'Abd al-Rahman al-Bazzaz, and of Islamic leaders in Egypt such as Ahmad Fu'ad al-Ahwani, Muhammad al-Bahi, and Shaykh Mahmud Shaltut, Rector of al-Azhar.[17]

Finally, before proceeding with my analysis, it may be noted that Egyptian policy apparently does not aim at the establishment of an Islamic state in Egypt or of an Islamic Arab empire in the traditional-legal sense of these terms. We should not conclude, however, that the Egyptian rulers are not actively interested in the sense of pride and feeling of solidarity that a successful revolutionary integration of the Arabs under Egyptian leadership can engender with the aid of Islam.

This Egyptian model for revolution, properly steeped in Islamic virtue (provided Islam is carefully accommodated to the prevailing socio-political conditions when necessary) becomes that much more appealing. As Nasir himself told the Preparatory Committee of the Congress of Popular Forces in 1962:

> Egypt has no choice but to be Arab . . . Arab Egypt's struggle for Arab unity is a historical responsibility, shouldered by the Egyptian people as per their capabilities and resources . . . They [other Moslems] have forgotten that [Islam] is the religion of justice and equality . . . Religion is against social tyranny; against exploitation in all its aspects. The Islamic religion was the first revolution which established the principles of socialism, and these pertain to equality and justice.[18]

Sir Hamilton Gibb has argued that a significant effect of the abolition of the Ottoman Caliphate in 1924 was a tendency among some Arabs to work for a revival of Mahdism, which would forcefully integrate the Islamic world.[19] Although Egypt's policy favours an eclectic but tactical use of neo-Mahdism, Nasir's regime combines the establishment of a just and equitable Islamic realm in the Arab lands with socialism and the requisites of a modern industrialised state. The radical revolutionary aspect of the regime is no departure from Mahdism, since the latter is by definition revolutionary in nature.

I

The abolition of the caliphate by Kemal Atatürk in 1924 — indeed, the dismantling of the Islamic edifice in Turkey by the disestablishment of the *Shari'ah* — had strong repercussions among Egyptians. Their concern for its fate preoccupied them for at least three years, and involved not only al-Azhar and the *'ulama*, but also the Palace, parliament, and other Arab rulers.[20] This Egyptian attitude was inevitable considering the pre-eminent position of al-Azhar and Cairo in the world of Islamic learning, as centres for the propagation and defence of the faith. The upholders of Islamic tradition represented in al-Azhar and its related organisations were obviously shocked by the abrupt, forceful disposal of Islamic institutions. At the same time, Western-trained intellectuals became involved in a debate about the fundamental nature, and necessity, of such institutions.[21] The attack upon Islam was massive, but the defence was no less vociferous. Egyptians once again declared their national concern with the problems of the Islamic faith and community. One may argue that today, however, there is no concern over such matters as the caliphate, and that Egyptians have actually led in weakening the bases of Islamic institutions by abolishing the *Shari'ah* or religious courts, by curtailing the vast activities of traditional religious orders (*Tariqat*), and by introducing modern secular-inspired reforms into the very seat of Islamic learning and culture — al-Azhar and its related organisations. How can we then argue for a significant relationship between Islam and Egyptian policy today?

The performance of the military regime since 1952 indicates that a revolutionary group of nationalist leaders, the 'Free Officers', is conscious of (1) the importance and efficacy of the Islamic link between their goals and the mobilisation of the community for their achievement; (2) the necessity of resuming the efforts of Muslims to reform their religious and traditional institutions to meet the requirements of a modern age; and (3) the natural and useful connection between religious belief and political duty, insofar as this connection can inspire and invigorate political performance for the attainment of the new leadership's objectives at home and abroad.

The first dimension of the Free Officers' political orientation became apparent early in their rule. The destruction in 1954 of their political rivals and enemies, the Muslim Brethren, did not result in a sweeping attack upon all forms of religious activity, institutions, or thought. Instead, the ruling junta iterated its respect for, and adherence to, Islamic faith and culture, culminating in the establishment of the Islamic Congress in November 1954.[22] The events of 1955 — the Israeli raid on Gaza, the formation of the Baghdad Pact, and the Egyptian-Czech arms deal — further pushed the Egyptian leaders into an Arab-Islamic frame of political orientation and articulation, culminating in the rigorous and systematic use of the religious sermon (*khutbah*) for political purposes. The pulpit of the mosque became once again, as in earlier times, the platform for communication from the leader to the public.[23] The Suez Crisis of 1956 further accentuated the feeling of an infidel attack upon Islam, and Egyptian leaders sought to acquire the heroic aura of Saladin.

The two other dimensions of Egyptian policy orientation are only now becoming clear. They can best be traced through a discussion of, first, the National Charter of May 1962, and its importance to both Egypt and the larger Arab-Islamic community; second, the renewed

importance of al-Azhar, as indicated by the Reform and Reorganisation
Law of June 1961; and third, the marked concern of writers and intel-
lectuals with establishing a basically Arab-Islamic political legacy for
Egypt.

II

However one may assess the record of Nasir's regime over the past ten
years, one must recognise that since July 1961, it has come forward
with recommendations at home (and declarations abroad) that, theoretically at least, indicate serious revolutionary intentions. It is not im-
proper, therefore, to consider their importance for Egyptians at home
and their possible impact on the other Arab countries. That Egypt puts
forth the claim to lead the modernisation of Arab societies in the Middle
East was made clear on 21 May 1962, in President Nasir's Charter to the
Egyptian people. Briefly, the Charter proposes a political programme
for Egypt's 'Second Revolution',[24] initiated by the promulgation of
socialist measures in July 1961. Here, however, we are more concerned
with those proposals of the Charter that relate to Egypt's aspiration to
Arab leadership in terms of leading Arab society to modernity and the
Arab peoples to unity. We are also concerned with the relation between
Islam as defined in our introductory remarks and this desired Arab
leadership.

The Charter recognises the inadequacy of the traditional (as distinguished from the reinterpreted) Islamic ethic for the advancement of
Arab society. It proposes that social change must be radical; that the
enemy of the 'Arab nation' is no longer imperialism in its naked form
of direct control, but disguised through local reactionaries. The 'socialist
revolution' in Egypt is now the principal weapon against 'reaction' (as
Nasir said on 23 December 1961);[25] Cairo is the centre of social revolution for the whole Middle East. Egyptian socialism will emerge victorious from the battle against reaction to lead in unifying the Arab world
and liberating it from capitalist exploitation and imperialist domination.

In the Second Revolution the struggle for Arabism (i.e. Pan-Arabism)
is identified with the struggle for socialism, and Nasir now becomes
the champion of social reform and, as we shall see, of Islam-sanctioned
social reform. Egypt is seen as the *avant garde* of the Arab struggle, the
base of Arab unity and of a progressive Islamic community; those who
are opposed to Egypt's new socialism are really against any progress in
the Arab world *and* against the strengthening of Islamic society. The

Second Revolution will build an economically, socially and politically strong Egypt, a model of national endeavour to be emulated and a pioneer in Arab development. Egypt will also represent a reforming and modernising Islam, whereas rulers like King Husayn of Jordan and King Sa'ud of Arabia represent stagnating and reactionary Islam. The Charter, moreover, does not stop at the distinction between two types of Arab government — progressive, led by Egypt, on the one hand, and reactionary on the other — but argues that it is incumbent upon the people to defeat the latter, preferably with Egyptian help. 'The UAR, firmly convinced that she is an integral part of the Arab Nation, must propagate her call for unity and the principles it embodies, so that it should be at the disposal of every Arab citizen, without hesitating for one minute before the outworn argument that this would be considered an interference in the affairs of others.'[26] Apart from the obvious implications of this statement, the Charter suggests the existence of 'Arab citizens' as distinguished from the citizens of the various independent Arab states.

Egypt's selection to lead the Arab countries and unite them by socialist example is, on the surface, a plausible one. That she offers the most successful revolution, so far, against the previous generation of Arab leadership, is undeniable. That the regime in Egypt has broken the power of landowning pashas is also a valid claim. That it has survived foreign invasion is proudly proclaimed. At the same time, the capital city Cairo, with its Azhar University, seat of Islamic learning *par excellence* for a thousand years, its secular state universities, mass communication media (radio, television, press, cinema), and its literary and publishing activity, make Egypt easily the most advanced Arabic-speaking Muslim country today. It is on these bases that Nasir's regime came forward in 1962 to reiterate boldly that an Arab nation really exists, stretching from Morocco in the west to the Arabian (Persian) Gulf in the east. What makes the Arabs one nation, according to Nasir, is (1) their recent experience of freedom from foreign domination, (2) their desire to accede to modernity with all its emblems of economic and social well-being, (3) their aspiration to strength and unity, and (4) their Islamic faith. The fact that disparities in development exist among them is only a phase in the revolutionary process that now grips the entire Arab world; those that are not independent will soon become so; those under archaic political regimes will achieve more radical political arrangements. What this implies is that the ideal is no longer a mere weapon against outsiders; it has been turned inward against a certain class of Arab political leaders. Egyptian political leaders now argue that

to be a loyal Arab one must be a progressive socialist. If, then, as Islamic
leaders in Egypt have recently opined, to be a good Muslim, an Arab
must also be a socialist, one can argue that it is a duty of all good Muslims to render the community of the faithful socialist and, thus, progressive. Although it is difficult to elicit a secular nationalism from an
Islamic base, it is not unreasonable to expect that the rectification of
the Islamic community along socialist lines becomes an extension of
the moral duty of all 'Arab citizens' in the Egyptian definition. The
eradication of 'unprogressive' regimes by 'progressive' elements is thus
no longer immoral, and constitutes neither illegal subversion nor heretical internecine warfare among co-religionists.

If the preceding fairly, if briefly, represents what the Charter envisages as the role and destiny of Egypt — namely, to be the first Arab
nationalist, revolutionary, and progressive socialist society and political
system in the Arab Middle East — it also sets up Egypt as the model for
revolution throughout the Arab countries. Our earlier reference to the
nature and objectives of such revolution indicates a vigorously novel
departure from traditional Islam. This may well turn out to be the case.
But it has already been argued that the revolutionary regime has not
been, and is not now, willing to declare a total detachment from Islam;
on the contrary, it is anxious to carry it forward. I will now, therefore,
turn to a consideration of one of the methods being used to do this,
and suggest in conclusion that such an alliance with Islam is, for the
time being, necessary for Egypt's Arab policy.

The case study will deal with the efforts of al-Azhar and religious
leaders, as well as of some Egyptian intellectuals, to attune a reformed
and activated Islam to the requirements of Egypt's bid for the progressive leadership of all the Arabs. At the same time, I shall try to show
that the political establishment welcomes this support from the recognised centre of religious education, for it considers it effective both at
home and abroad.

III

Early attempts by Egyptian nationalist leaders to motivate Egyptian
society toward the attainment of modern national goals necessarily
included a desire to reform the religious institutions, especially if the
dichotomy between secular and religious education were not to continue. The great Shaykh Muhammad 'Abduh sought earnestly to reform
al-Azhar. Many of his followers, especially members of the Ummah

Party, and others since 1911, succeeded in getting the Egyptian government to enact a series of reform measures to meet this problem. Shaykhs such as al-Zawahiri, Mustafa 'Abd al-Raziq, and al-Maraghi attempted in one way or another to push al-Azhar into the main stream of modern society.[27] It was not until 23 June 1961 that the Egyptian government decreed the most radical and sweeping reform measure affecting al-Azhar and all of its institutions. Law No. 103/1961 is epochal not only in its aim of revolutionising the whole character of religious education, but also for its possible effects upon society as a whole and its impact among Arabs everywhere. The exciting potential of its success may have permanent repercussions in the Arab countries, and indeed in all Islamic societies.[28]

Bearing in mind our original premise that the regime in Egypt is consciously and deliberately seeking to associate its revolution and objectives with a reinterpreted Islamic nexus, two initial questions may be asked regarding the importance of al-Azhar. First, what is the Azharite reaction and response to the law of June 1961? Second, what is the Azharite view of Nasir's Charter for National Action presented on 21 May 1962? Since it is impossible to deal with these two questions by a complete perusal of all Azharite expressions over the past two years, we shall confine ourselves to statements by leading Azharites, such as Shaykh Shaltut, Shaykh of al-Azhar; Dr Muhammad al-Bahi, until recently Chancellor of al-Azhar University, and Ahmad Hasan al-Zayyat, Editor of *Majallat al-Azhar* (*Journal of the Azhar*).

Basically, Law No. 103/1961 (to reorganise al-Azhar and its affiliated institutions as justified in the Explanatory Memorandum of Minister of State Kamal al-Din Mahmud Rif'at) first concedes the central importance of al-Azhar for the continuance of the nation's religious and cultural personality. Second, it emphasises the importance of Azhar graduates trained in the modern way, who will contribute to the welfare of the Arab nation by recommending 'a reform movement to bring al-Azhar closer to the modern age, while retaining its special characteristics and values for the preservation of the faith and the protection of the Islamic heritage'. Third, the government sees no contradiction in reorganising al-Azhar as a modern institution of higher learning, because 'Islam in its true meaning does not distinguish between religious and secular knowledge. It is a social religion which regulates the conduct of man in life . . . Every Muslim must be a man of religion and of the world at one and the same time.' Fourth, by training the man of religion to earn his livelihood in modern professional and technical vocations, Egypt will ensure that no Azharite will be isolated from his fellow-citizens in a modern industrialised society. Thus, the importance of renovating al-Azhar lies in the recognition of its central place and contribution to the achievement of the goals of the Egyptian revolution. According to the Minister, previous attempts at reforming al-Azhar were superficial. In the past, al-Azhar itself was forced into rigid, backward conservatism because it had to defend Islam against foreign attack. Imperialism tried to promote a dichotomy between the Islamic heritage and modern life. Now, while al-Azhar must remain basically the largest single Islamic institution in the world, it must also be in a position to elevate and revive Islam by expanding the scope of knowledge. In this manner, al-Azhar will produce religious leaders who combine practical and scientific training with their religious mission. Religion will no longer be their only profession. Finally, when al-Azhar takes its proper place in the work of building a new society, the old barriers between al-Azhar as the 'fortress of Islam' and other Muslims will come tumbling down.

The most radical departure from Azharite tradition proposed by the Reorganisation Law is the introduction of four modern colleges: Government and Public Administration, Industry and Engineering, Agriculture, and Medicine. These are added to the original colleges of Sacred Law, Theology, and Arabic Studies. The importance of al-Azhar's work in Arab and non-Arab Islamic countries is reflected in the establishment of an Academy for Islamic Research and a Department of Islamic Education and Missions under the jurisdiction of the Higher Council of the University, headed by the Shaykh of al-Azhar.[29]

The reorganisation of al-Azhar is obviously designed to bring the Azharite closer to the political élite by introducing him to modern education and by allocating to him specific tasks of national and international importance, not necessarily at variance with his Islamic belief and sentiment. The regime therefore argues that al-Azhar must be strengthened in order to lead in the liberation of the Islamic community, and thus to remain, as always, the 'fortress of religion and Arabism'. The political significance of this measure can be appreciated from the fact that the reorganised Azhar will be independent of the state university system, which is normally under the direction of the Ministry of Education. Instead, over-all supervision of al-Azhar's affairs is entrusted to the Presidency of the Republic.[30]

Al-Azhar has a primary role in the communication between Egypt and the rest of the Arab and Muslim world and as the leading Muslim interpreter of the Egyptian revolution and its aims. 'Our Cultural Centres in Benghazi, Tripoli, Rabat, Omdurman, Accra, the Philippines,

Afghanistan, the USA, Germany, Austria, Italy, Switzerland, Spain, Lebanon, Morocco, Pakistan, India, Indonesia, China, and other cities of the world, radiate the light of our civilisation and culture until it covers all the corners of the universe.'[31] The message of the Egyptian Revolution which the learned men of religion explain and spread throughout the Muslim Arab countries is merely a continuation of Muhammad's mission fourteen centuries ago:

> We Muslims possess a glorious revolution proclaimed fourteen centuries ago, in order to restore to humanity its human sentiment and dignity, and to give man his proper due. He [Muhammad] proclaimed his revolution to destroy despotism and to realise the high principles of God, namely, security and honour. This most grandiose of revolutions included many dimensions: a scientific revolution (*Iqra' fi ismillah al-khaliq*), a social revolution with which all men become equal before God, distinguished only by piety, and a spiritual revolution in the direct relationship between God and man . . . In the face of a world in conflict our answer must be: to return to our Islamic revolution proclaimed by the Prophet in 622, to inspire us by its scientific, moral, and spiritual import.[32]

If we can accept the argument that the Egyptian regime considers a modernised and revitalised Azhar essential to the success of its revolutionary policy at home and the propagation of its liberating message for the Arabs abroad, how does al-Azhar itself view this politically allocated task? To put the question differently, how does al-Azhar as the accepted interpreter of Islam for Egypt, and the respected religious opinion-maker for the wider Islamic community, consider the regime's concept of revolution, socialism and Arab unity? Briefly, according to the Azharites, their role is to revive the socialism that is present in the original Islamic message and turn its meaning today into a national belief. Hence, the reorganisation of al-Azhar is 'one of the greatest revolutionary works, and will have a great influence on society and the other Islamic and Arabic nations'.[33]

Officially, at least, the Azhar hierarchy views Nasir's revolution, especially the Second Revolution, beginning in July 1961, and including the National Charter, as the start of a new era. The revolution has brought al-Azhar back to its original role in the propagation of the Islamic message and the building of an Arab society 'whose principles were laid down in the Charter upon the firm bases of religion, character, knowledge, work, justice, and sufficiency in freedom, peace and

unity'.[34] Al-Azhar welcomes the revolution because 'revolution is of its nature, and socialism of its spirit'. It further accepts the new Arab socialist order decreed by the revolution 'as the whole accepts its parts
. . . and because the mission of Muhammad cannot deny just socialism, for it was his message which rendered the poor his due of the rich man's wealth'.[35] Nasir's Charter, which the people have vowed to fulfil, consists of 'words from God, which were not expressed by anyone before him in the old days or today, in the West or the East, namely, that what the tormented and oppressed on earth desire they have found in the Charter'. The Islamic message is not dead; the Charter has recaptured the light of Islam from 'Omar in Medina to the kingship of Muawia [Mu'awiyah] in Damascus, from the Empire of Rashid in Baghdad to the Republic of Nasser in Cairo'.[36] The National Charter is therefore a gift from God, the renewed call to God via Nasir.

Mahmud Shaltut, Shaykh of al-Azhar, is a good example of the Islamic propagandist for Nasir's revolution and for the Egyptian model of Arab nationalism and socialism. He has urged Arab-Islamic societies to disengage themselves from a declining and degenerate West on the one hand and an arrogant East on the other. He counsels them to return to the real 'national personality' given to them by God in His Islamic message. This return will lead to unity among them, since their disunity was in great measure due to their earlier mistaken adoption of a foreign personality.[37] Concerning the unity of the Arab nation, Shaltut has both written and voiced (in broadcasts) statements consonant with official Egyptian policy and coincidental with specific acts of policy. Thus, since the Azhar Reorganisation Law, the so-called Socialist Laws of July 1961, and the proclamation of the Charter by Nasir, Shaltut has tried to underscore the Islamic basis of unity and the deviant nature of oppression and exploitation.[38] Lest 'they burn in hell', he warns believers not to aid the tyrants, those who have not established equality between ruler and subject and who perpetuate class distinctions in Arab society. This view not only coincides with the political leadership's identification of Arab tyrants and exploiters on the Voice of the Arabs Radio and in Cairo's newspapers, but also reflects the religious leadership's blessing of the proposed socialistic aims of the Charter. 'In the month of Ramadan, when Muslims submit to the teachings of God and His Guidance, He orders them to be one nation which does not know conflict and division.'[39]

Islam, according to Shaykh Shaltut, decreed the idea of social cooperation among the members of the *ummah*. So far (i.e. before Nasir's revolution), the basic shortcoming of Arab Islamic states has been the exploitation of the needy. The revolution has come now to repeat the chastisement of 'oppressive capitalism', which, in Shaltut's conception, includes the following vices: the extension of the power of the rich by their exploitation of the poor; the contravention of the Islamic 'popular formula' which commands mutual aid in society; the undermining of belief; the corruption of society by the extended control of the materialist spirit and mentality; the prevalence of fear among all social classes; and the increase of crime. What the revolution proposes to accomplish through its Charter, both in Egypt and elsewhere in the Arab world is really similar to what Islam came to accomplish against the oppressive capitalism of Mecca — namely, to combat this 'oppressive capitalism' through the *Shari'ah*, which sanctions social cooperation and prohibits all kinds of material exploitation of one group of people by another.[40] From this one may assume that in his capacity as Shaykh of al-Azhar, Shaltut is not only informing Muslims everywhere that the socialist revolution intended by Egypt is not at variance with the faith, but — more significantly for Egyptian foreign policy — that it is a continuation of the sacred mission of Islam itself. At the same time, he is warning Muslim Arabs that it is un-Islamic and sinful to permit the existence among them of what Egypt identifies as tyrannical and exploiting regimes.[41]

Another interesting aspect of Shaltut's work in the service of Egyptian policy pertains to his conception of the role of al-Azhar after the reorganisation. 'Indeed, al-Azhar is the spirit of both the Arab and Muslim life; it is also a positive factor in their progress and development.'[42] He asserts that Egypt's position as leader of all Muslims is not a result of progress imposed from outside but rather of al-Azhar's uninterrupted work and fame. Al-Azhar is the protector of both Islam and Arabism. 'By promulgating the new law, the UAR government is aiming at making al-Azhar — as it was 1,000 years ago — the stronghold of the *religion of Arabism*. It wants Islam to be revived.'[43]

One may well ask if Shaltut is not reading too much into the intentions of Egypt's political leaders. Do they, in fact, want Islam to be revived? Or do they merely want to assimilate its institutions and leadership into the policy apparatus of their proposed revolution? The latter possibility has been obvious for some time now. The revival of Islam, however, presents serious problems. First, what kind of Islam will it be, and second, what kind of a revival is planned? Our original thesis stressed the idea that the Egyptian leaders are now committed to a systematic accommodation of Islam to political reality that can also be used to buttress their revolutionary ideology and its export to the

Arabs outside Egypt. The Azharites, on the other hand, seem on the surface to assume that Nasir and his regime are interested in restoring the eminent position of religious institutions in the councils of state. This assumption may be exaggerated and over-enthusiastic. Nevertheless, the present Azharite leadership is encouraged to view Nasir as the leader who will elevate and extend Islamic power, for they see Islam as a force that will soon influence the modern world and possibly counteract Communism in Africa and Asia.[44]

Ahmad Hasan al-Zayyat, Editor of the *Azhar Journal*, is perhaps the most extreme of the Azharites in his assumption that the Nasir revolution will become synonymous with (1) the redemption of Muslim Arab society and (2) the restoration of Islamic power and glory. In an open letter addressed to President Nasir on the occasion of the Festival of Education, al-Zayyat declared that after a long period of stagnation,

> God has willed that the Arabs should have a fourth Golden Age, to surpass the brilliance of the three previous ones. And so has appeared your age, Mr. President, in which . . . have been applied the principles of Islam. These were understood and believed in earlier periods but never applied. In your age government is by consultation, wealth is shared, people are equal, and they are the source of political power.[45]

He thus singles out Nasir as a man with a mission (*dhu risalah*), whose message for the unity of the Arabs radiates from his Charter.

A more consistent and systematic attempt to present the Charter and its socialism as, basically, Muslim developments in Egypt, and desirable models for political action by other Arabs, has come from the pen of Muhammad al-Bahi, one-time Chancellor of al-Azhar University. An Islamic writer who is primarily conservative, al-Bahi has, since 1957, argued for a course in Egyptian policy that would permit the centring of the Egyptian revolution on 'the tenets and virtues' of Islam. In doing so, he has not refrained from attacking the secularist modernists who would work for a totally new ethic deriving from the existential characteristics of an industrial and technological society.[46] Briefly, al-Bahi has insisted that Arab socialism is no more than a reiteration of Islamic values. If it also aims at the betterment of Egyptian and Arab society through productive work that combines material with spiritual power, the Charter becomes 'a covenant on ourselves to be believers in God, in ourselves and our humanity in the Great Arab Homeland in which we live'.[47]

Al-Bahi equates the central Islamic belief in one God with the socialist belief in human values of justice, cooperation, and unity, so that the message of a reorganised Azhar becomes simply one of reviving these human values. Then, to the questions of what the socialist society is, and what the role of al-Azhar is in it, al-Bahi gives what he considers to be Islamic answers. Socialism, he asserts, is no more than the 'solidarity and unity of a people in order to prevent the demolition of human dignity at any moment by means of the misuse of fortune, which surely leads to slavery or to social injustice . . . to realise equilibrium in society and cover the needs of the needy. Surely such a society will be a co-operative and united one.'[48] Socialism is thus synonymous with humanism, and, even if the new revolutionary society will not be an Islamic one in the traditional sense, it will at least be one that revives 'the conditions that Islam has called people to since its advent' – i.e., a society in which social injustice has been removed. To this extent, Arab socialism will be based on the religion, because Islam is the source of its human values. The attitude of al-Azhar, therefore, to both the Charter and the Reorganisation Law decreed by the political leaders of the revolution, must be one that considers it a duty to call people to the society contemplated by the revolution. Al-Bahi even argues that Nasir was prompted to decree Law No. 103/1961 by his appreciation of the central role which al-Azhar can play in building this new Arab socialist society.[49]

Still more revealing is the view in Azharite literature of President Nasir as a revolutionary leader. This view is significant because of its circulation among Muslims outside Egypt. The most consistent picture is that of Nasir as the 'natural leader' to whom the people have entrusted the task of re-establishing the true religious base of the Arab nation.[50] Al-Zayyat claims that as far back as 1935, while editing another journal, *al-Risalah*, he prophesied Nasir's 'coming'. Nasir has come, like the Mahdi, to stamp out corruption and tyranny. His fierce call to social justice and Arab socialism has reverberated throughout the Arab world and especially the Arabian Peninsula, as has been evident in the Yemen.[51] The new revolutionary society Nasir proposed in his Charter is in accordance with the spirit of the sacred law, because, 'according to the nature of the message of the Islamic religion, God promulgated it a socialist one'. Thus, the July 1961 laws derive from 'our cultural heritage and our merciful sacred laws, as well as from the nature of our peaceful Arab people'.[52]

One can also deduce from the writings of the Azharites that the Arab socialist revolution can be led only by a 'naturally selected leader' (Nasir), a head of state in whom people confide and to whom they give their oath of allegiance (*bay'ah*). All their hopes lie in him, for he is one of them and reflects the spirit of the nation. In the Azharite view, Nasir's revolution aims at the restoration of the early socialism of Islam.

IV

One may object to the preceding rather lengthy consideration of Azharite opinion on Egyptian policy. The Azhar was known to lend the support of its Islamic prestige and pre-eminence to Egyptian policy before 1952. Could not perhaps this extremist reinterpretation of Islam, especially its relationship to socialism and a revolutionary Arab nationalism, reflect unavoidable obeisance to the power of an authoritarian regime that does not permit the proliferation of ideas or the free expression of opinions at variance with accepted policy? Or could it not also be the Azharite way of forestalling the development of Egyptian policy (socialism, Arabism, etc.) in a completely secular direction and orientation? Is al-Azhar, that is, eager to get the Egyptian ruling class to accept the premises that their revolution has better chances of success and that their Arab policy can be more convincing to other Arabs, if both are steeped in the values and virtues of Islam? For, in Egypt today, there are individuals and groups identified with the regime who would prefer a completely secular base for the revolution. These might be loosely characterised as leftist writers, critics, economists, and journalists. They are products of the secular state school and university systems who, with the arrival of the Free Officers in power, have attained favoured positions in career and professional circles.

In the last two to three years the question of the role of religion in Egypt's revolution and policy has been brought into sharper focus by the appearance of a new debate among certain Egyptian writers. This centres its attention upon the meaning of the Arab-Islamic heritage. What is this heritage? If it is Islamic, must it also be Arab, and vice versa? Was this heritage one of intellectual weakness and stagnation regarding the ability of man to organise his life and carve out his destiny on earth, or was it a source of strength combining mind and work for continuous progress? Those Egyptians who take the latter position in this debate argue simply that man is the most important living being of the universe, as he is the strongest, by virtue of his intellect and perception. He uses his mind to devise organisation and order for his existence and uses his hands to build his material environment and destiny. They further argue that the most important feature of human society is its evolution and constant change, two aspects whose rate and character depend in the first place on man's physical and material environment. It appears that such a position sanctifies the human mind and capacity for physical work to support an existential, secular conception of society. If this is the case, Egyptians holding this view are seriously challenging tradition and religion, for they are really claiming that man has the ability to discover the unknown, as well as himself. They are also saying that these ideas should form the basis of modern education and culture if the Egyptian revolution aims to found a new and modern society.

What is interesting, though, about this position is that its advocates use Arabic-Islamic sources to advance it, namely, the writings of Ibn-Khaldun. They argue that Ibn-Khaldun's historical work had a definitely rational and sociological approach. If an Arab Muslim of the fourteenth century could attain that degree of sophistication, it is fatuous for modern Arabs and Muslims to languish in the quagmire of stifling tradition. On the contrary, this intellectual heritage constitutes the strongest tradition of rationality and, therefore, progress, which contemporary Arabs must adopt as a model for their programmes of educational and cultural development.[53]

The adoption of reason as the basis for human endeavour is not, however, a novel idea or view in Egypt if one considers the works of Shibli Shumayyil, Salama Musa, Lutfi al-Sayyid, or even those of Ahmad Amin and Tawfiq al-Hakim. What *is* novel in the revived call for rationality today is the near-deification not only of the intellect but also of man's labour — especially manual labour — as is apparent in the writings of Muhammad Sidqi.[54] Moreover, this new approach seeks to 'socialise' the misfortune of the farming peasant, the *fallah*, by bothering the conscience of the Egyptians, as both 'Abd al-Rahman al-Sharqawi and Yusuf Idris have tried to do in their writings.[55] The trials and tribulations of the hard-working, lowly public official and his family are projected into the daily awareness of the emancipated Egyptian and Arab nationalist in an effort to evoke his sympathy.[56]

Thus, even this secular debate to identify and assign a political and intellectual legacy for the revolutionary society is anxious to utilise profitably the Arab-Islamic connection. Al-Azhar and conservative Islamic groups may have no choice but to recognise the importance of an adapted and slanted Islam. Not only has the attack upon its earlier identification with rigid tradition lasted for almost seventy-five years, but it now emerges under the influence of ideas and ideologies that became widespread after the Second World War: socialism, Communism, and 'development'. Moreover, the government itself has ordered

by decree the religious leaders and their institutions to join the bandwagon of modernisation, so to speak. Thus, if a maverick shaykh, Khalid
Muhammad Khalid, can call for a religion 'in the service of the people',
the Shaykh of al-Azhar himself can reconcile socialism with Islam.[57] If
President Nasir can assert that Arabs are the only people who own a
qiblah (direction for prayer), and that 'the pilgrimage should have a
potential political power', a Muslim nationalist associated with the
revolutionary aims of Egyptian policy can popularise the central importance of the religion as a factor in Arab nationalism.[58]

V

So far we have tried to show the association and accommodation of
Egypt's Arab policy with Islam and the measures taken by the Egyptian
regime to mobilise the institutions and men of religion to explain this
association in its various dimensions to the rest of the Arab world. Relevant to this explanation is the relationship of Islam to revolution and
to socialism, to Arab nationalism and unity. The political establishment
also decided that this explanation cannot be formulated effectively for
both Egyptians and Arabs without the reform of religious institutions
and, more significantly, without the reformulation of religious beliefs
themselves, in modern parlance, reflecting the realities of power. I beg
to submit that herein lies the possible contribution of Nasir's Egypt to
the resolution of the as yet ambivalent attitude of the Arabs regarding
the role and place of Islam in the evolution of a modern Arab society,
nation, and state. If successful, Egypt may conceivably secure a measure
of pre-eminence, if not hegemony, among radical Arab movements.
However, to equate this chance of success with ultimate Egyptian control of all Arab lands would, at this time, be a serious mistake.

The debate among Arabs so far regarding nationalism has raged
among four major groups: (1) those who insist upon an Islamic base
of solidarity and political action among all Arabs; (2) those who reject
the Islamic base completely in favour of a secular formula of popular
sovereignty; (3) those who wish to activate the Islamic base within the
framework of modern policy orientations in such a way as to render it
an efficacious mover to nationalist action throughout the Arab lands;
and (4) those who do not consider this connection at all, but who react
instinctively and emotionally as Muslims.

The third group appears of choice and necessity ascendant — even
dominant — at the present time. The mistake of the older, more enthus-

iastic secularists, who wished to reject the Islamic ethos, is being avoided, and there seems to be popular recognition that strength is to be derived from the revival of one's own heritage. For even when we speak of language, culture and history as factors in Arab nationalism, we find that, for the Arabs, all three have been closely connected with Islam. Under these circumstances, there seems to be a return to the idea of strengthening the Arab, but essentially Islamic, community. This return, however, does not represent a complete reversal in Egyptian thinking. Rather, it seeks to avoid the pitfalls of both apologia and fundamentalism and to concentrate instead on freeing Islam from the shackles of its own traditional inertia through reinterpretation. But reinterpretation is specifically a theological task, and what one perhaps confronts in Egypt is an attitude of accommodating Islamic ideas to the situation in which the community finds itself. This attitude, I beg to submit, is most interesting, and pregnant with possibilities, for Islam could always be accommodated, despite the argument that the gate of *ijtihad* has been closed for centuries, and *ijtihad* really pertains to theological interpretation. The accommodation of Islam, however, to the practical situation of the community is particularly within the reach of forceful and successful rulers: *man ishtaddat wat'atuhu wajabat ta'atuhu* (It is a religious duty to obey those who are powerful). Ever since Muhammad 'Abduh's first serious attempts to reform Islamic dogma, there has been a split in the ranks of the Egyptian *'ulama'* regarding the reform of Islam and related problems of modernisation. Although it is fair to say that the use of the *'ulama'* for political purposes is a basically un-Islamic practice, their gradual bureaucratisation by the Muhammad 'Ali dynasty and state established a tradition in Egypt of the control of the men and institutions of religion by whatever regime is in power. Similarly, the control of *awqaf* (endowments) by the state deprived al-Azhar and its affiliated institutions of their financial independence, thus also placing them under state control.

It is difficult to assume that the Azharites are really evolving any systematic political or revolutionary ideology based on Islam. Their educational and other activities rather represent an attempt to accommodate Islam to the requirements of an authorised policy. It is therefore safer and more accurate to speak of Egyptian policy than of Egyptian ideology. The latter is hard to ascertain from the record of the military regime so far, according to the accepted criteria of ideological formulation. What the Azharites are doing in the final analysis is nothing more or less than the bidding of the ruler.

In 1957 I argued that 'developments in the Arab countries tend to undermine the identification of national aspirations with a revived and active Islam'.[59] By 1961-2, on the strength of evidence coming from Egypt, I was forced to abandon this position and to argue instead that until patriotism, as distinguished from nationalism,[60] crystallises among members of the Arab communities, a nationalist interpretation of Islam remains the most efficient formula of consensus.[61] If Islam can also be interpreted in such a way as to sanction the policies and ideas required to revolutionise and modernise Arab society, its instrumentalism in politics is augmented for the benefit of those who use it. But it is often dangerous to develop or extract political theories from religion. In addition to being the most perfect religious message of God to man after a succession of imperfect revelations, Islam is singularly distinguished from other religions as a sacred juridical system. Essentially, it does not prohibit theoretical speculation about the nature of society, politics, and human behaviour. But, since it represents the most perfect revelation of God to man and the most satisfactory legal system for the regulation of the affairs of man and society, speculation about such matters is by definition limited to a process of deduction from given data and premises. Thus, the most advanced and systematic intellectual activity in Islam has consisted of compiling learned works on the sacred law. When the sacred law was discussed in relation to the state and the head of state — namely, the caliphate — it provided the basis for Muslim juridical thought and an interest in constitutional law. Any theoretical political speculation on the nature of the state and authority has been characterised by idealisations of political types.

Intellectual activities (even intellectual movements) in Islamic societies, particularly those that dealt with the state, power, and authority, have often, if not always, emanated from established authority (i.e., from the ruler). And this was particularly the situation in nineteenth-century Egypt. For a while, one might argue, the Western-influenced and Western-educated liberals, such as the late Ahmad Lutfi al-Sayyid and his colleagues at the turn of the century, essayed genuine speculation upon theoretical questions of politics, society, and man. But this kind of speculation and intellectual endeavour was completely outside the fundamental religious framework of Islam, and was short-lived. By 1930, enlightened liberal thought was discredited in Egypt and a variety of authoritarian mass movements and religious fundamentalist ideas came into fashion. With the rise to power of a military junta in 1952, free speculation upon basic issues of power and political organisation was prohibited. Speculation and theoretical exercise once more emanate from established authority, or from the ruler. The latter, moreover, has decreed the casting of Egyptian policy in a dual but not mutually exclusive direction — a presumably modern socialist one, whose principles and inspiration derive from an outside, non-Islamic source, and a local traditional one, Islam.

The fact that the ruler finds it necessary to do this, given his declared intention of bringing about revolutionary change both in Egypt and the rest of the Arab world, is an indication and admission of the significant and basic relationship between Islam and his policy abroad. It is in this relationship, I suggest, that one can take a long-range view of the use of Islam as an instrument in Egyptian foreign policy.

Notes

1. See *The National Charter of the United Arab Republic*, 21 May 1962 (Cairo: UAR Information Department, 1962).
2. See Albert Hourani, *Arabic Thought in the Liberal Age, 1798-1939* (London, 1962); Nadav Safran, *Egypt in Search of Political Community* (Cambridge, Mass., 1962); and Jamal M. Ahmed, *The Intellectual Origins of Egyptian Nationalism* (London, 1960). One of the main themes in my forthcoming volume, *A History of Modern Egypt, 1800-1960*, deals with this response. See *The Modern History of Egypt*, London, 1969, 1976. Second Revised Edition, *Egypt From Muhammad Ali to Sadat*, London, 1980, 1983.
3. Professor Vernon McKay has written extensively on Islam in Africa.
4. *Collected Speeches of President Nasser*, January-March 1960.
5. Ibid., April-June 1960.
6. Ibid.
7. Ibid.
8. Ibid., October-December 1960.
9. See Muhammad Ibrahim Hamzah, *Ishtirakiyat al islam wa al-ishtirakiyah al-gharbiyah* (Cairo, 1961), no. 12 in the series 'Dirasat fi al-Islam', issued by the Higher Council for Islamic Affairs, Ministry of Endowments. In his tract, Hamzah refers (p. 7) to the Prophet Muhammad as *'al-ishtiraki al-awwal'* ('the first socialist').
10. The term 'religious institution' as used here does not mean the existence of an organised religious hierarchy or priesthood such as exists in Christianity, but rather denotes the majority of religious leaders and teachers, as well as the religious and educational institutions and organisations, which are primarily concerned with teaching and maintaining the Islamic faith and tradition. An institution or organisation similar to the church does not exist in classical Islam.
11. See his 'An Interpretation of Islamic History', *Journal of World History*, vol. 1 (July 1953), pp. 39-62.
12. See Ahmad Hasan al Zayyat, editor of the *Journal of the Azhar*, in an editorial entitled 'An Open Letter to the President', proclaiming the Fourth Golden Age of Islam under President Nasir, in *Majallat al-Azhar*, vol. 34 (January 1963), pp. 573-5. 'The light of your judicious, balanced, and calm Charter will extend to every person and every land, as was extended the word of God, because it [the Charter] is the truth which God has placed in His *shari'ah* and the programme (*manhaj*) which He devised for all His creatures.' The other three Golden Ages in Islam, according to al-Zayyat, were: the Age of al-Rashid and his son al-Ma'mun in Baghdad, the Age of al-'Aziz and his son al-Hakim in Cairo, and the Age of al-Nasir and his son al-Hakam in Cordova.

13. The writer has argued this point intensively in the essay entitled 'Islam and Revolution' from which this chapter is adapted.

14. For example, the Cairo-versus-Mecca radio war as manifested in the psychological warfare and propaganda emanating from the Voice of the Arabs Radio in Cairo, on the one hand, and anti-Nasir broadcasts of Radio Mecca on the other.

15. Events in Europe during the 1920s and 1930s undoubtedly encouraged these trends and tendencies.

16. See his *Umm al-qura* (*The Mother of Cities*) (Aleppo, 1959). See also Muhammad Ahmad Khalafallah, *al-Kawakibi, hayatuhu wa ara'uhu* (Cairo), and Sami al-Dahhan, *'Abd al-Rahman al-Kawakibi* (Cairo). For an excellent discussion of al-Kawakibi's work, see Sylvia G. Haim, *Arab Nationalism: An Anthology* (Berkeley and Los Angeles, 1962), Introduction, especially pp. 25-9.

17. Ahmad Fu'ad al-Ahwani teaches philosophy at Cairo University. In December 1960, the Ministry of Culture published his tract, *al-Qawmiyah al-'arabiyah* (*Arab Nationalism*) (no. 27 in *al-Maktaba al-thaqafiyah* series of the Ministry); in this he discusses the role of religion in the genesis of an Arab national ideology. Dr Muhammad al-Bahi was Chancellor of al-Azhar University until September 1961. Now Minister of Endowments, he continues to act as Chancellor of the University. Shaykh Shaltut, Imam and Rector of al-Azhar Mosque, publicly declared the Islamic sanction of Egypt's socialist laws of July 1961, in a long pronouncement published in the official newspaper, *al-Goumhouriyya* (*al-Jumhuriyah*), 22 December 1961. (Shaykh Shaltut died in Cairo on 16 June 1964.)

18. See *Khutab al-ra'is Jamal 'Abd al-Nasir*, November 1961-February 1962, pp. 107, 113.

19. See his *Modern Trends in Islam* (Chicago, 1947), pp. 106-29. The other two tendencies, according to Gibb, were for (1) a Pan-Islamic idea of a spiritual caliphate, and (2) a complete dissolution of the institution and its replacement by modern national sovereignty.

20. See Ahmad Shafiq Pasha, *Hawliyat Misr al-Siyasiyah* (Cairo, 1925, 1929), vol. I, pp. 119-21; vol. III, pp. 40-391. See also Elie Kedourie, 'Egypt and the Caliphate 1915-46', *Journal of the Royal Asiatic Society*, parts 3 and 4, 1963, pp. 208-48.

21. See Shaykh 'Ali 'Abd al-Raziq, *al-Islam wa usul al-hukm'* (Cairo, 1925); French translation by L. Bercher, 'L'Islam et les bases du pouvoir', *Revue des études islamiques*, vol. 7 (1933), pp. 353-91, and vol. 8 (1934), pp. 163-222; and A. Sanhoury, *Le Califat* (Paris, 1926).

22. For a brief appraisal of the Islamic Congress, see the writer's *The Egyptian Army in Politics* (Bloomington, Indiana, 1961), chapter VII. In his *The Philosophy of the Revolution*, President Nasir projected the thought, 'The Pilgrimage should have a potentially powerful significance.' Writing elsewhere, Nasir asserted that the Arabs are the only people who own a *qiblah* (direction of prayer). See *al-Hilal*, vol. 65 (January 1957), Special Issue: 'Our Arab Nation'.

23. For example, President Nasir's well-known introduction to his public rally speeches, 'As is my practice and custom, I always try to keep you abreast of what is happening.'

24. The writer originally used the term 'Second Revolution' in his 'Nasser's Second Revolution', *SAIS Review*, vol. 6 (Spring 1962), pp. 3-9.

25. Victory Day Speech, Port Said, UAR, *Arab Political Encyclopedia*, Documents and Notes, Tenth Year, December 1961 (Cairo, Information Department), pp. 131-2.

26. See *Charter*, p. 94.

27. See the interesting biographical work of Dr Fakhr al-Din al-Ahmadi al-Zawahiri, *al-Siyasah wa al-Azhar* (*Politics and al-Azhar*) (Cairo, 1945), which is presumably based on the memoirs of Shaykh Muhammad al-Ahmadi al-Zawahiri,

Shaykh of al-Azhar, 1929-35. See also Shaykh 'Ali 'Abd al-Raziq, *Min athar Mustafa 'Abd al-Raziq* (Cairo, 1957). There are numerous works by Egyptians on the history of al-Azhar and the various attempts at reform. Bayard Dodge, *Al-Azhar, A Millenium of Muslim Learning* (Washington, DC, 1961) lists the various reform measures and laws, but is not useful as an analytical treatise on al-Azhar and its problems. See also, 'Azhar', *Encyclopaedia of Islam* (new edition, 1960), vol. I, pp. 813-21.

28. The text of the law, together with the Explanatory Memorandum of the Minister of State, are readily available in *Majallat al-Azhar*, vol. 33 (July 1961), pp. 237-64. A French translation of the Explanatory Memorandum is found in *MIDEO*, vol. 6 (1959-61), pp. 474-84.

29. Writing in 1962, Hasan al-Ashmuni stated that there were 3,022 Egyptian teachers abroad in twenty Afro-Asian countries in 1959-60, and that the number of foreign students studying in Egypt in the same year numbered 14,349. 'Thus', he says, 'the Arabs have retrieved their glories.' See his tract, *Mujtama' una al-jadid wa al-Shari'ah al-islamiyah (Our New Society and the Shari'ah)*, no. 23 (12 November 1962) in the series *Dirasat fi al-Islam*, of the Higher Council for Islamic Affairs, Ministry of Endowments (Cairo, 1962), p. 74. In February 1959, al-Azhar published a 64-page brochure, *al-Azhar fi sutur*, aimed at non-Egyptian readers and audiences. It contains statistics about Azhar enrollments and offerings to foreign students.

30. The regime also has paid special attention to the efforts of the Department of Islamic Affairs and Studies of the Ministry of Endowments, which sponsors essay and book competitions among Muslim students in Egypt and elsewhere. The Department's journal *Minbar al-Islam (The Pulpit of Islam)*, founded in 1960, complements the *Journal of the Azhar* in many ways. It also publishes a series of popular monographs on Islamic subjects. (See *MIDEO*, vol. 6 (1959-61), pp. 470-2.) An interesting series of lectures delivered at al-Azhar by leading Egyptian writers, teachers, and scholars, under the auspices of Shaykh Shaltut, the Rector, was published in Cairo in 1960. The theme of most of these is the relationship between Islam and the requirements of a modern society.

31. Al-Ashmuni, p. 75.

32. Friday Sermon by Anwar al-Sadat in al-Azhar on 22 March 1959, reported in *al-Ahram*, 23 March 1959.

33. See Muhammad al-Bahi, 'al-Quwa al-sha'biyah wa kaifah tu 'abba' nahwah al-ishtirakiyah al-'arabiyah' in *Majallat al-Azhar*, vol. 33 (January 1962), pp. 926-39.

34. See Ahmad Hasan al-Zayyat, 'Am jadid 'ala Azhar jadid' in *Majallat al-Azhar*, vol. 34 (June 1962), p. 3.

35. Ibid., p. 2.

36. Ibid.

37. See his 'al-Ishtirakiyah al-samawiyah li al-ummah', *Majallat al-Azhar*, vol. 34 (January 1963), pp. 576-9.

38. See his editorial 'al-Imam wa al-istiqama tariq al-amn wa al-salam', vol. 34 (October 1962), pp. 6-9.

39. See his editorial, 'al-Shakhsiyah al-diniyah lijama' at al-muslimin', vol. 33 (April 1962), pp. 1291-5. Shaltut's approach to the Islamic community in this editorial is similar to President Nasir's interpretation of the significance of the pilgrimage and the *qiblah*.

40. See his editorial, 'Mawqif al-islam min al-mustaghillin', vol. 33 (March 1962), pp. 1168-75.

41. This view is more strongly expressed by Ahmad Hasan al-Zayyat. See his 'al-Jazirah al-'arabiyah tantafidu marratan ukhra', *Majallat al-Azhar*, vol. 34 (November 1962), pp. 325-88, in which he openly discusses the situation in the

Yemen and the 'tyrannical' ruling houses of Jordan and Saudi Arabia.

42. See his English editorial, 'The Message of al-Azhar After Its Reorganisation', *Majallat al-Azhar*, vol. 33 (January 1962), pp. 16-20.

43. Ibid. In a speech at the Ibn-Khaldun festival, Shaltut laid greater stress on the Arabism of the religion when he said: 'The Arab *ummah* was the nucleus of the elite leadership of the Islamic community when it carried Islam's message and spread it eastward and westward.' See 'Kalimat al-imam al-akbar fi mahrajan ibn-Khaldun', pp. 907-9.

44. See the interesting article by Mahmud Hoballah, 'al-Islam wa al-alam', *Majallat al-Azhar*, vol. 34 (January 1963), pp. 593-600.

45. See his editorial, 'Sayyidi al-ra'is', *Majallat al-Azhar*, vol. 34 (January 1963), pp. 573-5.

46. See especially his *al-Fikr al-islami al-hadith* (Cairo, 1957).

47. 'An Idea and Its Utilization', *Majallat al-Azhar*, vol. 34 (July 1962), pp. 16-20.

48. 'The Duty of al-Azhar Toward the Mobilization of the National Power', vol. 33 (April 1962), pp. 14-23.

49. Ibid. Al-Bahi argues further that the overall objective of the revolution, the Charter, and the Reorganisation Law of al-Azhar is to gear Islamic values to the modern world. Thus, he ends his article: 'Praise be to God for the advent of the revolution and its leaders.' In his article 'al-Tadayyun dururaton li-hayat al-ummah wa al-afrad', *Majallat al-Azhar*, vol. 33 (March 1962), pp. 1250-5, Muhammad al-Nawawi considers Nasir as the leader who is recapturing the true religious base of the nation.

50. Al-Bahi also argues that the leaders of the revolution which aims to mobilise national power toward socialism must be 'naturally selected'. This is also the thesis of Hasan al-Ashmuni, namely the reconciliation of the socialist laws of July 1961, the programme of the National Charter with Islam. Muhammad Hamzah, on the other hand, considers the revolution as the force that will restore early Islamic socialism. See his, *al-Ishtirakiyah al-islamiyah wa al-ishtirakiyah al-gharbiyah* (Cairo, 1961), *Dirasat fi al-Islam* Series of the Higher Council for Islamic Affairs, Ministry of Endowments, no. 12, pp. 99ff. Al-Ashmuni, moreover, argues that Egypt's new socialist and revolutionary society is based on the *Shari'ah*; that the socialist laws of July 1961 were inspired by the heritage of Islamic values; in short, that the majority of legislative acts by the revolution since 1952 are consonant with the spirit of the sacred law – a link between the past and the present. As for al-Bahi's 'naturally selected leaders' for the revolution, Ashmuni supports this view by arguing that the revolution and the new society are led by a head of state who through the *bay'ah* acquires the confidence and trust of the people. Conversely, the people place all their hopes in him, as he is one of them.

51. Al-Zayyat claims that in April 1940, he said in his journal *al-Risalah*, 'O God we ask Thee for the shepherd who will turn away the wolf . . . who will reconcile faith with reason, and private with public interest and welfare . . . All these attributes O our Lord will be found in one man, closest to the expected Mahdi and the promised Jesus.' Nasir presumably fulfilled this entreaty to the Heavens in 1940, so that all al-Zayyat and Egyptians have to do now is repeat the formula, 'We ask the Lord to prolong Your rule and strengthen Your power,' i.e., the rule and power of President Nasir. As usual, there is no conception of a limited duration for the tenure of public office or power by one man.

52. Al-Zayyat, vol. 34 (January 1963), pp. 573-5.

53. See, for example, the interesting book by Rushdi Salih, *Rajul fi al-Qahirah* (Cairo) and his article 'Tarikh ibn-Khaldun yantami li al-hadarah al-'arabiyah wa al-lughah al-'arabiyah', *al-Kitab* (October 1961), pp. 28-39.

54. See, for instance, his *al-Aidi al-khashina* (Cairo, 1958).

55. See, for example, al-Sharqawi, *al-Ard* (Cairo, 1954); an English translation, by Desmond Stewart, *Egyptian Earth*, appeared in London in 1962; and Yusuf Idris, *Hadithat sharaf* (Beirut, 1958). Al-Sharqawi has recently published an interesting book, *Muhammad Rasul al-hurriyah* (*Muhammad, Apostle of Freedom*) (Cairo, 1962). See a critical review of this book in *Majallat al-Azhar*, vol. 34 (June 1962), pp. 106-9.

56. See the famous trilogy by Najib Mahfuz, *Bayn al-qasrayn*, *Qasr al-shawq*, and *al-Sukkariyah* (Cairo, 1956-7). Generally on the intellectuals, see the writer's 'al-Muthaqqaf al-'Arabi wa al-mujtma' al-hadith' ('The Arab Intellectual and Modern Society'), *HIWAR*, vol. 1 (May-June 1963), pp. 41-51, and the response to it in the Cairo newspaper *al-Goumbouriyya*, 13 and 19 June 1963.

57. See Khalid Muhammad Khalid, *al-Din fi khidmat al-sha'b* (Cairo), and Shaykh Shaltut in *al-Goumhouriyya*, 22 December 1961.

58. Ahmad al-Ahwani, *al-Qawmiyah al-'arabiyah* (Cairo, 1960).

59. 'Recent Developments in Islam', *Tensions in the Middle East*, P.W. Thayer (ed.) (Baltimore, 1958), p. 178.

60. For an interesting distinction between these two concepts, see Bernard Lewis, *The Middle East and the West* (Bloomington, Indiana, and London, 1964), Chapter 4.

61. See 'Dilemmas of Political Leadership in the Arab Middle East', *American Political Science Review*, vol. 55 (March 1961), pp. 103-11; and 'Foreign Policy of Egypt', *Foreign Policy in World Politics*, Roy C. Macridis (ed.) (2nd edn; Englewood Cliffs, NJ, 1962), pp. 335-59.

4 THE RISE OF THE CLERISOCRACY

Just before noon one Monday morning in June 1940 Italian aircraft bombed the Iraq Petroleum Company's Storage Tank Farm in Haifa Bay, Palestine. There were then no anti-aircraft defences in place, and the raid was over in a matter of minutes. One of our neighbours was a charming Muslim lady, living with her daughter. On hearing the deafening rumble of bombs dropped from an appreciable height, she grabbed her Koran and dashed out to an olive grove opposite the house, where she proceeded to read — recite — for protection against what she thought was a terrible natural catastrophe. A week later, on a Friday noon, *Il Duce*'s airforce was back, this time to bomb other installations in the industrial complex of the Kishon river. As it coincided with the Friday noon prayers at the main mosque in East Haifa, the faithful came out to applaud the Italian raiders, the enemies of their enemies, the British.

As a young teenager, I was impressed first by the deep, transcendent faith of my neighbour, placing all her trust for her physical safety in the protection offered by the revealed word of God — as well as perhaps ascertaining her Islamicity were she to meet her Maker — and second, by the reckless expression of defiance of the mosque congregation. But I could not then understand the significance of any of this. With hindsight, I could suggest that the two episodes encapsulate the oft-quoted depiction of Islam as 'religion and state' (*din wa dawla*), spiritual and temporal, other- and this-worldly. Thus my neighbour exemplified the Muslim's strict adherence to the faith which admonishes that there is no way or power without God, and the gesture of the mosque congregation the religious expression of a political perception or view.

Later, as an undergraduate in Cairo in February 1946, I witnessed one of the most massive and bloody demonstrations against the British. I had been blithely sitting in a philosophy class when the clash between demonstrators on one side and Egyptian police and British forces guarding the Kasr el-Nil Barracks on the other in nearby Midan Ismailia (after 1952, Tahrir, now Sadat) resulted in several casualties — dead and wounded. Demonstrators urgently demanded our assistance, screaming '*shahid, shahid*' (martyr, martyr). Those who had fallen were martyrs in the Holy War (*jihad*) against the British.

Source: *Encounter*, vol. LVIII, no. 3 (March 1982), pp. 68-76.

The use of religion by Muslim rulers and their opponents in nationalist political activity is at least a century old. That is why perhaps in the late nineteenth century European writers wrote about 'Islam inflamed' and 'the revival of the East'. Today they write about 'the resurgence of Islam', 'Islam on the march', 'the dagger of Islam', and so on. To some extent, this is due to the loss of political control by Europeans over Muslim lands and their perception of a threat emanating from the attempt by Muslim rulers in the last two decades, say, to assert their influence in local, regional and world affairs. But it is also due to the fact that religion has been used by Muslims to confront, resist and thwart the encroachments of European power and ideas, and the economic, cultural, social and political changes which these brought, and continue to bring, in their wake.

This personal digression is intended to highlight the overwhelming feeling and sense of religious community and identity among Muslims, the cohesive bond of faith and its social force, as well as its potency as a political idiom and weapon. But it is also meant to suggest that, in the final analysis, it does not matter what non-Muslims say about Islam, whether in interpreting its meaning or its political import. It has meaning only for Muslims, and its use in political discourse and action can be determined only by them. The outsider can merely try to assess its impact or effect on those who do not share the faith, by studying its history, observing the economic, social and political behaviour of its practitioners, and by trying to gauge, as well as understand, what it is that Muslims seek or want.

Clearly there are Muslims today who seek to restore lost power by recapturing an idealised glorious past and establishing a 'true' Islamic state and society; that is, one that is regulated and governed exclusively by the religious or sacred law (the *sharia*). To do this, however, they must come to grips, more successfully than their predecessors have in the past, with a very old and difficult problem — that of the relationship between power and religion, or temporal authority and the faith, or religion and state. To this extent, the crisis in Islam is one that concerns Muslims; they alone can resolve it, if at all.

The collision between Islam as the focus of popular loyalty and the determinant of mass political perceptions and aspirations on the one side and the modernity borrowed by the official and intellectual classes from the West on the other, produced spiritual tension, intellectual disorientation, social dislocation, political conflict, turmoil and upheaval. Its apparent consequences have been unsettling in an area of great economic and strategic interest to the rest of the world and particularly to the two rival superpowers, the USA and the Soviet Union. The prospect of social upheaval and political instability greatly preoccupies the Western industrial states which are so heavily dependent for their energy supplies on the very core of the Islamic world: Arabia, the Gulf, Libya, and Iran. For this reason Westerners are now very concerned – perhaps obsessed – with what they see as the 'revival' or 'resurgence' of Islam, for they perceive this as a looming threat on the horizon of an international economic and political order originally devised and controlled by the West.

To be sure, Islam in the last two decades (as claimed, represented, projected or led, by a variety of rulers and leaders who do not necessarily agree with one another) has begun to assert itself in international politics and the internal affairs of most Islamic states. On the former plane, this is the result of the proliferation of independent states after the Second World War and the fantastic enrichment of some of them from oil revenues. On the latter, it is a consequence of the failure of imported, or borrowed, Western ideologies, chief among them nationalism and socialism – as well as models of development and modernisation – to take root in Islamic societies and provide the kind of institutions and processes which can cope with a vast array of economic and social problems, and change. Alien 'truth' of infidel provenance failed to fire the imagination of the faithful Muslim masses, to provide a substitute basis for their social cohesiveness and national unity, or to tackle the problems of modernity. For a long time, in fact since the ninth century, mainly despotic rulers were obeyed but kept at a safe distance, partly because Muslims had developed a comfortable social order based on an intricate network of personal and group loyalties and obligations. At the same time, rulers had not undertaken complex functions, beyond taxation and the defence of the realm. Nor had they made unfulfillable promises. They may have been usurpers and illegitimate satraps in the eyes of many of their subjects. What counted, however, is that the social order was legitimate because it was governed by the law of God.

Modern integrative notions of society and politics produced a dichotomy, and caused a disparity between an emulative 'modern' political arrangement and a traditional social order. The failure of the former at a time of rapid economic growth, vast demographic change, social dislocation and spiritual and intellectual disorientation, was apt to provoke a return for answers to the traditional native idiom of religion; not, dare one say, a reaction that is unique or peculiar to Muslims in the annals of human experience. Thus in an article in *Commentary* (January 1976), Bernard Lewis wrote of 'The Return of Islam' in this sense. He emphasised the point that an entire civilisation has religion as its primary loyalty, underlined the universality and centrality of its faith, and drew attention to the association from the start of that faith with power: the believers constitute a community and polity; religion, not nation or country, is the basis of identity and loyalty. Looking briefly at the record of the secular nationalist movement, he observed that as nationalism became more popular and radical, it also became less secular and more religious. He concluded that Islam is a powerful but as yet undirected force in politics, since it has yet to find its own convincing leadership.

Edward Said criticises Lewis for implying that Islam has 'returned' to confront and challenge the West as a hostile force. Said's main argument is:

> that the canonical, orthodox coverage of Islam that we find in the academy, in the government, and in the media is all interrelated and has been more diffused, has seemed *more* persuasive and influential, in the West than any other 'coverage' or interpretation. The success of this coverage can be attributed to the political influence of those people and institutions producing it rather than necessarily to truth or accuracy . . . this coverage has served purposes only tangentially related to actual knowledge of Islam itself.

In *Covering Islam*, the third tract of his 'critique of the West' trilogy,[1] Said claims that the purpose of those Western reporters on Islam (academics, government officials and journalists) is not simply to 'cover' Islam in the manner of reporting about it, but to give it a biased interpretation by covering its true meaning to suit the political predilections and power-purposes of the West.

For Said all knowledge in the West is affiliated with power. He accuses Western media, government officials and academics of constructing an 'Image of Islam' calculated to elicit the hostility of Western societies. He states that after the Second World War the USA took over the earlier British and French imperial role in the Middle East. That it acquired a global role as defender of Western interests there is no doubt, but the record shows, as Elie Kedourie has argued on the basis of massive documentation, that it did so with a curious anti-imperialist ideology.[2] Said declares:

> I do not believe as strongly and as firmly in the notion of 'Islam' as many experts, policy-makers and general intellectuals do; on the

contrary, I often think it has been more of a hindrance than a help
in understanding what moves people and societies.

Theoretically one may agree with him for, after all, phrases like 'Islamic
resurgence' or 'revival of Islam' reflect an intellectual approach to the
problem of Islam in society and politics, as well as in ideological discourse, but do not help in describing or explaining actual change, its
level, intensity and direction. Yet the Muslim himself believes in the
construct and idea, and many of his concerns, aspirations, and dislikes
are couched in this idiom, whether one is dealing with events in Iran,
Pakistan, Libya, Saudi Arabia, or the activities of militant Islamic
groups in Egypt and elsewhere. And this is clearly what many Western
students, as well as Muslim students, are reporting and studying.

The point is amply illustrated by V.S. Naipaul in his *Among the Believers*.[3] He quotes the *Tehran Times* as follows:

> The history of Pakistan and the Islamic Revolution in Iran is a re-
> minder of the power of religion and the hollowness of secular cults.
> How the world works is the concern of science, and how society is
> to be governed is the affair of politicians, but what the whole thing
> means is the main concern of Iran and Pakistan. Politics is combined
> with religion and Islam. Iran and Pakistan can join hands to prove to
> the world that Islam is not just a faith of the past, practising ancient
> rituals.

Khomeini's tolerant tone in January 1979 when he appealed to the
Christians of the world while still in exile was replaced by his strident
fulmination in August after his triumph in Iran:

> The governments of the world should know that Islam cannot be
> defeated. Islam will be victorious in all the countries of the world,
> and Islam and the teachings of the Koran will prevail all over the
> world.

But Naipaul also alludes to the Muslim's ambivalence towards change
which has come mainly from the outside, i.e., the West:

> It was of the beauty of Islamic law I heard a third Iranian speak.
> But what was he doing studying law in an American university?
> What had attracted these Iranians to the United States and the civil-
> ization it represented? . . . it was more than a need for education and

skills. But the attraction wasn't admitted; and in that attraction, too humiliating for an old and proud people to admit, there lay disturbance – expressed in dandyism, mimicry, boasting, and rejection.

Khomeini may be the interpreter of God's will, leader of the faithful, but he also expressed

> all the confusion of his people and made it appear like glory, like the familiar faith: the confusion of a people of high medieval culture awakening to oil and money, a sense of power and violation, and a knowledge of a great new encircling civilization. That civilization couldn't be mastered. It was rejected; at the same time it was to be depended on.

In fact, it is the modernity which the radical Muslim anathematises and rejects which has radicalised him; a point closely argued by Elie Kedourie, and by many of the contributors to *Islam and Power*.[4] The editors of this slim volume in fact argue that 'Muslim reawakening does not simply reflect the reaffirmation of Muslims in their faith, but rather expresses deep-seated social concerns that are reflected in a situation of a 'society-in-crisis'. At the same time, they emphasise the static Islamic concept of history and the restorative nature of the militant Islamic movement, which holds that 'progress . . . must have as its aim the restoration of the true community'. They also view the activation of political Islam as part of the process by which Islamic communities try to accommodate themselves to the modern world. Naipaul concludes his Islamic journey by opining that 'in Iran and elsewhere men would have to make their peace with the world which they knew existed beyond the faith'. The life that had come to Islam, he discovered,

> had not come from within. It had come from outside events and circumstances, the spread of the universal civilization. It was the late twentieth century that had made Islam revolutionary . . . It was the late twentieth century – and not the faith – that could supply the answers – in institutions, legislation, economic systems.

American stereotypes about Islam, especially over the Iran crisis (1979-81), were not really constructed by orientalists or academics. Possibly the vacillating American policy, the initial mistake of depending on an 'alliance' with a despot, and mindlessly providing him with a huge arsenal (given the tension, instability and endemic conflict the Middle

East region generates, all alliances are precarious), contributed to the reaction. The USA as Satan and Western Imperialism as the Enemy are not strictly recent epithets of abuse, or expressed hostility, by Muslims.[5] Thus in discussing Iran, Edward Said refers to 'the attempted coup, directly encouraged by the United States' General Huyser in late January 1979'. The contributors to *The Security of the Persian Gulf*, edited by Hossein Amirsadeghi,[6] show that General Huyser, on the contrary, was anxious to forestall such an eventuality. Furthermore, throughout the USA-Iranian relationship, especially after the oil crisis of 1973-4, it was the Tehran tail that wagged the Washington dog. Besides, as the crisis mounted in 1978-9, Iranian generals were so mistrustful of one another that their intrigues precluded a successful coup. Finally, the problem of mutual perceptions which Edward Said rightly raises would be illuminated by the reverse exercise to 'Orientalism', namely, 'Occidentalism': how the Muslims have viewed, and view, the West.

It is only natural for a non-Muslim like Said to de-emphasise the notion of Islam. But as I stated earlier, it does not matter what non-Muslims say; Muslims themselves proclaim Islam as their prime concern and the new force in their search for cultural reassertion and political rehabilitation.

It is of course correct that one cannot consider Islam – transcendent, mystical or immanent – as a monolith. Its history abounds with a diversity of religious, social and political adaptive experience. In fact, its political pluralism has been its most salient feature, ranging in diversity from Central Asia to West Africa and from North Africa to Indonesia and the Philippines. Nevertheless the core of the faith, which requires a Muslim to live according to the precepts of the sacred law (a law which must inspire not only his spiritual life and guide his personal conduct but also regulate his relations with other men) is common to all Muslims everywhere. For the immanentists among them, the faith further enjoins the believers actively to seek to realise on earth the divine pattern of the universe decreed and revealed by God in His revelation to His Apostle. This is what Khomeini, albeit in the Shiite version of Islam, is about; this is what Gaddafi has called for in his 'Third International Theory'. It is fortuitous no doubt that riches from oil[7] can push forward the claims of this recipe.

The pluralism one found within Islamic societies has, however, been eroded by modernity; it remains on the interstate or international level. There are several states that are Islamic in the sense that the majority of their populations are Muslim, and the recognised official religion of the state is Islam (giving rise to communal and sectarian problems).

Ernest Gellner argues in *Muslim Society*[8] that 'cultural and religious pluralism' were 'tolerated or exploited by the weak traditional state', but that 'it is difficult to sustain in the modern, post-independence situation'. He is referring to the integrationist demands of the modern nation-state and the pulverising capabilities of the powerful centralised state. But he constructs his theoretical model for a sociology of Islam almost entirely on the basis of Ibn Khaldun's *Muqaddima*.[9] This, as he concedes, is relevant to the peculiar condition of the tribal segmented society in the Maghreb, and he admits that it cannot explain the Ottoman phenomenon. Nor can it deal with the core area of Islam, especially during the Abbasid period, when the separation between state and society was complete by 850 AD. The recent works by Patricia Crone and Roy Mottahedeh make this clear.[10] Gellner also overlooks Ibn Khaldun's treatment of the caliphate and the imamate, the central feature of leadership in an Islamic community.

The basis of the Islamic state, as Professor Ann Lambton asserts in *State and Government in Medieval Islam*,[11] was 'ideological, not political, territorial or ethnical and the primary purpose of government was to defend and protect the faith, not the state'. Although Ibn Khaldun argued that power or domination and authority 'are the rewards of social cohesion', his *Muqaddima* is replete with the assertion of the supremacy of the divine law which ultimately guides and determines events. The course of history which Ibn Khaldun examined was what it was because man deviated from the law of God by his sin of pride and greed. Even his not very original cyclical conception of history and the history of states is the consequence of mankind's refusal to follow the *sharia*.

Thus in developing a theoretical model for the sociology of Islam Gellner fails to examine Ibn Khaldun's historical approach to political association and the state, or his emphasis on the shortcomings, beyond founding a kingship, of *asabiyya* (social cohesion), which, without religion, can provide no unity. In short, while Ibn Khaldun was keen to understand the nature and causes of historical events, he also asserted that religion is the most powerful creative force of civilisation.

Several writers and commentators on recent events in Iran and other Islamic countries have argued that the rise of Islamic militancy, the upheaval in Iran and other developments, are the result of despotic rule; that Muslim nations have for long been afflicted by despotic regimes because of the influence and domination of colonialism. No one can deny that the late Shah and his father before him were so-called modernising despots; but so also were Muhammad Ali of Egypt, the

Ottoman Sultans, the Qajars and most other Muslim rulers, before colonialism appeared on the scene. The ruler in Islam is absolute; his autocracy is theoretically limited only by the requirement to observe the
religious law. There are no notions of popular participation in rule or
the sharing of power. An absolute ruler is acceptable to the faithful so
long as he is a Muslim and allows the religious law to regulate society.

Power in the Islamic state derives from the faith, and Muslims are
unwilling to share it with others. Muslims exclusively possess religious
truth and power, since according to the Koranic Sura: 'Power belongs to
God, His Apostle, and the believers.' This fusion of power and sanctity
evaporated less than a few decades after the Prophet's death. Yet the
illusion was perpetuated, and sacred title to power by Islamic rulers
remained, in the face of its having been acquired by force. The religious
teachers ignored mundane history while the jurists accommodated themselves to its exigencies, by insisting that the caliph is the sole source
of religious and political authority and imposes religious and political
uniformity on the community and state. Inevitably the distance, even
separation, between religion and state, state and society grew, without
however — beyond the well-known juristic rationalisations — reformulating the relationship. Or as Naipaul put it vividly and baldly:

> The glories of this religion were in the remote past; it had generated
> nothing like a Renaissance. Muslim countries, where not colonized,
> were despotisms; and nearly all, before oil, were poor.

Quoting one of his Iranian interlocutors, Naipaul reports him as asserting that

> All Muslim people tend to put their faith in one man. In the 1960s
> the Shah was loved. Now they love Khomeini.

Most of the writing on Iran indicates that Khomeini used the Shia
concept of the illegitimate, unjust ruler to overthrow the Shah, but
according to his concept of the *wilayet el-faqih* (guardianship of the
jurist),[12] he used that in conjunction with a virulent, uncompromising
anti-Americanism to institutionalise an Islamic republic and then transform it into a one-party fundamentalist theocracy, or to coin a term,
clerisocracy.

Yet, as Professor Kedourie has argued, the radicalism of Khomeini
— and Gaddafi — differs from that which infected the Middle East after
the First World War. So the intimate connection between Arabism and

Islam, or nationalism and socialism and Islam, differs to the extent that it has made use of more recent European ideological trends, for instance, the doctrine that the Muslims 'were among the truly proletarian nations in the world, the real victims of European capitalism'. Gaddafi's 'Third World theory' proclaims the poor peoples of the south as 'the downtrodden victims and eventual heirs of the rich peoples of the north'.

In Khomeini's case, the Man of the Pen has not only become the Man of the Sword, but he has also donned the mantle of the Expected Imam in Shia doctrine, ready to lead the believers towards an era of righteousness and justice. It avails little to argue that a paralysed economy in Iran will sooner or later undermine the Islamic venture of Khomeini. This may well turn out to be the case. In the meantime, his followers are not those who miss the earlier economic bonanza – they hardly enjoyed it; they are not the consumers of luxury goods. It is, on the contrary, the new elite of clerics around Khomeini, the needed monstrous bureaucracy and the indispensable military institution which will not be able to keep modernity at bay, or Iran insulated from the modern world, as Khomeini would wish. The projected permutations of the evolution of the struggle for power among these diverse forces in Iran today have been discussed by Rubin, Amirsadeghi and others. Shahram Chubin and his colleagues also consider, in *Security in The Persian Gulf*,[13] the implications of superpower strategy and conflict in South-west Asia and the Gulf. For the moment, as Muhammad Heikal puts it in *The Return of the Ayatollah*,[14] in the Middle East it is usually 'one-man' rule.

It is not only radical contenders of Islamic revival and their drive for power who preoccupy Western writers and policy-makers. The richest oil state in the Middle East – in the world – with an income of over 300 million dollars a day, Saudi Arabia was founded and exists today as an Islamic state in which the recognised regulating principle is the *sharia*. A renewed alliance between the Al Saud family and the puritan Wahhabi movement at the turn of the century enabled Abdul Aziz Ibn Saud, the founder of the present dynasty, to establish his kingdom. Robert Lacey, in a most readable narrative,[15] emphasises this alliance, highlights the story of the Al Saud family with its contradictions of fierce loyalties and intense rivalries, and wonders at the paradox of a strict tribal-religious ethos surviving alongside modern finance, commercial enterprise and real – also *rial* – politik.

The crucial point he misses is supplied by Christine Helms, who, in *The Cohesion of Saudi Arabia*, a rather original geographical approach to the rise of the Saudi state,[16] concludes that the recognition of boundaries rather than religion was the crucial factor in the final establishment of the kingdom. The Saudis, that is, by the early 1930s, defined their state on a territorial basis. What neither author refers to is the fact that Ibn Saud learned from his neighbours (and then enemies), Hussein and Faisal, that a ruler's writ is best secured over territory whose boundaries are internationally recognised. What Lacey offers in characterisation of people and places in Saudi Arabia, including princes and their palaces, Helms complements with an analysis of the relation between environment, ecology and the determination of power, loyalty and obligation.

A somewhat different portrayal of this pillar of the Islamic community and the second 'pillar' in American foreign policy before the fall of the Shah — now a key state in America's strategic consensus in the region (note how all three key states, Egypt, Israel and Saudi Arabia, are different) — is offered by Arnold Hottinger, Middle East correspondent of the *Neue Zürcher Zeitung*, in his chapter on 'Political Institutions in Saudi Arabia, Kuwait and Bahrain', which forms part of *Security in the Persian Gulf*. Tribal loyalties, reinforced by the bonds of a militant puritanical religious movement, enabled Ibn Saud to create his kingdom and, for a long time, maintain its unity and cohesion. Hottinger forcefully argues that both these foundations of the kingdom's stability are being eroded by money; that the 'chasms in Saudi Arabia are growing wider and deeper', and that religion is becoming a divisive influence or force. Much of this is due to the fact that the 'country is already split between rich and poor. The ruling class is deeply corrupt . . .' The pressure of money, Hottinger argues, is so great that the rulers must spend it for, among other projects, the transformation of Bedouins into labourers, or the introduction of general conscription into a national army. Both of these developments, Hottinger believes, will spell disaster for the ruling family. There are neither religious teachers independent of government control with a political leadership role, nor, as yet, a sizable middle class to challenge the Al Saud's legitimacy. A 'national army' could.

Yet it was Faisal who, for primarily regional political reasons, inaugurated Saudi Arabia's Islamic policy. At base, this policy was neatly elementary: to bring Islam, along with petro-wealth, into regional and international politics. The World Muslim League of 1962 was followed in the mid-1960s by an Islamic bloc to counter Nasser's radicalism and his threats to the Kingdom via south Arabia.

Muhammad Heikal is possibly right when he links this phase of the 'resurgence' of Islam to the Arab defeat in the 1967 war with Israel. Only in the view of Faisal it was not quite an Arab defeat, merely the rout of secular radical Arab socialism as purveyed and led by his rival

Nasser, and the equally secular champions of Pan-Arab socialism, the Ba'th in Syria. Generously subvented publicists attributed the defeat to deviation from the faith of Islam. For the Saudi, Kuwaiti and other oil-rich states it meant not only the discomfiting of their rivals but the chance to devalue secular radical notions and promote an Arab solidarity based on the most prominent feature of Arabism – Islam. The balance of power shifted in their favour as financiers of the new solidarity and brokers of inter-Arab power. They rid themselves of the Nasserist threat in south Arabia and, in the 1970s, found his successor more amenable. By 1973-4, they believed they had achieved a turning point in world affairs and changed the fortunes of the Middle East with a policy which asserted the Islamic voice in the affairs of practically every Middle Eastern state and in those of world councils, backed of course by the power of the oil embargo (or the threat of one) and petrodollars.

And yet the Saudi Islamic state venture is caught in the same revolutionary trap or political conundrum: their financial power is not paralleled (let alone buttressed) by any visible social, political or military capability. To develop too fast is to court sedition; not to be involved in the murky waters of inter-Arab politics is to leave the arena free for their rivals. Much of their expanded role in the region has been thrust upon them by the disengagement of Egypt from the inter-Arab political arena, the turmoil in Iran, and the currently stalemated ambitions of Iraq in the Gulf and the Fertile Crescent. The Saudis must not only compete for Islamic leadership with Khomeini and Gaddafi by subverting Islamic summits, cultural centres abroad, banks and other activities, but they must also ward off, as Hottinger suggests, potential sedition at home, and the encroachment of other Arab contenders for regional leadership. In the meantime, they expose their claim to Islamic leadership to the charge of a close alliance with imperialist America.

Historically, Islam was vindicated by political success, especially in the period from the seventh to the seventeenth century. Its military ascendancy and success in establishing a vast empire, comprising a diversity of peoples and cultures, proved the truth of Islam's message. Soon after, Islam suffered an uninterrupted series of defeats at the hands of Christian Europe from North Africa to South-east Asia, from Central Asia to the Near East. The victors may have been British, French, Italian and Russian imperialists, but to the average Muslim, to the doctors of Islamic law and local Islamic leaders, they were the infidel enemies of Islam.

Since Islam is not scornful of temporal power, as the Christians were at one time, and since it must prevail in the regulation of man's worldly order, this massive and consistent loss of power to non-believers inevitably undermined Muslim self-respect and generated doubts in some of them of the truth of the Muslim revelation itself. Those who tried to restore self-confidence and power by emulating Western societies have not been successful, and are now being challenged by those who demand the rejection of the path of modern civilisation and the return to a strictly Islamic norm. In this clash, or struggle, there seem to be several protagonists. Some label themselves Mahdis, others Supreme Guides, and still others Imams.

Throughout 1981 militant Islam in Iran and elsewhere in the Middle East dominated the news in the Western press. It preoccupied policy-makers because it endangered the stability of a strategically important region and jeopardised energy supplies to the industrial states. Whereas eighty or a hundred years ago, in the heyday of imperial power, it was contained and defeated, today it has triumphed — for the time being at least — in Iran. It challenges the state structures and the authority of rulers from North Africa to the Philippines. The message, though, is the same: Muslims must live in states governed by the law of God as revealed to his Apostle Muhammad. It is the duty of every Muslim to help bring about the pattern of the universe revealed by God to the believers, reject all other alien and infidel patterns, especially the pattern represented by the modern civilisation that evolved in Europe and spread to the rest of the world. Thus militant Islam today rejects all culture that is not Islamic and seeks to liberate (as well as insulate) Muslim society from its deleterious influences.

In the last six months, militant Islam in Iran has claimed the lives of some 3-5,000 young and old people who were considered to be 'enemies of God' and of the Ayatollah Khomeini, the supreme spiritual guide of the Islamic republic of Iran. In Egypt, it clashed violently with the Christian Coptic minority, attacked men and institutions of the state, and finally took the life of the country's President, Anwar Sadat, who dared curtail the activities of its followers and punish its leaders.[17] In Syria it has waged a relentless war of sabotage and assassination against the heretical Alawite rulers of that country.

Vast demographic change throughout the Middle East in the last twenty years, rapid economic growth, and astronomical revenue from petroleum (nearly 50 per cent of the world's proven oil reserves lie in the Muslim world) have had dislocating social consequences and produced disturbing psychological and political disorientations, undermining not only the traditional social order but also destabilising existing political arrangements. In such conditions, including the failure of existing regimes, partly emulating alien models, to cope with the pressing complex problems of modernity, militant Islamic movements have attracted the young, the under-privileged, the destitute, and even some of the better-off, whose expectations are greater than ever before in a mass *restorative* movement, in a nostalgia for the past and in a return to a native idiom.

Islam, which since its appearance has been a social force that welded together peoples from different countries and diverse cultures into a powerful community of believers to produce an illustrious civilisation, failed to provide a formula for a flexible political order which could cope with change. It never quite managed to establish an acceptable relation between religion and state, power and belief. It insisted on the possession of both power and a universal religious truth, that is, on the sanctity of power. Soon, however — by the ninth century if not earlier — mundane history, with its concrete events, separated society from the state as an organisation of power. Militant Islam today seems to want to rejoin them, by force if necessary. In this militant populist attempt lies one of the greatest factors for turmoil in the Middle East, because militant Muslims believe in the fusion between power and faith.

Whether militant Islam can restore Islamic society to its classical ideal — or even whether its adherents may one day exercise legitimate power in the several, diverse Islamic states — is not at all certain. But that it will continue to galvanise the Muslim masses against things non-Islamic is certain, thus challenging the national-state and international order as we have known them since 1945. On the other hand, one may soon discover that even militant Islam is about no more than the game of power. Whichever it turns out to be, it cannot be ignored as an assertion of cultural identity and an expression of a deep felt nostalgic desire to restore to the community of believers the power which it once possessed. In the meantime, it has generated a dichotomy between those relatively quietist transcendentalist Muslims who are willing to accommodate themselves with modernity on the one hand and those activist immanentists among them who reject such accommodation on the other.

Although not a new development — indeed, historically at times of deep crisis, it is a recurring phenomenon — militant Islamic movements at this juncture of world affairs and power relations between states, whether successful or not, can have serious consequences not only for Muslims themselves but also for the rest of the world. For they tend to polarise Islamic societies and that world, as well as sharpen the distinction between the Muslim and non-Muslim worlds.

Notes

1. Edward Said, *Covering Islam: How the Media and the Experts Determine How We See the Rest of the World* (Routledge and Kegan Paul, 1978). The other two volumes are: *Orientalism* (1978) and *The Question of Palestine* (1979).

2. Elie Kedourie, *Islam in the Modern World* (Holt, Rinehart and Winston, and Mansell Publishing, 1980).

3. V.S. Naipaul, *Among the Believers: An Islamic Journey* (André Deutsch, 1981).

4. Alexander S. Cudsi and Ali E. Hillal Dessouki (eds.), *Islam and Power* (Croom Helm, London, 1980).

5. See especially the Notes to Ali Merad, 'The Ideologisation of Islam in the Contemporary Muslim World' in *Islam and Power*, pp. 37-48.

6. Hossein Amirsadeghi (ed.), *The Security of the Persian Gulf* (Croom Helm, 1981).

7. J.A. Allan, *Libya: the Experience of Oil* (Croom Helm,

8. Ernest Gellner, *Muslim Society* (Cambridge University Press, 1980).

9. Franz Rosenthal, translator, *The Muqaddima* (1958).

10. Patricia Crone, *Slaves on Horses* (Cambridge University Press, 1980); Roy Mottahedeh, *Loyalty and Leadership in an Early Islamic Society* (Princeton University Press, 1980).

11. Ann Lambton, *State and Government in Medieval Islam* (Cambridge University Press, 1981).

12. See Abbas Kelidar, 'Ayatollah Khomeini's Concept of Islamic Government' in *Islam and Power*.

13. Shahram Chubin (ed.), *Security in the Persian Gulf* (Gower Publishing Company, for the International Institute for Strategic Studies, 1981).

14. Muhammad Heikal, *The Return of the Ayatollah* (André Deutsch, 1981).

15. Robert Lacey, *The Kingdom* (Hutchinson, 1981).

16. Christine Helms, *The Cohesion of Saudi Arabia* (Croom Helm, 1981).

17. See 'Sadat's Last Interview: Egypt on the Eve of the Assassination', *Encounter* (January 1982).

PART TWO: INTER-ARAB AND REGIONAL POLITICS

5 INTER-ARAB RELATIONS

Many Arab states are the fragmented successors of the Ottoman Empire, and subsequently of the British and French dominions in the Middle East. As such, they are riddled with obsessive and violent nationalisms, and governed by unstable individuals or groups who invariably achieved power by force. Today, the survival of most of these rulers depends on perhaps three main factors: (1) a tight and ruthless internal control of the three essential structures of state power: the armed forces, the security apparatus and the bureaucracy; (2) the maintenance of a client relationship with a superpower patron; and (3) a claim to satisfy perhaps unattainable national aspirations and popular expectations.

Even without the Arab-Israel conflict of the last twenty-seven years, the Arab Middle East would have been a conflict-ridden and conflict-generating area. The aspirations and pretensions of Arab nationalism, with its visions of Pan-Arabism and Arab unity, would have clashed — as they did — with the interests of the several Arab states which, except for Egypt, were literally put together from the debris of the collapsed Ottoman Empire. The lid on that cauldron was kept down (if not tightly shut) by the presence of the new European hegemonies, Britain and France, for a quarter of a century (1920-45). Their withdrawal or eviction — not, incidentally, without American encouragement[1] — ushered in a new era of unstable, conflict-ridden inter-Arab relations from that time on, and more specifically from 1955 to 1967. This condition was aggravated by the varied and different political evolution of the several Arab states, as well as by their disparate economic and social development.

Several of these states, for instance, contain within their territories large ethnic, tribal and sectarian minorities which are, in most cases, economically deprived and politically underprivileged. Frequently, these seek a greater share in wealth and power, often autonomy. Among them are the Kurds in Iraq, the tribes in South Arabia and the non-Muslim tribes in the southern Sudan. Until this year there was, for example, a Kurdish-Arab civil war in Iraq, a guerrilla war in Dhofar, supported by the radical regime in South Yemen against the ruler of

Source: A.L. Udovitch (ed.), *The Middle East, Oil, Conflict and Hope* (D.C. Heath and Co., Lexington, Mass., 1976).

Muscat and Oman who, in turn, is assisted by Saudi Arabia, Iran and Britain.

As a result of this diversity and heterogeneity, Lebanon experienced a dreadful communal war in 1958, almost a hundred years after its first one. Yet another and even more terrible one is now in progress. Such civil strife in Lebanon also reflects the delicate and awkward relationship of that country to the rest of the Arab world. In addition, an attempt to undo an Arab state or regime in the name of Arab national revolution led to a bloody civil war in Jordan when the Jordanian army crushed the Palestine Resistance Movement's armed bands in 1970-1.

Iraq, for example, has harboured irredentist designs on neighbouring Kuwait. Under a treaty provision, newly-independent Kuwait sought and received British military assistance in 1961 when it feared Iraq might invade its territory. A similar crisis could arise in the future, involving this time Saudi Arabia and Iran, as well as, indirectly, the Soviet Union, the current superpower patron of the Baath regime in Baghdad, which is also keen on achieving a position of influence in the Gulf. Potential crises, with both regional and international repercussions, can occur over irredentist claims and counter-claims between Saudi Arabia and the Union of Arab Emirates, especially oil-rich Abu Dhabi, and this could also involve other local powers, in particular Iran. Similarly Saudi involvement in North Yemen against the radical regime of South Yemen would generate flashpoints of inter-Arab conflict which could attract, say, Egyptian involvement, as well as that of outside powers.

These prefatory remarks and cursory, random illustrations of variety, diversity, and sources of actual or potential conflict in inter-Arab relations, suggest the absence of an Arab world monolith. That there can be instances of a convergence, or commonality, of interests among a number of Arab states over a particular issue, and therefore a common policy, cannot be denied. It is therefore important that outsiders who must respond to these instances be fully aware of their provenance, intricate, and complex motivation, and possible effect. They must be seen in their proper perspective, not as the manifestation of an ideological or other phantasmogoric monolith.

The ready articulation and official promotion of something called Arab nationalism or Arab socialism will remain a prominent activity of individual Arab states. But Pan-Arabism and its variant of Arab unity are, for the time being, dead issues. This, in effect, has been the impact and consequence of the failure of Nasserism on inter-Arab relations since 1967. In partaking of a common Islamic heritage (which, incidentally, remains at the heart of Arab nationalism) with its universalist pretensions, and past confrontations with the non-Islamic world, Arab rulers and states, as well as individuals, will continue to perceive their collective interest in terms of the solidarity of the Community of the Believers and its struggle for power, prestige and dignity *vis-à-vis* the outside world. The tensions they experience in their relations with the non-Muslim world and their feeling of alienation from it will continue to influence the Arabs' response to events. Stated more simply, they are committed to a different scale of values, virtues and ethic, regardless of the imported secular rationalisations they may adumbrate for that commitment. This fundamental perception of a major confrontation between the Islamic and non-Islamic worlds aside, the Arab Middle East will continue to suffer the dissonance and conflict of local rivalries and differences between its several states, rulers, communities and factions as much in the Maghreb as in the Fertile Crescent, the Arabian Peninsula, Egypt and the Gulf.

Patterns of Inter-Arab Relations since 1920

The dominant feature in the modern history of inter-Arab relations is the struggle for leadership in the name of Arab unity. Ideologically, that is, regional Arab politics have been concerned with the problem of Arab unity, the supreme, or ultimate, objective of Arab nationalism. Closely linked to this, since 1948, has been a collective position towards Israel. Theoretically, the two issues are interrelated, but practically quite separate. Moreover, they often obfuscate and gloss over the more practical problem of relations between Arab states, governments or regimes and leaders. Since the mid-1950s, regional Arab politics and inter-Arab relations have also been concerned with the relationship of the Arab states to outside powers and their positions in the rivalry between the superpowers.

Having postulated Arab unity as a desirable end, its attainment in the last twenty or thirty years has been constrained by the power struggle between the major Arab protagonists: the Hashemites in Iraq and Jordan before 1958, the Egyptians both under their monarchy and republic, and the Saudis. Until 1958, or even later, the Arabs could argue that their efforts in the attainment of unity were thwarted by colonial powers in the region, i.e., Britain. But even after these departed from the area, the struggle for hegemony among some of the Arab protagonists has continued undiminished.

Before 1920, inter-Arab relations were confined to the Fertile

Crescent area, where the victorious Entente Powers had defeated the Ottoman state and put an end to its dominion. Separatist Arab movements converged within the orbit of the Hashemite-led Arab Revolt of the Hejaz, to provide the first governing cadres in the new British and French mandated territories of Iraq, Syria and Transjordan.

Until 1936, there were only two fully independent Arab states, Saudi Arabia and the Yemen. The others, including Egypt, enjoyed semi-independent status in a treaty or tutelage relationship with one or the other of the dominant European powers in the area. The independent ones were virtually isolated from Arab affairs, whereas the foreign power-dominated ones sought a greater measure of independence.

The manifestations of rivalry in the struggle for leadership between them however can be traced back to this earlier period. The independent Arab Kingdom of the Hejaz under the Sherif Hussein, for example, was literally undone and integrated by the Saudis in 1924. Soon after that, in 1926, a political row over pilgrimage arrangements to the Holy Shrines in Mecca and Medina, broke out between Egypt and Saudi Arabia. It involved some use of force. The dispute, however, was linked to the issue of the caliphate to which the Egyptian monarch aspired. The blatant aggrandisement of Saudi Arabia at the expense of the Hashemites was being countered by the other major contender for regional, or Arab, power, Egypt. The chosen arena for this struggle was the issue of Islamic solidarity, the caliphate, and related matters.

There were, moreover, disputes between the Saudis and Iraqis over tribal activity which were not settled until 1936. The Iraqis for their part, after *formal* independence in 1932, sought a wider Arab role by improving their relations with Arabia, the Yemen and Egypt. This was in part the inevitable response of a Hashemite ruler in Baghdad and his governing class of Sunnis who were and still are the politically dominant minority in Iraq over a politically underprivileged and suspect heterdox, Shia, majority.

The Arab far west, the Maghreb, was too far removed from the centre of inter-Arab relations and politics in the Arab east, the Mashreq. Algeria, Tunisia and Morocco were all under French control, whereas the buffer country of Libya was under Italian colonial rule. Yet even there an Islamic revivalist and reformist movement, influenced mainly by trends in the Arab east, made its appearance as a prelude, if not as the progenitor, of the later struggle for independence from French colonial rule.

On the whole, the presence of Britain and France restrained inter-Arab relations and rivalries. The Arab countries themselves were wholly occupied with the task of freeing themselves from the control of their European masters. Their foremost national priority was the attainment of complete independence.

By 1936, international conditions and other considerations prompted Britain and France to negotiate new treaty arrangements with their mandated and other client countries in the Arab Middle East, with a view to allowing them a greater measure of independence. In Iraq this had already been accomplished in 1930-2; Egypt, Lebanon and Syria followed suit in 1936. But it was another issue altogether which brought these relatively weak Arab political entities into the wider arena of regional politics and inaugurated a new phase, or cycle, of the struggle for Arab leadership. This was the Palestine question which, until 1937, was more or less a local matter between the Arab and Jewish communities in Palestine and the British Mandate authority.

A Royal Commission, appointed in 1936 to look into the question of Palestine, recommended in 1937 the partition of the country into Arab and Jewish areas. Meanwhile, the local Arab rebellion, which began with a six-month general strike in April 1936, by October of that year had invited the mediation of Iraqi political leaders in its settlement. In the following year, a conference of leaders from the Arab countries at Bludan (Syria) marked the first 'official' or formal involvement of those states in the Palestine question.

Egyptians, Saudis and Yemenis may not have been equally deeply concerned over the fate or problems of the Palestinian Arabs. They were more interested in checking the influence of Iraqi, Transjordanian and Syrian politicians in the affair. But the involvement of all these countries in the Palestine problem was given official recognition at the end of 1938 when the British government announced the convening of a conference to which would be invited not only representatives of the two rival communities in Palestine but also those of the Arab states. This unilateral act by the British so to speak 'regionalised' the issue, and rendered it prey to inter-Arab political rivalries. The latter were to surface more thunderously in the 1948 Palestine War. Furthermore, it limited the freedom of British action over Palestine, and granted the right of intervention by the Arab states in the conflict. From a local conflict, Palestine became a regional one, and Egyptian, Hashemite and Saudi rivalries were injected into it.

Similarly, the exigencies and requirements of wartime policy prompted Britain to encourage greater Arab political cooperation and cohesiveness. In the face of the military dangers in 1941-2, the British government encouraged and inspired Hashemite-sponsored schemes of Fertile

Crescent and Greater Syria unity. For instance, Abdullah's Greater Syria plan (Syria, Transjordan, Palestine) and Nuri's Fertile Crescent Union (Iraq, Syria, Transjordan) were opposed by both Egypt and Saudi Arabia since they would have meant the domination of an important Arab area by their rivals, the Hashemites. Eventually, Britain supported the less contentious scheme of a League of Arab States which was also preferred by Egypt and Arabia. In recognising the sovereignty and independence of the member states, the League allowed for the containment of the struggle for power among the Arab states. But it also recognised the major protagonists for Arab leadership at the time as being Egypt, Iraq and Saudi Arabia. Until his assassination in 1951, King Abdullah of Jordan dominated the inter-Arab squabble over Palestine. But his own plans were thwarted in the end by Egypt and Saudi Arabia, using for that purpose the Palestinian followers of the Mufti, Haj Amin al-Husseini who, until 1959, resided in Egypt.

On the whole though, during this period, all the Arab states, especially the weaker ones, were interested mainly in the security of their territory and the maintenance of their independence regardless of how diluted. Saudi Arabia and the Yemen for a long time preferred a state of near-isolation from inter-Arab affairs so long as the more active among the Arab countries did not encroach upon their interests. It was a period of limited inter-Arab activity. What there was of it was confined to the Palestine question and inter-Arab relations arising from it, which mainly involved Iraqis, Syrians and Transjordanians. Otherwise, the major interest of the Arab actors in the Middle East scene was still the attainment of complete independence or the ending of special relationships with an outside power.

The patterns of inter-Arab relations after the Second World War can be observed in four periods: 1948-58; 1958-67; 1967-73; from 1973. In considering these patterns or trends, one must bear in mind several major developments that are relevant: the increase in the number of independent Arab states (Libya, the Sudan, Kuwait, Tunisia, Morocco, Algeria, South Yemen, Bahrain, Qatar and the Gulf States); the rise of military despotisms (i.e., the accession of soldiers to political power) in several of these states since 1949 (Syria, Egypt, Iraq, the Sudan, North Yemen, Algeria and Libya); the so-called radicalisation of regimes and the Arab nationalist movement under the impact of (a) military regimes; (b) parties, or movements, with ideological pretensions, e.g., the Baath in the Fertile Crescent area, and the Palestinians; (c) the use of single-party state organisations (which are not really parties, only agencies of state control) by military regimes, as in Egypt, Iraq, Syria, Algeria and

Libya; (d) the failure of Western attempts at regional defence or other mutual security arrangements, and the re-entry of the Soviet Union into the Middle East; and (e) the continuation of the conflict with Israel, involving three wars after the armistice agreements of 1949.[2]

1948-65

Between 1948 and 1958, inter-Arab relations were dominated by the two traditional rival centres of Arab power, Egypt in the Nile Valley and Iraq in Mesopotamia. They struggled against each other firstly for the control of Syria and Jordan, or failing that, in order to prevent one another from exerting exclusive influence in either of those countries. Until 1952, the contest occurred within the framework of the Arab League. Syria, in particular, was an attractive arena for this struggle in view of the rapid succession of ephemeral military governments after March 1949. Yet until 1955 both contestants were constrained by the presence, however weak, of a foreign power, namely, Britain. The Palestine question was in abeyance, with Jordan having emerged as the major Arab beneficiary of the 1948-9 war.

By 1955 there were certain developments which tended to increase the number of protagonists for Arab leadership, and that led some of them to shift the ground of their respective roles in inter-Arab relations without, however, changing the nature of the struggle. Once Egypt had resolved the question of its relationship to Britain (1954), it felt free to turn its attention to its role in the region. Almost simultaneously, the introduction of a Western-sponsored security or defence arrangement (the Baghdad Pact) supported by the Hashemites in Iraq, elicited a sharp Egyptian reaction. Egypt interpreted this step as an attempt on the part of its erstwhile British occupiers to isolate Cairo in the Arab world and deny it a position of leadership in favour of its arch-rival, Iraq. Positive neutralism, adopted by Nasser as a slogan, if not a policy, after Bandung in 1955, inaugurated a campaign of anti-colonialism in the Arab world aimed at the elimination of the remaining Western presence in the region from North Africa to the Gulf. It also served to attack and discredit Nasser's main rivals, the Iraqis, for Arab leadership. The 'battlefield' was to be mainly the Fertile Crescent, particularly Syria and Jordan.

The emergence of the radical Arab Baath in Syria, Lebanon and Jordan, vociferously opposed to the Hashemites and the West, facilitated Egypt's eventual, although temporary, triumph over its Iraqi adversary. Egypt succeeded in preventing Jordan from joining the Baghdad Pact, and pressed that nation to sever its special relationship with Britain. Syria then joined Egypt in an 'organic' union to form the United Arab Republic, and Lebanon blew up in a bloody civil war. The opposing regime in Iraq was overthrown by a military coup, and so was the regime in the Sudan.

Despite Egypt's defeat in the Suez War of 1956, Nasser in the late fifties emerged triumphant in this contest to lead a movement of Arab unity whose primary objective was the eviction of imperialism (i.e., Western influence) from the Arab Middle East. Saudi Arabia, meanwhile, fearing either Iraqi control of Syria in the mid-fifties, or Syrian-Egyptian control over Jordan, reconciled its differences with Egypt, only to resume its more traditional opposition to Cairo two years later.

Although some of the protagonists in inter-Arab relations in 1958 were newcomers to the game (the Iraqi military rulers and the Syrian Baath), Egypt in the end could not overcome the traditional, strategic differences in state interest between them. A period of sharp conflict between Cairo and Baghdad, from 1959 to 1963, followed, despite their mutual commitment to Arab unity and opposition to imperialism and its agents among the conservative, or reactionary, Arab rulers in the Middle East. It involved the alleged Egyptian subversion in the Shawwaf Mosul uprising of February-March 1959, Egyptian accusations of Iraqi surrender to communism, and other even less edifying mutual recriminations.

The vaunted ideological agreement between Nasser's Egypt and its Baathi clients and partners in Syria could not overcome the more serious differences between them in the UAR (1958-61). These eventually brought about the secession of Syria from the union, leading first, to the widespread devaluation of the idea of Arab unity; second, to the loss of Egyptian prestige; and third, to a more active opposition to Egypt's policies by her foes in Arabia, Tunisia and elsewhere in the Arab world. One of the difficulties arose from the fact that Egypt, on one hand, was not in Syria strictly for ideological reasons, but also for the pursuit of its state interests in the Arab Middle East. On the other hand, neither the Baath nor the Syrians generally were prepared to forego their own pretensions or claims to Arab leadership, or their state.[3]

In the meantime, Egypt had forged a new relationship with the Soviet Union which, since 1955, allowed its leader, Nasser, to preside over a virulent anti-Western campaign and to improve his position in the struggle for Arab leadership over that of his adversaries, particularly those who were supported by the West. He managed to establish radical, revolutionary nationalism as the basis of Arab unity while at the same time using it to promote further Egypt's claim to leadership. He combined, that is, Arab revolutionism with Egyptian state interests. He grabbed and retained the initiative of Arab leadership for a decade (1955-65) against the Baghdad Pact, the Eisenhower Doctrine, Iraq's so-called separatism under Qassem, Syria's secession from the UAR, and Saudi opposition and hostility in South Arabia. He succeeded, at least in his own eyes, in preventing the isolation of his country from the region.

The rejection of Egyptian leadership expressed in the Syrian secession, Iraqi insistence on independent opposition, and Saudi Arabia's and Jordan's quiet resistance, constituted a defeat for Nasser's Arab policy. He retreated to his corner to brood and ponder over his next step. The result within a year was the proclamation of an Egyptian National Charter (1962), which was not as significant for Egypt as it was for its declaration of war on Egypt's enemies. In the face of Egypt's differences and quarrels with Syria and Iraq, Nasser scorned normal dealings with governments and regimes, and the kind of Arab unity that might result from a collaboration with them. Instead, he declared that Arab unity would be attained by a Socialist revolution throughout the Arab world. The declaration implied a call to Arabs in other countries to rise against their reactionary rulers, and suggested they could expect Egyptian help in their sedition and subversion. The polarisation of the Arab world was now complete. What this also meant was that Egypt would resume its struggle for Arab leadership, armed with the new weapon of Arab national socialism, and backed by its new superpower patron, the Soviet Union.

The polarity was given a bloody expression in the Yemen War, the events in Aden and South Arabia in the period from 1962 to 1967. The focus of inter-Arab relations shifted to the Arabian Peninsula, and the protagonists in the struggle for Arab hegemony became Egypt and Saudi Arabia. Historically, of course, Egypt had been concerned with the protection of its eastern flank, especially the approaches to the Red Sea between South Arabia and Suez. While flaunting its ideological commitment to Arab revolution anywhere by its immediate support of the Sallal regime in Sanaa, Egypt was at the same time responding to a perception and consideration of its strategic needs and interests. Cairo's response to both these concerns, moreover, carried the prospect of discomfiting its rival in the Arab struggle, Saudi Arabia. The initiative in inter-Arab relations was somehow retrieved.

By 1963, however, inter-Arab relations generally had reached a low ebb. Egypt was at odds with Syria, Saudi Arabia, Jordan, Tunisia and even Iraq. Syria was at odds with Iraq; Algeria came to blows with Morocco over a border dispute; Tunisia and Morocco quarrelled over the recognition of Mauritania.

Soon, though, the combination of the stalemate in the Yemen, changes in regimes in Damascus and Baghdad and the catalyst of Israel's challenge in diverting Jordan river waters imposed on inter-Arab relations and the main protagonists in them an interlude of reconciliation. Presidents of republics and fellow ideologues could agree to disagree; and monarchs were no longer monsters to be ostracised by the Arab community of nations. All this presaged a period of Arab summit meetings at which adversaries were temporarily reconciled in the face of the common danger.

But this was preceded by perhaps a last attempt on the part of the so-called revolutionary Arab Socialist states of Syria and Iraq (both of them, in 1963, under Baath control) to seek a union of sorts with Egypt. These efforts came to nothing, not only because of the accumulated mutual distrust between the three parties involved, but also because Egypt was literally tired out. Its army was bogged down in the Yemen quagmire, its African policy had failed and backfired, and it preferred, in any case, to remain free to take the initiative of wider Arab leadership on its own at the propitious moment.

The outcome of the summit meetings in Cairo in January and September 1964 and in Casablanca in 1965 was a beginning in the settlement of the Yemen conflict between Egypt and Saudi Arabia, a reconciliation between Egypt and Jordan, and Egypt and Tunisia. But it also afforded Nasser the opportunity to re-establish Egypt's leadership in dealing with the Arab-Israel conflict in a way that suited its own purposes. The seeds of future conflict, however, were also sown in these summits. In order to deal with the matter of Israel without recourse to war, Egypt convinced its sister-Arab states to organise the Palestine Liberation Organisation (PLO). This immediately worried King Hussein of Jordan and, as it turned out, not without good reason. As for the hoped-for settlement of the Yemen War, it soon foundered on the rocks of indigenous Yemeni tribal factionalism which neither regional patron power of the local adversaries could easily manage or control.

A further radicalisation of regime in Syria (February 1966), the activities of the PLO, Jordanian anxiety and unease, and the temporary campaign led by Nasser in his old firebrand style against West Germany over the recognition of Israel, all seemed to erode the apparent achievements of the summits. By 1966, the era of Arab reconciliation was over. A realignment of conservative monarchs against radical regimes occurred.

The old mutual abuse between Cairo and Riyadh was resumed, exacerbated further now by the new Saudi King Feisal's campaign to construct an Islamic bloc, to which King Hussein of Jordan immediately lent his support. Syria almost clashed with Iraq over a dispute about transport royalties from the Iraq Petroleum Company (IPC) oil pipeline which passes through Syrian territory. King Hussein was having his problems with Ahmad Shuqeiri and the PLO, who were now supported, and exploited, by his enemies, the Syrians. The struggle for power between Egypt and Saudi Arabia that year, moreover, presented the Syrians with a golden opportunity to seek the pivotal security of a *rapprochement* with Cairo, especially in view of their difficulties with neighbouring Iraq, and the border tensions created by the activities of their Palestinian clients. It is, incidentally, a safe rule of thumb to assume that when Cairo and Riyadh are feuding, Damascus will seek an alignment with Egypt. The same is true of Cairo in these circumstances. In 1966, then, inter-Arab relations were characterised by a return to the 1958-61 alignments of Cairo-Damascus-Sanaa versus Riyadh and Amman.

In this atmosphere of Arab dissension and mutual recrimination, Egypt had resumed the leadership of radical regimes. This time around, however, Cairo did not enjoy the same control over its even more radical Syrian junior partners (with whom Egypt had concluded a military alliance in November 1966) which she had in the days of union. Thus, for their own purposes of embarrassing the Iraqi regime that had tried to improve its relations with Cairo in 1964, and in order to intimidate King Hussein, the Syrians encouraged Palestinian activities against Israel, launched from East Jordan.

In these circumstances, Nasser felt obliged to prove his concern for the Palestinians and to assert his leadership of the Arab revolution, whatever that was. With his army stuck in the Yemen, his economic problems at home getting worse, and in the face of a virulent Saudi-led and -financied campaign against him (which he incidentally suspected was inspired by the Americans), he believed the time had come for a showdown. The rest was all downhill towards the abyss of the June 1967 debacle.

Whether or not Nasser really intended to go to war in June 1967 is a question that falls outside the scope of this survey.[4] What is certain though, in relation to inter-Arab relations, is his determination to assert his leadership and control over the Arab political arena. When it was clear that his brinkmanship would result in a third Arab-Israel war, King Hussein of Jordan, eager to protect and improve his standing in the inter-Arab political galaxy, abandoned his fellow-monarch Feisal and his conservative camp, and signed a military pact with his enemy of the day before, Nasser.

A major consequence of the 1967 defeat for inter-Arab relations was its effect on the Cairo-Riyadh confrontation. The immediate question was that of a settlement with Israel. Nasser could not, of course, contemplate such a step without wider Arab support, primarily because his prestige had been shattered. At this juncture Nasser's arch-rival King Feisal came forward at the Khartoum Conference with magnanimous (and, for Nasser, devastatingly humiliating) offers of generous financial support, on condition that Nasser carry on the implacable struggle against Israel. Feisal, in short, had brought Nasser to his knees. Not only was Egypt soon to exit from the Peninsula, but Saudi Arabia was to embark, thanks to its inordinate wealth, on the road to Arab pre-eminence.

After the Six-Day War

The 1967 War ended the sharp polarisation of the Arab states between radical and conservative, and reconciled monarchies and republics in the agony of shame and defeat. But it also ended a decade of Egyptian primacy in Arab affairs under Nasser, and an era of inter-Arab subversion and war in the Yemen. It allowed countries like Jordan to rehabilitate their standing among the Arab states and to protect their independence. Most importantly, it allowed a weightier role, on the basis of wealth, for the more conservative rulers of Arabia in inter-Arab affairs. Equally significant, although in the short term less important, was the emergence of the Palestine Resistance Movement in a more radical form.

The conflicting interests of different Arab states, however, were not less apparent. Egypt, Jordan and, to a lesser degree, Syria, were clearly anxious to recover some of their occupied territories. This common interest brought their two rulers, once bitter enemies, closer together. Both, in a way, became dependent on the financial assistance of a major rival in the struggle for Arab leadership: Saudi Arabia. One may view the willingness of rich oil-producing states in the Peninsula and the Gulf to aid Egypt, Syria, and the Palestinians since 1967 as a matter of paying protection money to troublemakers in the hope and expectation that they will behave. Oil-rich, but otherwise weak, states such as Saudi Arabia, Kuwait and the Gulf Emirates have been, in effect, doing this since the early sixties. Kuwait's £150 million Fund for Arab Economic

Development, for example, dates from 1962. The fact remains that King Feisal at least emerged as the most serious contender for Arab primacy. For the time being he had destroyed the prospects of another Egyptian thrust into the peninsula or its affairs.

Even though by 1969 Egypt, or Nasser, had chosen to withdraw from the inter-Arab arena as a prelude to accepting the Rogers Plan, he nevertheless thought it necessary to forge a convenient relationship with the new maverick regime of Qadhafi in Libya, as an alternative axis for his Arab initiative and as a counterweight to the conservative rulers.[5] No Egyptian ruler in fact can allow the initiative in inter-Arab affairs to pass exclusively, or for too long, into the hands of a rival Arab leader.

The threat posed by the Palestinians to certain Arab regimes derived in part from the struggle between their several patrons: Syrians, Libyans, Iraqis and the sheikhs. But their most immediate, credible threat to Jordan was removed by forceful, bloody military action in 1970-1.

It was inevitable after Nasser's death, the impasse on the Suez Canal, the deteriorating relations with the Soviet Union and the eventual rupture between Cairo and Moscow, that Egypt should seek a working, profitable alliance, or accommodation, with a rich Arab state, permitting it greater freedom of action in the regional Arab and international arenas via the Middle East conflict. Once again, the interest of the state of Egypt (as distinguished from any ideological preferences or pretensions of the Egyptian regime) asserted itself in the policy of seeking to reclaim the initiative in the Middle East. The growing support of the Palestinians by Syria, Libya and Iraq could well produce certain unwelcomed changes in the Fertile Crescent area and thus a shift in the Arab balance of power. This was a dangerous prospect for Egypt, which it could not tolerate. It is in this context that the forging of the Cairo-Riyadh axis before the October War must be viewed.

Aftermath of the October War

The October War did not lead to the abatement of the inter-Arab rivalry for leadership. It did, however, affect the form and level of the conflict, for it introduced a somewhat different pattern of Arab alliances and alignments, and changed perceptions of Arab capabilities and limitations as well as priorities. Inter-Arab relations are now to a great extent dominated, or at least influenced, by the availability of the so-called oil weapon. Some have argued that with this vital commodity and the fantastic revenues from it, the Arab states can hold the industrial world in their power, even to ransom. After all, the argument goes, a group of states belonging to a single cultural group have access to this seemingly perfect weapon. They can, for a variety of purposes, hold the industrial (primarily the Western) world responsible for the occupation of parts of their Arab national territory by Israel and, therefore, use it to press them to abandon it. Others may feel that with this weapon the Arab states acting in concert, or in a sub-regional constellation of power, can challenge a rival Western civilisation over influence, power, and domination. They can possibly also challenge the hegemony of either or both of the superpowers.

One detects in recent Arabic writings, and particularly statements by Arab officials for home consumption, a resentment of all the past real and imagined ills and injustices visited by the West, from the Crusaders to the nineteenth century imperialists, upon Muslim Arab society. There is in these utterances a sharp tone of defiance and an allusion to revenge, which project the 'Arab Restoration' at hand.

In terms of inter-Arab relations one can identify, among others, three fundamental changes wrought by, or at least ensuing from, the October War. First, the balance of political influence, if not power, among the Arab states has shifted from the radicals to the conservatives, and from the Fertile Crescent and Egypt to the Peninsula. An important corollary of this is the proposition that haphazard radicalism is unproductive both in terms of Arab advancement and of bringing about Israel's defeat. Second, an unholy alliance between two of the strongest contenders for Arab hegemony, Egypt and Saudi Arabia, has been forged. Third, a partial way out of the thorny issue of the Palestinians has been found.

In the November 1973 and October 1974 Arab Summits (Algiers and Rabat) a formula for the integration of the Palestinians into the 'official' pattern and mainstream of inter-Arab relations was found, albeit at the expense of King Hussein of Jordan.[6] Briefly, the formula was as follows: The PLO agrees to abide by the leadership of the Cairo-Riyadh axis in return for its recognition as the sole legitimate representative of the Palestinian people and its inclusion as a party to, and essential ingredient of, any Middle East peace settlement.

The question which remains is whether this formula heralds, or even envisages, the abandonment of the previous Arab position which held that peace with Israel is impossible. Needless to say, according to their declarations, this remains the position of Libya, Iraq, even Algeria, and the extreme organisations within the PLO. The assumption, never publicly expressed, is that the leading contenders for Arab leadership, Egypt and Saudi Arabia, would accept peace with Israel if it can be reconciled with Palestinian rights, which rights, they go on to assert, can be defined only by the Palestinians themselves, not by other Arabs. To what extent, however, these paymasters and current mentors of this political arrangement, or authors of this formula, can control their new Palestinian partners, is not certain. What is clear is that for the time being inter-Arab relations are marked by an Egyptian-Saudi axis, an Egyptian-Syrian *rapprochement* over the PLO, an implacable opposition to the new constellation of Arab power by Libya and Iraq, a split within the PLO between its presumed 'establishment' and its more extreme members and the alienation of Jordan from the whole arrangement.

The perceptions of the October War and its achievements by the Arabs is an interesting, revealing, and relevant factor in inter-Arab relations. For the Egyptians it constituted a new departure that provides for them room for manoeuvre, both in regional Arab and international diplomacy. They believe that by crossing the Canal they broke the impasse in the Arab or, more accurately, Egyptian-Israel conflict, extricated themselves from total dependence on the Soviet Union, and, by extension, restored their relations with the USA. On the Arab front, they countered radical accusations of timidity and ineptitude, thus regaining their prestige and initiative in the struggle for Arab leadership. More typical is the perception of the *solidarity* achieved among some Arab states on the basis of a convergence of their interests in coordinating the use of financial, oil and military resources in a common policy for the prosecution of the October War and its diplomatic aftermath. They believe that they achieved the diplomatic and political isolation of their enemy Israel; that is, they have attained the only condition in which they could fight against Israel with any hope of even partial success.

With Saudi backing, Egypt's option for gradual or piecemeal negotiations with Israel became more acceptable to other Arabs. More significant for inter-Arab relations, Saudi support permitted Sadat of Egypt a certain authoritative cogency in Arab councils and gave Cairo an opportunity to moderate Syrian and Palestinian attitudes. This was shown particularly clearly in the November 1973 Algiers Summit and in the eventual disengagement agreement between Syria and Israel on the Golan. Closer to home, it made it easier for Egypt to deal with the wild Colonel Qadhafi of Libya and, in many ways, isolate him from the mainstream of Arab affairs.

But the situation was fraught with dangers and uncertainties. The Rabat Summit of October 1974 stirred the undercurrents of inter-Arab conflict. Winning international public opinion to the side of the Palestinian or Arab cause in the Middle East conflict restricted Egyptian freedom of action and only precariously bridged the widening rift between Syrian and Egyptian interests, not to speak of the alienation of Hussein and the repercussions in Jordan that it caused. Syria's position in the Golan Heights seemed to limit Egypt's options in another round of disengagement negotiations with Israel over Sinai. Then Arafat's unexpectedly strident and uncompromising address in the UN General Assembly in November 1974 highlighted the differences in perception among the Arabs of a lasting settlement of the Middle East conflict. More dangerous to Sadat was the reaction at home to, and unease about, Egypt's over-dependence on a conservative ally like Saudi Arabia, and its impact on Egyptian society, as well as to the alacrity with which Sadat embraced the American diplomatic and economic *démarche* that jeopardised Egypt's military arrangements with the Soviet Union.

The vital Cairo-Riyadh axis between the two major local Arab centres of power in the Middle East will probably hold so long as their respective interests relating to the Middle East conflict and the region as a whole are served. The Saudi regime is mainly interested in improving its chances for Arab leadership, and this is, in turn, linked to its ambitions in the Peninsula proper.

For Egypt, the axis gives its rulers time to retrench at home, and allows the recent successful isolation of Israel, with its attendant difficulties, to erode their adversary's power. Unlike Syria, a state that could be self-sufficient without having to play a wider role in the region, Egypt, *not for ideological reasons*, must view the conflict with Israel not simply as a territorial dispute, but as a long-term contest for the strategic and economic control of the core eastern area of the Arab Middle East. It is this *state* interest of Egypt which leads one to believe that regardless of its moderation ('Egypt is the least Arab of the Arab States') Cairo cannot — perhaps will not — under whatever ruler easily accept a permanent accommodation with its most obvious rival in the region, Israel, unless it is clearly to its advantage.

It was common after the Arab defeat in the Six-Day War of 1967 to argue a shift in Arab priorities. It was, for example, widely held that the Arabs had revised their policy in relation to Israel, from one of destruction to one of containment. Is one to assume that after the October War the priorities have given this policy its original order, from containment to destruction, not necessarily by war, but by economic pressure, political and diplomatic isolation, as well as by international pressure? That the 1967 defeat had a profound impact on inter-Arab relations there is no doubt. The overwhelming, dominating presence of Nasser in these relations was permanently diminished and his role in them undermined. Smaller and weaker states secured their legitimacy and independence: they felt safer from the subversive effects of the struggle for Arab leadership. Whereas the emergence of the Palestine Resistance Movement tended to radicalise the region and threaten and mesmerise Arab regimes as well as the international community, established Arab states became more determined to resist its disruptive intrusions and defend their regimes. Egyptian regional influence, however, could not be exercised single-handedly, but only in collaboration with another — and alternative — credible Arab leader whose influence was based on wealth. Together they were able to push to the background the vaunted old style Arab nationalism of the radical variety and instead project Arab *solidarity* between independent Arab states that have the resources to pursue credible policies. Above all, the Cairo-Riyadh axis showed that less radical, even conservative, Arab rulers or regimes could successfully promote and defend Arab interests, even when such rulers are associated with the 'imperialist' USA. The central position of Egypt in Arab affairs since the Second World War was not ended; rather it acquired a partner, Saudi Arabia, a country that also aspires to regional power.

The October War and its aftermath put an end to the ideologically phoney but otherwise earnest inter-Arab contest inaugurated by Nasser in 1958 between monarchies and republics. In any case, ideological agreement between Arab radicals in the decade 1958-67, or at any other time, did not and does not preclude serious conflict between them as states or regimes. This was the case of Syria, Iraq, Yemen and Libya in their relations with Egypt.

One must expect, though, efforts at sub-regional arrangements both by Egypt and Saudi Arabia in anticipation of future disagreements, even a rupture, between them. To this end Egyptian interest in Libya will remain keen. Saudi Arabia is already seeking to 'organise' its lesser sisters in the Gulf in a common policy. Although the immediate thrust of these Saudi peninsular moves is directed against Iraq to the north and Iran to the east, any successful local groupings of oil-rich states (Kuwait, Bahrain, Qatar, Muscat and Oman, the Gulf Emirates) under Saudi leadership will provide little comfort for the other aspirants to Arab leadership, whether in Egypt, Libya or the Fertile Crescent.

Qatar for all practical purposes is a Saudi 'satellite', and its integration in the future is not a fanciful projection. In the Levant, a parallel prospect is the reduction of Lebanon to a Christian enclave, with part of the north going to Syria, and part of the south to Israel – assuming the latter still exists. Jordan, on the other hand, might conceivably be dismembered, with its southern territories from Kerak to Aqaba going to Saudi Arabia and a small section of its northern part being grabbed by Syria. In view of the Iranian-Saudi Arabian antithesis in the Gulf, Iraq may manage no more than a 'buffer state' role.

The present political map of the Arab Middle East may not be a permanent one, in view of the nature and main features of inter-Arab relations presented above. The sharp new differences perforce engendered between the very rich oil-producing Arab states and those less naturally endowed are a major factor in this instability or impermanence.

The Cairo-Riyadh axis and the outcome of the October War muted, for a while, the more shrill polarisation in the Arab world that had been promoted by Nasser and his followers for over a decade. The apparent shift this brought about locally and regionally from 'radicalism' to 'moderation', and in the Arabs' external orientation away from the Soviet Union, is an ephemeral, transient by-product. Thus, the assassination of King Feisal, 'the architect of Arab solidarity' and financier of the anti-Soviet push in the Arab world, was unexpected. The same impermanence, incidentally, attaches to another prominent, local architect of a 'permanent future' in the Gulf, the Shah of Iran.

All UN member states (including some of the Arab ones) that clamoured for the recognition of the PLO did so on the assumption and expectation that with such recognition the Palestinians would finally agree to negotiate with an Israeli state, however small in size. This, so far, has not been the case. The other assumption was that the Arab states that count in the region, e.g., Egypt, Saudi Arabia, Syria and even Jordan, were already willing to recognise an Israeli state, and would therefore be able to cajole a politically and internationally respected PLO into coming to the conference table. This too, in my view, could be a mistaken assumption, perhaps a hopelessly fanciful one. There will always be a vast number of Arabs who will not accept an Israeli state in the Middle East, even if it were miniscule in size, because of their particular conception of Islam and the history of Arab-, or Muslim-, Jewish coexistence.

Regardless of the limited objective of Dr Kissinger's efforts, namely, a further disengagement in the Sinai, its implicit long-term corollary has to be a peaceful accommodation between the two countries. This has been and remains mainly a Western (and, reluctantly, Soviet) objective. No Arab state, or ruler, has really accepted it *unequivocally*. The long-term objective of all the Arab states, including Egypt, which supports the declared objectives of the Palestinian movement, is for the region to be freed of a sovereign independent Jewish political entity – the state of Israel. And this, incidentally, is not necessarily synonymous with the physical extermination of that state's population, since the Arabs have historically accepted and do today accept coexistence with sectarian, ethnic, and other minorities, as long as these do not lay claim, aspire to, or attain, a sovereign political existence.

It was suggested at the time that the breakdown in the negotiations of March 1975 occurred over the matter of further Israeli territorial concessions in Sinai. The Israelis, in turn, claimed that these could not be made without an Egyptian declaration of non-belligerency, which the Egyptians refused to offer as a counter-concession. Ostensibly, the justification for this Egyptian refusal was that non-belligerency can be attained only after Israel has withdrawn from all Arab territories. Arab interpretations of what this entails abound: pre-1967, 1947 Partition boundaries, etc.

Sadat, in a closed session briefing of the Arab Socialist Union (ASU) Central Committee on 18 July 1972, justified his expulsion of Soviet personnel from Egypt in part by the following:

> There is between us and the Soviet Union a fundamental disagreement on principle regarding Israel . . . Despite the sincere Soviet stand in supporting the Arab states in their struggle against Israel, and specifically in their demand to remove the traces of aggression which occurred in 1967, the Soviet Union still recognises Israel and believes in the importance of protecting her existence. The Soviet Union (unlike us) is not concerned with international legality and its violation when Israel was founded on Arab land in 1948.

Moreover, after the October War, as far as can be gauged from public statements and published materials (October-December 1973), most Arabs were convinced of their long-term advantage in the fight against Israel.

In short, there still remain certain minimal entrenched positions on both sides of the conflict which are not negotiable: security for the Israelis; unwillingness to recognise a Jewish state for the Arabs, unless Israel withdraws from all Arab territories (*all* is as yet undefined) and satisfies the rights of the Palestinians (as yet undefined, nor agreed upon, by the Arabs).

At the same time, the Arabs have tended since the October War to use oil as a tactical weapon not simply to press Europe and the United States toward an anti-Israeli policy, and to divide Europe from the United States over that policy (the so-called Euro-Arab dialogue), but very much as one against Jews in the Middle East and elsewhere.

Dr Kissinger's successful 'shuttle diplomacy' in August-September 1975 generated further conditions of renewed inter-Arab conflict. The political implications of the second interim agreement over Sinai between Egypt and Israel are dangerous. This has significantly introduced two important elements of regional conflict, one being the exposure of Egypt to Arab attack, resulting in a sharper polarisation of the Arab states, the other consisting of the more direct involvement of the USA as the patron power of two adversaries in the conflict, Egypt and Israel, and as a convenient target of attack by other Arabs and the Soviet Union. Upon the conclusion of the agreement, the USA was immediately accused by the Arabs opposed to separate agreements between Egypt and Israel as wishing to strengthen conservative Arab regimes in the Middle East; to isolate Egypt from the rest of the Arab world; to secure the existence of Israel by forging a closer alliance with it; and to deny the Palestinians their legitimate rights. On the other hand, the second Egyptian-Israeli interim agreement could attract the remaining two Arab 'confrontation' states, Jordan and Syria, to a policy of actively seeking a similar accommodation with Israel.

Inter-Arab conflict, however, persists not so much over Israel (although tactical differences between certain Arab states over this issue and between them and the Palestinians have always been present) as over the resurgence since October 1973 of a pressing Islamic impatience with the careful tactics of the so-called moderates: thus Libya's impatience with Egyptian diplomacy in the Middle East conflict and the Palestinians' involvement in a fear-dominated confessional system in the Lebanon.

There is a renewed contest between the Arabs over 'Islamicity', similar to the one over radicalism and socialism a few years ago. Sadat of Egypt and Feisal of Saudi Arabia helped suppress a Communist coup in Khartoum in July 1971, only two months after Sadat had suppressed his own Nasserite radicals at home. The lip-service paid by Arab leaders since the October War to the analogy between the struggle against Israel and that of their Muslim ancestors against the Crusaders eight and nine hundred years ago has encouraged extremist calls for holy wars and Islamic revivals, such as the one emanating from Qadhafi of Libya. In short, the Islamic euphoria and a new psychology of confrontation with an alien world that has kept Arab genius down, provides still further sources of inter-Arab conflict.

It is clear that if Egypt has been and remains unable to control the Arab Middle East, neither can any other Arab state, however rich. Differences over local issues and fear between states and communities within them will persist for the foreseeable future and so mar and complicate domestic and inter-Arab politics. From time to time internal explosions, such as the food riots in Egypt, communal conflict in the Lebanon, Syrian-Iraqi contests, tribal rivalries in Arabia and the Gulf, border and other disputes in the Maghreb, will occur. Those Arab states without revenue from oil will remain dependent on outside economic aid and the diplomatic patronage of one or other of the great powers.

It is, in fact, the essentially Islamic-Arab rejection of an alien Jewish state in the area which enables Egypt, for instance, to remain the most influential state among them, by virtue of its dexterous manipulation of the Middle East conflict's local dynamism. The Arabs are divided over most issues. But the potency of a perception since October 1973 of the destruction of the myth of Israeli invincibility, the recruitment of the USA and Europe as a result of the oil weapon as concession-extractors from Israel, and the inevitable triumph of the combination of Arab numbers and money, renders the belief in the superfluousness of a permanent peace with Israel irresistible.

Major Areas in Inter-Arab Relations

On the basis of the preceding brief survey of the patterns of and trends in inter-Arab relations, one may outline some of the major problem areas and main elements of potential conflict which could affect inter-Arab relations and impinge upon United States interests in the region.

Economic Considerations

The following conditions affect inter-Arab relations:

1. A division between rich oil-producing states, on one hand (Saudi Arabia, Kuwait, some of the Gulf States, Iraq, Libya and Algeria), and, on the other, those states not so naturally endowed (Egypt, Jordan, Lebanon, Morocco, the Sudan, Tunisia and the two Yemens). Bahrain, which is also oil-producing, is, as an island, in a special position. The mixed composition of its population (Arab and Persian) and its location, as well as Iran's irredentist claims upon it, impose upon it a circumspect stand *vis-à-vis* its Arab neighbours. Muscat and Oman, moreover, also oil-producing, equally maintain a peripheral involvement for the time

being. But its current domestic turmoil and its possible outcome may inevitably push it into the mainstream of Arab peninsular affairs.

2. In addition to the basic division, there is also the fact of the disparity in development between these two groups of Arab states. The richest among them are also, by and large, the least developed economically, socially and politically. Many of them, such as Kuwait and the Gulf States, employ in their current programmes of development vast numbers of expatriates from other Arab states, in particular Egypt (medical, engineering and educational services), Palestinians, especially in Kuwait (educational and entrepreneurial projects), Iraq (mainly political refugees in administrative services), and the Lebanon (banking, financial and contract enterprises). These constitute not a wholly comforting or reassuring intrusion for the Peninsula and Gulf States.[8]

3. Syria and Iraq can conceivably become economically self-sufficient states given the size of their populations and resources. Syria, however, will continue to depend, to some extent, on financial assistance from some of the oil-producing states (Saudi Arabia, Abu Dhabi) in the prosecution of the struggle against Israel. Lebanon, on the other hand, has an economy which rests largely on financial and related services, and is also dependent, to some extent, upon its ability to attract capital and contracts for these services from the richer Arab states, and upon its continued ability to extend these services throughout the region. Both Syria and Lebanon have oil-pipeline terminals on their coasts. They would be interested in maintaining the flow of income from them. (A glut of oil on the world market led to the closing down in 1975 of the pipeline terminal in Lebanon.) Iraq and Saudi Arabia are also interested in the security and continued use of these pipelines. To this extent, the economics of overland oil transport is a factor in these inter-Arab relations. With the re-opening of the Suez Canal, their importance may diminish.

4. Egypt and Jordan are the least favourably placed in the oil game. By virtue of the September 1975 interim agreement with Israel, Egypt has regained control of its oil wells in the Sinai, and Cairo may yet strike it rich with major oil finds in the Western Desert. For the time being, Egypt remains dependent on massive financial assistance from the oil-producing states, and Cairo is not sanguine about the prospects of capital investment for economic development in her own country from them. Inevitably, the current dependence constitutes a constraint upon Egypt's freedom of action in relation to Israel and the wider area of inter-Arab relations. The reopening of the Suez Canal may improve its economic situation, as it may also infuse some life into the Aden

complex in southern Arabia. For the time being Egypt may have to make do with the economic palliative of the American offer of some $800 million in economic aid as part of the September 1975 interim agreement 'package' with Israel. Meanwhile, there are those who argue that the reopening of the Suez Canal may free Egypt from the 'collective' Arab constraint regarding its policy towards the Middle East conflict. On the other hand, a future rehabilitation of the Egyptian relationship with the Soviet Union and the intensive use of the Canal by the Soviet fleet may lead Egypt's rulers to adopt a more aggressive, intransigent, and strident position over the Arab-Israel conflict.

5. The structural differences in the economies of Arab states (state-controlled, private enterprise, etc.) constitute a relevant factor in inter-Arab relations. It is not, therefore, only the disparities in resources, but also the different economies which must be considered.

6. Libya is perhaps heard of only because of its oil revenues. It has used and, under the present regime, will continue to use, its income from oil to create for itself a role in inter-Arab relations out of all proportion to its other capabilities, which are almost nil. With a very small population, it can afford to do so. But this also suggests an inter-Arab 'bribery' contest with regard to the Palestinians and in the pursuit of state rivalries, as, for example, between Libya on one side and the Peninsula on the other, or as between Libya and Egypt, or Libya and Morocco.

7. Generally, then, the recent accumulation of astronomical financial reserves from oil revenues affords some of the Arab states greater influence in inter-Arab relations than they would otherwise possess. Such influence, however, reflects vulnerable power. In most of the oil-rich Arab states this 'economic' or financial power is not underpinned by the credible infrastructure one normally associates with powerful states. In the meantime, the division between the rich and poor Arab states (although some of them are more advanced in other respects) could initiate a new phase of inter-Arab conflict. Despite the existence of the odd regional Arab economic institution, such as the Arab Development Fund and similar organisations, until now the full use of Arab resources for regional economic development has not occurred. Most of the capital flow from oil-rich states into the Arab region so far has gone to finance the conflict with Israel, as well as to 'useful' political groups in several countries. Oil money has always been, in passing, a weapon of subversion in other Arab states, and the 'oiler' of several propaganda campaigns in the press and other media.

8. If, however, the pattern of inter-Arab relations has been one of

independent states resisting integration into subjugation under a wider Arab arrangement, led by one or another of the protagonists for hegemony in the region, their economic behaviour may well continue to rest on that basis. A scramble for resources by those not possessing them when the opportunity arises is not unlikely. A case at hand is Morocco's claim to the Spanish Sahara that may develop into a first-class inter-Maghrebi row.

9. If by some good fortune the Arab-Israel conflict is peacefully settled or resolved, one can expect a deterioration in inter-Arab relations with economic overtones. So far, the rich Arab states, for their own purposes, can use their financial resources for the maintenance of the conflict at relatively little expense to themselves and, in the meantime, derive maximum benefit in the struggle for Arab leadership.

10. So far, only Egypt, among these states, really entertains hopes of a wider inter-Arab economic role by virtue of its relatively vast human (educational, technical, industrial) resources. The Syrians and Iraqis could conceivably compete. So far only the Lebanese have done so credibly. To this extent also, Egypt will maintain an interest in an integrative kind of Arab economic development as long as Cairo perceives a leading role for itself.

Political Considerations

Despite the appearances of Arab solidarity after the Rabat Summit of October 1974, the centrifugal tendencies and other tensions in inter-Arab relations remain, albeit muted for the time being. Strategic calculations may have changed since the October War. There has been a transformation of the balance of power in the core Arab Middle East. At least the Arabs perceive this to be the case and that is what counts in dealing with them, for it entails the matter of Arab 'bargaining power' in the conflict with Israel and in their relations with outside powers. Having discredited Arab radicalism and its usefulness in the struggle against Israel, Egypt at least contends that the successful recruitment of the financial resources of the rich Arab states helped it perform a 'miracle'. The myth of Israeli superiority and invincibility, according to Cairo, was shattered. The quick 'recruitment' of the USA, first extracting concessions from Israel and second, a new economic relationship with Egypt and Saudi Arabia, was achieved. As for the Arabs generally, they believe that the combination of military action and economic pressure by virtue of the oil weapon did the trick in October 1973. The USA, according to Arab perceptions, has been committed to the role of concession-extractor from Israel as well as the provider of economic and other assistance to some of the Arab states. All this, the Arabs believe, was achieved in return for an Arab promise of continued energy supplies, new investment opportunities, etc. There have been, however, no known, clear, and unequivocal undertakings by the Arabs on the matter of the permanent acceptance of America's client, Israel, as a sovereign independent state in their midst. There are, indeed, many Arabs who believe the USA, in its new relationship with them, will help them achieve in relation to Israel what they themselves have not been able to in the past twenty-six years. Seventeen of those years have been crowded with Soviet help. The ambivalence over this *ultimate* issue in the conflict will plague inter-Arab relations as well as relations between Arabs and the outside world, particularly the USA and the Soviet Union. It is the kind of gnawing uncertainty which breeds suspicion and distrust among Arabs, and between Arabs and outsiders.

Negotiations for the peaceful settlement of the Arab-Israel conflict have not, so far, progressed beyond the stage of disengagement agreements. In the meantime, a vastly accelerated rate in the importation of arms not only by the principal adversaries in the conflict, but also by those Arab states on its periphery, could lead to the further escalation of the conflict and the outbreak of hostilities, as well as to serious domestic trouble in some of the Arab states. Then the American offer in 1974 of nuclear reactors to Egypt and Israel could trigger a chain reaction in other Middle Eastern states. It has already pushed Iran, on the periphery (and with India in mind), to follow suit, by rumoured negotiations with French suppliers. The Soviet Union may well offer nuclear arrangements to Iraq and/or Syria. Algeria may feel obliged to seek similar arrangements with France or the Soviet Union. What the impact of such developments on inter-Arab relations, let alone the Arab-Israel conflict, will be, is difficult to say, but the prospect is daunting.

Arab insistence on the satisfaction of the 'legitimate rights' of Palestinians and the continued clashes between Palestinian terrorist infiltrators and Israeli security forces sustains the tension in Arab-Israel relations. But it also exacerbates inter-Arab relations, depending on the perception of interest individual Arab states have in the crisis. If, for example, Israel and the PLO remain at odds, the tendency will be for an Arab regional realignment. The PLO will be inclined to blame the policy of the Cairo-Riyadh axis for failure to reach its objectives. The Libyan-Iraqi loose alliance will also attack the Egyptian-Saudi constellation. Meanwhile, the Jordanians, having abandoned the West Bank to the PLO, will move to split the Palestinians settled in East Jordan.[9] Together with the probable failure of the PLO to regain the West Bank from Israel within a reasonable period of time, all these problems will lead to another cycle of inter-Arab differences – and disarray.

The tactical manipulation of the Palestinians both by the Soviet Union (for its own purposes) and the Arab states is bound to continue, hindering further peaceful negotiations. Until recently, one could not dismiss, for instance, the possibility that the Cairo-Riyadh policy of sponsoring the PLO regionally and internationally, and the threat of the further use of the oil weapon was one of procrastination in order to gain enough time during which Israel would collapse without recourse to another round of hostilities. Domestically though, Egypt, as it turned out, was unable to afford too long a hiatus between the first interim agreement with Israel in 1974 and the second in 1975. Nor, incidentally, was Cairo able to resist for too long the offer of sizeable US economic and financial aid. One cannot rule out the possibility, however, that in the future Egypt may abandon its Saudi paymaster and present ally in favour of a return to the old close relation with the Soviet Union, a development which will affect the pattern of inter-Arab relations, and influence the evolution of the Arab-Israel conflict. For the time being, Egypt has sought to strike a balance between an opening to the West in the hope of regaining Sinai, involving a guarded and cautious movement toward an accommodation with Israel on the one hand, and a continued attachment to the general Arab position regarding a final settlement of the Middle East conflict, on the other.

Continuing Trends and Patterns in Inter-Arab Relations

The Arabian Peninsula and the Gulf

In addition to being the richest oil-producing area in the Arab Middle East, this is also, in contrast to the Fertile Crescent and the Maghreb, the centre of traditional, conservative, tribal-dynastic states. The Arab side of the Gulf has only recently (1971) emerged as independent of a protecting power. It is, therefore, exposed to the momentum of local, or regional, powers that may seek to dominate and control it, as, for example, Saudi Arabia and Iran. Saudi Arabia at the centre of the Peninsula may seek to dominate the Union of Arab Emirates and South Arabia, i.e. both Yemens. In doing so, it may come into conflict with Iraq and Iran. It will, in the meantime, resist what appear even now to be Iranian 'salami tactics' (to achieve immediate goods without revealing the long-term policy) in the lower Gulf (Muscat and Oman) in order to assert its own gradual domination. One must note in this connection the presence of sizeable Iranian communities in Dubai and the other Gulf states, as well as in Kuwait and Bahrain. Saudi activities in the Gulf, however, are not altogether welcome. One observes a form of resistance to them on the part of the Emirates, particularly when one considers the lavish use of funds by Abu Dhabi, especially in support of the Palestinians, Syrians and other so-called Arab causes; or in the now nearly indiscriminate distribution of largesse among propagandists in the West. All the same, on a broader front, Saudi Arabia with its vast wealth, will continue to assist such rulers as Qabus of Muscat and Oman in resisting domestic sedition, and will also continue to manipulate the Arab-Israel conflict to its advantage (as it has since the Khartoum Conference in 1967) in the context of inter-Arab relations.

Such widespread inter-Arab activities based strictly on money, however, invite the mistrust of other Arabs. This remains the case especially in view of Saudi Arabia's relation to the United States. Nor is the ability to exercise such influence in inter-Arab affairs a permanent feature of Saudi Arabia's role in the region. The uncertainties that surround the future and fortune of the Saudi family and establishment after Feisal's assassination by his nephew are too great, and the consequences too complex, to permit any prognostication. For the moment, however, in the absence of a genuinely strong, rather than merely rich, local or regional power able to maintain stability, the Gulf at least remains a potential centre of conflict that attracts the interference not only of the local contestants but also of outside powers.

The Fertile Crescent

The problems that have historically plagued relations between Syria, Iraq, Lebanon and Jordan remain. In view of the developments discussed in an earlier section, Jordan may introduce a new factor in relations with the Palestinians which will affect Syria and Lebanon, too. Until the beginning of 1975, Iraq had been too busy with the Kurdish War to concern itself with Syria and Jordan, or even Kuwait. Despite the recent recognition of the PLO, Lebanon will continue to face difficulties in its relations with the Palestinians, whose administrative, political, propaganda and military headquarters remain in that country. The recent clashes between the Christian Phalangists and the Palestinians in Beirut in April-May 1975, are a grim reminder of these difficulties. Whereas in 1958 the civil war was in effect contained and the political crisis eventually sorted out, today the massive Palestinian factor intervenes to threaten the delicate and precarious Lebanese communal system. It adds tremendous weight to the existing Lebanese Muslim community. Moreover, if the Libyan inspired inflammatory articles in the Libyan-aided Beirut paper, *al-Safir*, are any indication, the explosive situation in the Lebanon tends to attract the interference of the more extremist and less responsible Arab rulers. In addition, in the latest clashes, the Phalangist and Liberal Christian militia proved as well, if not better, armed and trained as their Palestinian adversaries. Suspicion between the two camps is deeper than ever before and, consequently, armed clashes could easily recur.

As long as Syria under Assad cooperates with the Cairo-Riyadh axis, Iran will counter it with a more intransigent stand associated with distant Libya. In view of the closer relations between Syria and Iraq with the Soviet Union, Cairo and Riyadh will seek to minimise their impact on inter-Arab relations. Until the spring of 1975, however, Iraq faced a separate problem with Iran on its eastern frontier in connection with the Kurds. Now that it has ostensibly buried its differences with Iran, it is assumed that it will play a more active role in inter-Arab affairs. If the recent dispute with Syria over Euphrates waters is any indication, it may not be too peaceful or constructive a role.

Typical of volatile, unsettled inter-Arab relations in this connection has been the recent flare-up between the Damascus and Baghdad Baath regimes. Reminiscent of their quarrel over pipeline oil transport nearly ten years ago, the dispute over the distribution of Euphrates Dam waters was in fact the epiphenomenal expression of deeper, more serious differences between them. The Iraqis had been, for some time, unhappy about arms supplies to the Kurdish *peshmerga* coming from across the Syrian border as late as February 1975. A complicating factor was the Iraqi suspicion that the Soviet Union might have been the source of these supplies, which increased Iraqi resentment already aroused by Soviet participation in the construction of the Euphrates Dam at Tabqa. The usual Iraqi inclination to attack any ruler in Damascus who had negotiated and accepted an accord, even a limited one of military disengagement, with Israel, was a further point of friction. Meanwhile, President Assad's action in arresting several Iraqi Baathi political refugees in Damascus for allegedly passing to Baghdad versions of his secret deliberations with Dr Kissinger leading to the May 1974 disengagement agreement with Israel on the Golan, increased the tension between the two regimes. Underlying all these events was the long-standing suspicion and occasional feuding between Baghdad and Damascus, dating from the 1920s and, particularly, the 1950s, when the Baath came to power.

A recent dimension of the Iraqi-Syrian 'dispute' was provided by the *rapprochement* between Syria and Jordan, prompted by developments in the Arab-Israel conflict, namely, the second interim agreement between Egypt and Israel in Sinai. Iraq immediately expressed its hostility to the Syrian-Jordanian alignment. At the same time, Iraq, which is interested in greater revenue from its oil, has equally differed and disagreed with sister oil-producing Arab states over oil policy.

Generally, the Fertile Crescent will remain a contested area in the struggle for leadership not only between Iraq and Syria, but also between Egypt and Saudi Arabia. It might conceivably also become the centre of confrontation, demarcating the boundaries of influence between the superpowers. With Syria, Jordan and Lebanon contiguous to Israel, 'the enemy of the Arabs', these states are exposed both to the vagaries of hostilities and the political gyrations of 'Arab policy' against Israel. They are relatively small countries. Consequently, wars can quickly reduce their respective size. In a way, they are seen by the major protagonists in the struggle for Arab leadership (Egypt and Saudi Arabia) as buffers between themselves and Israel. This is the meaning and true import of the appellation 'confrontation states' used by the Arabs to denote the array of frontline states in the struggle with Israel. None of them enjoys the strategic depth and bulwark of a Sinai or Suez Canal.

The survival of the Fertile Crescent states so far has been due first, to the influence of foreign powers in the area, and second, to Arab factionalism in the struggle for leadership. Conversely, these states themselves, realising that their survival depends on extraneous forces, played an appropriate role in both inter-Arab rivalry and the contest between the great powers.

The region will remain, for some time to come, a contested one among the Arabs, among indigenous movements for its unification, and between the powers. Israel for its part will seek to maintain its threat of an overwhelming military deterrent — and domination — over this immediate area.

Egypt

Although a part of the Arab east, Egypt in fact sits astride the two parts of the Arab world, the east and the west. It must avoid isolation from either and must therefore be involved in the affairs of both. Its national state interests and security in fact dictate a regional role for Cairo in Arab politics. In the past, with a British connection, Egypt projected a leadership role in Arab affairs primarily through the Arab League. Later, with Soviet backing, Cairo was able to increase the intensity and widen the scope of its Arab role, albeit with indifferent results. In the east, Egypt has faced its rival, Saudi Arabia, both in the Fertile Crescent and South Arabia.[10] In the west, despite the so-called special relationship between Nasser and Algeria until the overthrow of Ben Bella in 1965, Egyptian interests require that it exert some influence over contiguous Libya, or failing that, prevent a powerful Maghrebi rival from exerting its own there. To this extent, Libya, under whatever regime, will be confined to a buffer role between the Maghreb and the Mushreq, and particularly in any rivalry between, say, Algeria and Egypt. Divided internally between east-oriented Cyrenaica and west-oriented Tripolitania, and governed by a cabal of officers open to sedition, Libyan policy must balance itself on the tightrope linking the Arab west to the Arab east. This was, in fact, also the case under the Sanussi monarchy. Neither Algeria nor Egypt would tolerate a Libya that is more than a buffer.

Unlike the Arab east, but like the Maghreb, Egypt must also consider its African periphery. This is especially relevant in relation to the Sudan, where an Arabised political élite governs a vast country exposed to the dangers of separatist sedition by the non-Arab, non-Muslim south and its African hinterland.

Theoretically, Egyptian hegemony, at least over the eastern Arabs (e.g., the Fertile Crescent), and the attainment of primacy over the Arab region as a whole can be secured by an accommodation with Israel. One could argue that Egypt and Israel are the two states in that core area of the Middle East which might conceivably entertain 'imperial' ambitions or designs. Without a permanent or final accommodation between them, one will always check and frustrate the other. As it is not possible, for the moment, for Egypt to proceed toward such an accommodation, it must be satisfied with an uneasy Saudi partnership in inter-Arab affairs. But this remains an insecure, shifting alliance. It has, moreover, engendered domestic political divisions in Egypt, between those in favour of the Saudi alliance (and, by extension, the American association), on the one hand, and those against it, as well as the general resentment among Egyptians of oil-rich Arabs and their suspicion that these Arab states are not forthcoming with the financial or economic assistance Egypt requires.

A dimension of this current split within Egypt is its exploitation by the weaker, though very rich, Libya. Colonel Qadhafi's Arab-Islamic ambitions aside, the steady deterioration of Egyptian-Libyan relations since 1973 is a result of this situation. The very recent irresponsible Soviet offer of arms and a nuclear reactor to Libya should also be viewed in this context. President Sadat's quick, vigorous attack on these developments underlines the tension between the two countries.

The dynamism of continuing local inter-Arab conflict has been, in fact, highlighted by the abrasive Libyan-Egyptian relationship. Mutual accusations and recriminations in the press of the two countries have not been elegant in thought or expression. Name-calling has been a common occurrence. Sadat was recently described in Libyan public print as the master, the one who thinks he is a twentieth century Caesar. Where is the money we have deposited in his banks? Can the Pasha face the people and tell them where he has hidden the money? He will not be able to do so because Cleopatra has spent it all on her dresses, on lavish wedding ceremonies for her daughters and on her trips to Europe. The Pasha then comes and accuses us of cutting off financial aid to Egypt. Of course we did, but only when we had become convinced that our money was going into special private pockets and into European bank accounts. The master should know that we know all about him and his kind and revealing the truth about their thefts and treacheries to the Arab masses we shut their mouths. Retorting in press interviews, Sadat referred to Qadhafi as a sick, unreliable man, possessed by the devil.

Meanwhile, in Egypt there has been a growing revulsion against other Arab states. This manifests itself both on the official, practical level and the popular, emotional one, and constitutes a new potential source of inter-Arab discord. Thus, the parlous, depressing economic situation in the country is generating its own scapegoats and villains, from Nasser's disastrous promotion of a privileged 'class' to the newly rich Arabs of the Peninsula, the Gulf and Libya. The Sadat regime appears to be trying to put the blame for its economic difficulties on the Nasser legacy. At the same time, members of the National Assembly, not without encouragement from the top, are arguing that whereas the October War raised the income of the Arab oil states from £15 billion to nearly £70 billion a year, over half the Arab investments have been going to the United Kingdom and the USA, another 45 per cent to Western Europe and a meagre 5 per cent to developing countries. They suspect oil-rich Arab states are reluctant to commit long-term investment to Egypt due to a combination of uncertainty about political conditions and fear of another war.

Among the general public, feelings of resentment against Saudi, Kuwaiti, Libyan and other oil-rich visitors to their country run very high. Incidents reflecting this feeling occur daily in Egypt.

Inherent in the Arab alignments and realignments of the October War and its aftermath are the seeds of new, perhaps different, inter-Arab discord and conflict.

Generally, the economic needs of a populous, relatively advanced Egypt add to the urgency of its pursuit of a major role in inter-Arab relations. A popular view is that Egypt can, in fact, opt out of Arab affairs altogether. Theoretically, and on the face of it, this is a valid suggestion. Actually, events in 1975 seem to corroborate it. Validity, however, is not synonymous with practicality or the pressures of reality. Whether under the Pharoahs, one observes, or throughout the Muslim Fatimid, Mamluk or Albanian dynasty domination, Egypt has always had to engage from time to time in a regional policy.

Wider Considerations

I have already argued that, since the October War, the tendency in inter-Arab relations has been one of eschewing the old objective and ideology of Arab unity in favour of solidarity, based on a convergence of the interests of individual Arab states. This was manifested in the use of the oil weapon (the coordinated policies of Egypt, Saudi Arabia and Syria) against Israel, and against its European and American friends. Nevertheless, the most likely development in the immediate future will be one of the consolidation of several *loci* of Arab power, for example, Saudi Arabia in the Peninsula allied with Egypt for a while, Algeria in the Maghreb, and possibly Syria and/or Iraq in the Fertile Crescent. To this extent the whole area of inter-Arab relations and relations between Arab and non-Arab states in the Middle East, as well as with Europe and the superpowers, will remain dangerously problematic.

Relations between the Arab states will continue to carry the seeds of inter-Arab dissension and diversion over (1) the Arab-Israel conflict; (2) economic matters; (3) regional and sub-regional rivalries, and (4) relations with Europe and the superpowers. Equally critical will be the relations between Arab and non-Arab states in the Middle East. The controversy over oil prices, oil production and the confrontation between Iran and the Arab states in the Gulf, all constitute sources of tension and potential conflict. Recently, however, the dispute between Iran and Iraq over the Kurdish issue and other matters of difference between them have been formally, if temporarily, settled.

On 6 March 1975, Iran and Iraq signed an accord which formally composed a number of long-standing differences between the two countries. The immediate effect of what soon came to be known as the Pact of Algiers was the collapse of the Kurdish insurgents once they lost their main source of support in Tehran. Thousands of hapless Kurdish refugees streamed across the border into Iran, or trekked further up into the wild heights of their mountain fastnesses.

For the Baath regime in Baghdad the advantages of the timely accord with Tehran were immediately visible and crucial. It freed their army from a costly endless struggle against a determined and tenacious adversary very much at home with irregular warfare. This alone was an attractive enough gain for the Iraqi regime to be willing to make several concessions to the Shah. But the Pact entails certain dangers that may still come to plague Baghdad in the future.

For many years, in addition to his support of the Kurdish irregulars, the Shah organised and financed several seditious elements, inside the Iraqi armed forces and among the vast numbers of the Shia community in Iraq. In the light of his policy in the Gulf, he has been concerned with military developments in Shatt al-Arab at the top of the Gulf. Meanwhile, he has been involved in Oman.

The Shah probably perceives the recent agreement with Iraq as helping him to accomplish several objectives. By sacrificing the Kurds, he believes he has acquired greater flexibility within Iraq through his sympathisers and 'agents' among the Shia community. He may also feel that he is in a better position to curb, if not neutralise, Iraqi or Baath activities throughout the Gulf. While pressing the Iraqis, as well as embarrassing them, over the Soviet naval and air station facilities in Umm Qasr, he can extract Iraqi recognition of an Iranian naval presence in Shatt al-Arab. Among the more concrete gains has been the agreement on interim steps in relation to some ten thousand former Iranian residents of Iraq who had been expelled. Even more significant has been the major concession the Shah extracted from Iraq by persuading that country to abandon its claim on the oil-rich province of Khuzistan, and so-called al-Ahwaz, in which lie the oil towns of Abadan and Ahwaz. There were some two million Arabs in the province when the British, after the First World War, attached it to Iran. Until then it had formed part of the Ottoman Empire and comprised parts of southwest Persia, south-east Iraq and a small part of Kuwait, and enjoyed 'home rule' under Sheikh Khazaal's family. In 1960, the Iraqi ruler, Abdul Karim Qasim, launched a campaign to liberate 'Arabistan' as the Iraqis referred to the province, and formed the 'Al Ahwaz National Popular Front'. In 1969, Saddam Hussein, vice president of the Revolution Command Council, launched an active campaign of subversion in Khuzistan as the main thrust of Iraq's conflict with Iran. Nearly 6,000 Khuzistan Arabs were recruited and trained in Iraq. Financial help for these 'freedom fighters' of Arabistan and Iraqi officers was infiltrated into the province. All of this was stopped by the Pact of Algiers.

Both Iran and Iraq believe that their accord frees them to withstand the Soviet presence in Iraq and Syria. This is in line with the Shah's policy of closing the Gulf to the interference and/or presence of outside powers. Yet an indication of the attraction of this area for such powers has been the alacrity with which the Shah of Iran followed up the Pact of Algiers by talks with the deputy prime minister of China, Li Hsiennien. A joint declaration issued last April was heavily tilted against the Soviet Union and the presence of all outside powers in the area.

The agreement between the two countries is, however, also a source of inter-Arab differences. Syria and Libya, for example, have been more sympathetic than other Arab states toward the Ahwaz National Popular Front and its solicitation of Arab support. That is, they have been critical of Iraq's accommodation with a non-Arab regional power that has clear ambitions in the Gulf and the region as a whole.

Israel and Iran might still find it convenient to combine in a common anti-Arab cause. Even though Iran has not extended even *de facto* recognition to Israel, the contacts and cooperation between them have been extensive, not to mention the oil supplies Israel received from Iran via tanker to Eilat. The Arabs, incidentally, already allude to this Iran-Israel collaboration, and have from time to time alleged the existence of a United States–Israel plan, in collusion with Iran, to frustrate Arab objectives.

Similarly, Israel enjoys formal relations with another non-Arab Middle Eastern state, Turkey. The confrontation between Greece and Turkey in the Eastern Mediterranean, whether over oil rights in the Aegean, or over Cyprus, both so close to the Middle East conflict, is worrying. The Greeks and Arab states have already bargained and horse-traded with each other over their respective conflicts. One cannot, therefore, completely rule out a greater involvement of Turkey and Iran in Arab regional affairs.

The USA and Inter-Arab Relations

Essentially, the USA seeks to:

1. prevent the Middle East from becoming the exclusive sphere of influence of its rival superpower, the Soviet Union, for that would immediately threaten its interests in the security of Europe (NATO), the Gulf, Africa and the Indian Ocean;
2. maintain an influence in the region which will
   a. guarantee the flow of oil to the West,
   b. guarantee the integrity and independence of all states in the area,

    c. provide an outlet for US economic activity (development investment, trade and commerce),

    d. exercise via bilateral agreements with Middle Eastern states some control over the use and impact of their huge reserves on the international monetary system.

3. maintain the strategic role of the US Sixth Fleet in the Mediterranean, still the main American deterrent in southern Europe and the Middle East.

The USA must pursue the above objectives and protect these interests for the next few years in the following context of inter-Arab relations:

1. The centre of wealth, if not, strictly speaking, economic power, in the Arab Middle East has shifted from its core to the peripheries: Arabia and the Gulf in the East; Libya and Algeria in the West;

2. There has never been and there is not now a monolithic political entity called the 'Arab Middle East', and the USA must not approach it as such. Rather the tendency is for the existence of several, competing *loci* of Arab power, and a preference among Arab states for bilateral arrangements with one another and with outside powers. Joint or collective Arab policies toward others is predicated on the convergence of the respective interests of the several states;

3. The more permanent, even constant, sources of inter-Arab conflict remain. There are, as indicated, different interests and perceptions which both historically and existentially separate, and divide, say, the Arab east from the Arab west, Saudi Arabia from Egypt or the Fertile Crescent. All these factors remain important for the region's future evolution. Added to these are agreements and disagreements among Arab states over, for instance, the role of the USA in their region, and their relations to it. They are all reconciled to the fact that it will compete for influence in the Middle East against the Soviet Union, and that it will, furthermore, work to prevent Russian domination. The weaker among the Arab states, and perhaps all of them, are not opposed to the American interest in safeguarding the independence and integrity of all states in the area. The disagreement arises both with the USA and among themselves over whether this principle should also apply to Israel. There is sharp disagreement between them over American economic activity in their region. This, however, flows partly from their disparate respective interests and varied relations with patron powers or superpowers. Considering the central position of Saudi-Egyptian collaboration to the area, American attention, in its political and economic manifestations, to these two countries, seems for the moment wise.

4. Arrangements are still made with rulers and regimes open to sedition and coups. This condition in itself renders relations between Arab states, as well as between them and external powers, especially difficult. Because of it, Arab power too remains vulnerable, though difficult to assess, and its potential effectiveness unpredictable. So far it has manifested and expressed itself through the use of the oil weapon in connection with the conflict with Israel. The Arabs, that is, succeeded in making America's major interest the guarantee of the flow of oil from the Middle East to the West contingent upon a reconsideration of her relations with the Arab states as opposed to Israel. The weaker West Europeans, heavily dependent on Middle East oil, appear to have bowed to Arab pressure.

5. In the event that Western dependence on Middle Eastern oil over the next five years is not appreciably reduced, and there is a resumption of Arab-Israeli hostilities, the Arabs may well use the oil weapon again. In those circumstances it is likely that Italy in Europe will collapse, and Britain could come close to the brink. If such an eventuality occurs, the USA may have to consider a role for itself other than that of peacemaker − not for the defence and preservation of Israel, but for the protection of the Western Alliance in Europe. In this connection, it is fair to suggest that any superpower deals with the Middle East will not occur because of its intrinsic local value, but because of the superpower's concern with the defence of Europe, as well as its interests in the Indian Ocean.

6. The Arab-Israel conflict is only one of several existing and potential ones in the region. Developments in the Gulf may entail some conflict between Arabs locally, and regionally between Arabs and Iranians. These may attract some form of superpower intervention. The rebellious, unsettled regions of south Arabia already command the attention of China and the Soviet Union. Related to developments there is the prospect of conflict over control of the Horn of Africa and the Indian Ocean.

In the Arab Middle East, inter-Arab relations themselves remain a labyrinth of intricate and often irreconcilable elements. In the past, as a rule, divisions, differences, and local conflicts were contained within and under an imperial arrangement. Today, in the absence of such an arrangement, local states which can dispose of wealth can generate more deadly conflict, dangerous not only to the region's stability but also to that of the rest of the world. Aware of the rivalry between the two superpowers, the Arab states today believe they can 'win' because neither the USA nor the Soviet Union can impose its will or peace over them. Is this, however, the case?

I believe that the resolution of the Arab-Israel conflict will not solve the Arab-Jewish antithesis and enmity in the Middle East. The Soviet Union, one is told, does not need Middle East oil; the West desperately does. How far is the Soviet Union prepared to risk an armed confrontation with the West merely in order to deny the latter access to oil it does not need?

In October 1973, the USA embarked upon the arduous and delicate role of peacemaker in the Middle East. It faces the monumental task of juggling all the disparate and competing elements of the Arab and Middle Eastern reality. Its basic assumption, at least in dealing with the Arab-Israel conflict, is that at some point peace will be concluded between the Arab states and an independent sovereign Israel. I have tried in this chapter to emphasise the dubious validity of this assumption and, therefore, the fragility of the whole enterprise. America's partners in *détente* may refuse to cooperate fully in the task of peace-making in the Middle East. Recently, they have loudly publicised their support for the PLO even after Arafat's uncompromising speech in the United Nations. Meanwhile, they seem, on the face of it at least, about to recover their 'losses' in Egypt with a military presence of sorts in Libya. The old advantages of shore base facilities for the Soviet fleet in Mersa Matruh and Bernis may soon be reproduced in Libya. In addition, they continue to chip away relentlessly at the strategic corners and peripheries of Western defence arrangements in the Mediterranean basin. They procrastinate over the Geneva Conference while they press the Egyptians over their loan repayments.

Reported American economic arrangements with some Arab states, regardless of how ingenious, guarantee very little, if anything at all. The question is, therefore, in view of these difficulties and possible complications in peace-making, what other options does the USA have that it is prepared to take a risk with in defence of its interests in the Middle East?

Optimists today insist that the newly-acquired respectability of the PLO will breed eminent reasonableness in Yassir Arafat; that with the assistance of other Arab states he will prevail over his detractors and enemies — the 'rejection' front — within the movement. They hope that all of this will eventually lead to his coming to terms with Israel, settling for a state of sorts somewhere on the West Bank and/or Jordan and the Gaza Strip. What is often overlooked is the fact that before any of this can take place, Jordanian action over the Palestinians will infuse new elements of inter-Arab conflict. Also, civil strife among Palestinians on the West Bank is already in evidence. There are, furthermore, too many loose gunmen about. Moderation and compromise on the part of Arafat may place him in what I would call an 'Abdullah role' regarding the Palestine question. When that happens, his life will be exposed to a bullet.

Even if the Palestinians acquire a state on the West Bank and Gaza, it is perhaps, on present evidence, too much to hope that, because it is viable only on the basis of a close economic-political relationship with Israel and Jordan, it will live in peace with its Jewish neighbour. It could conceivably invite a Soviet presence in whatever guise in the hope of realising its goal of a 'secular democratic Palestinian state', i.e., one that will take the place of Israel.

One thing is certain in the immediate future. To settle or not to settle with Israel, and what kind of settlement this should be, will become a central issue of discord and dissension among the Arab states. The rumblings in Egypt already surveyed are only one indication of this. In April 1975, a leading Egyptian journalist, Muhammad Sid Ahmad, who is considered to be a Marxist, published a book, *After the Guns Have Been Silenced*.[11] In it, he makes the bold, extraordinary and, among the Arabs, first and singular, proposal that they should now come to terms with Israel, and permit it a developmental role in the region, implying that the Israelis, with their knowledge, skills and advanced technology, can contribute greatly to the development of Arab societies. The Beirut weekly *Al-Hawadith* (30 March 1975), probably financed by the Kuwaitis and Saudis, published a blistering attack on the book and its author, rejecting his proposals, implying that they constituted treason.

President Sadat, on the other hand, has contended since the October War that that war proved finally and conclusively that the Arab-Israel conflict cannot be resolved by war. The reason is that the superpowers will not permit the local adversaries to settle their conflict in this way. What President Sadat wishes to convey to the world is that his country is now committed to the search for peace. This may sound logical, but it cannot be taken as the reflection or expression of an everlasting reality. If, according to Sadat, Egyptian and Arab strategy is not to surrender 'an inch of Arab land' and not to compromise over or negotiate away the rights of the Palestinians (as yet undefined), the tactics of peacemaking, buying time, or whatever, about which Arabs can differ and quarrel with each other, relate only to current conditions. Conditions, alas, may change in the next five or ten years.

For the foreseeable future, inter-Arab differences and conflict will continue, whether over Israel, the piecemeal or Geneva Conference approach to a settlement, over natural, economic and financial resources, over Islamic or less native views of the world, over communal, sectarian and ethnic matters. This is a feature of the area that will remain more or less a *constant*. The question of American choices or options in the future, therefore, is one that must first of all be resolved on the basis of this fundamental reality: inter-Arab relations cannot be placed on a spectrum of linear development, moving from hell to paradise or vice versa. Rather their course is partly cyclical, partly jerkily spiral, and always resting occasionally at some 'grey' area. Secondly, American choices must be made on the assumption that what the Arabs want or desire is not always – if ever – what Americans desire; in fact, the two desires may be diametrically opposed and radically different. Finally, if the Arab Middle East is important to the United States for the security of Europe, NATO and the Western Alliance, as a source of energy supplies and transport, trade routes and communications in the Mediterranean and Indian Ocean, then the only choice Americans can really have is to maintain their strategic (military and political) capability in the area. This capability, whatever its detractors say, was amply demonstrated in 1971 in connection with the Jordan-Syria clash. Alas, in a conflict-ridden area, even a superpower as technologically advanced as the USA still needs to consider, and respect, some of the unfashionable strategic concepts and practices of the nineteenth century. Often, one has the distinct impression that this is exactly what the rival superpower does.

Notes

1. Here I refer to the tendency of American policy after the last war to favour – and encourage – nationalist, anti-colonial movements, the involvement in Egypt in the period 1949-53; the heyday of what I would call the American inclination to 'fix' things. At that time Americans seemed to think that by 'fixing' a big boy among the Arabs, he, in turn, would fix the rest. Foremost example was American enthusiasm for Nasser.
2. Here only an outline of these patterns and trends is presented. For a more detailed exposition of the events illustrating these trends, I refer the reader to my *Conflict in the Middle East* (George Allen and Unwin, London, 1971), in particular Chapters 2, 4, 5-6 and 8.
3. In explaining why Nasser broke with the Syrian Baath leadership during the Union (1958-61), Muhammad Hasanein Heikal suggested, among other reasons, that Nasser could not very well allow a member of one of the minorities (i.e., Michel Aflaq, a Christian Arab) to govern a predominantly Muslim country like Syria. See Fuad Matar, *Bisaraha an Abdel Nasser: hiwar ma Muhammad Heikal* (*Frankly Speaking about Abdel Nasser: a dialogue with Muhammad Heikal*) (Beirut, 1975).
4. See Mohamed Heikal, *The Road to Ramadan* (London, 1975) and General Salah el-Din al-Hadidi, *Shahid ala harb '67* (*Witness to the war of '67*) (Beirut, 1974)

5. Heikal, in *Road to Ramadan*, argues that Nasser considered Libya as providing the 'defence depth' Egypt needed in a war with Israel, and that he began laying plans for another war on the morrow of the 1967 defeat.

6. Hussein's willingness to abandon the West bank to the PLO is, in my view, based on two factors: (a) he knows the Israelis will vigorously resist its falling under PLO control, in which case Arafat's prestige will suffer; (b) he has satisfied for the moment the demands of his own East Jordanian establishment to relinquish the West Bank.

7. Organisational Directive of the ASU Secretariat, August 1972. Reproduced in Fuad Matar, *Nasserite Russia and Egyptian Egypt* (Arabic) (Beirut, 1972), pp. 196-201.

8. For a general treatment of the shambles of economic development (planning, investment, savings, industrialisation), see the devastating monograph by the Egyptian economist Galal A. Amin, *The Modernization of Poverty, The Political Economy of Nine Arab States, 1945-70* (Brill, Leiden, 1974).

9. The recent proposals for constitutional amendments in Jordan indicate Hussein will ask those of Palestinian origin to choose between Jordanian citizenship and Palestinian status. If a majority of them opt for the former, a similar move by Lebanon is possible as regards its 300,000 Palestinian residents. This will seriously weaken the PLO.

10. There are those who interpret the present Egyptian-Saudi alliance in part as one aimed against a possible Iraqi-Syrian constellation in the Fertile Crescent under Soviet influence.

11. Dar al-Qadaya, Beirut, 1975. English translation, *After the Guns fall Silent* (Croom Helm, London, 1976).

6 REGIONAL POLITICS

One may approach the problem of regional politics by a consideration of the impact of the Egyptian-Israeli peace treaty and the Arab opposition to it. Second, one may suggest patterns and trends in developments, especially the shift of the focus of conflict further east to the Gulf and South-west Asia. Third, one could attempt to identify potential problem areas or crisis points. An initial assumption is that, because of its political geology or morphology, the Middle East region naturally generates both local and international conflict and will continue to do so in the foreseeable future. And, because of the vital interests of foreign powers, especially the superpowers, the Middle East attracts outside involvement.

The epochal shift that occurred in the political and strategic balance of the Arab-Israeli conflict is a result of Egypt's policy and the not too surprising, indeed anticipated, reaction of the Arab states. This shift is of great importance whatever may be the outcome of the attempt to implement, by negotiation, the provisions of the Egyptian-Israeli peace treaty. Among the factors that one ought to consider in this connection are, first, Egypt's massive presence in the Arab world in spite of the political differences between her and other Arab regimes; second, Egypt's ability to formulate policy based on her national or state interest and related to her historically important function in the region; and, third, the absence so far of an alternative and enforceable policy of peace or war on the part of other Arab states. The mutual distrust, conflict of interest and rivalry among the Arab states, especially between Iraq and Syria, the original leaders of the anti-Egyptian front, make it still possible for Egypt to continue her peace policy.

Having concluded that their experience of the last thirty years has been one of a counter-productive policy, bloodied as they have been by a terrible war in October 1973, and aware of the horrors of yet another one, the Egyptians believe they still have a role to play in the region. This, however, is somewhat different from that of the past. They will play it in future while trying to maintain a balance between their national interests on one hand and their wider interests as members of

Source: George Wise and Charles Issawi (eds.), *Middle Eastern Perspectives: the Next Twenty Years* (The Darwin Press, Princeton, N.J., 1980).

an Arab cultural entity and community of nations on the other. In a way, therefore, one finds, temporarily at least, the proposition that Egypt can be isolated from the rest of the Arab world somewhat absurd.

The strategic and political importance of the shift that has occurred at the very core of the Arab-Israeli conflict is balanced, however, by serious threats to this Egyptian peace policy. Yet, for the time being, the singular choice the Egyptians have made to relinquish war as a policy in dealing with Israel is having an impact on inter-Arab politics. One consequence, as mentioned, has been the realignment of several Arab states against the new Egyptian policy, but within a traditional historical context of the Fertile Crescent versus Egypt. There has also been a reorientation in the external policies of the region's states. Egypt, for example, has reoriented her policy since 1972 towards the West. Even without the Soviet invasion of Afghanistan at the end of 1979, there could still have been an array of regional forces between Mesopotamia and the Nile Valley, especially if one bears in mind that in 1978-9 there was renewed interest on the part of Egypt in closer cooperation with the Sudan.

It could be argued that the oil-rich states of Saudi Arabia, Kuwait, the United Arab Emirates and Libya on the peripheries have tried to influence and maintain in balance the regional antagonism between Cairo and Baghdad. It could also be argued that this shift has been underway since the 1973 war. Egypt perceived that a break in the conflict was possible only by shunting aside for the moment the Palestinian and inter-Arab factor in its relations with Israel and reorienting its external policy towards a closer relationship with the West.

Egyptian policy led to a split in the Arab League and the severance of diplomatic relations between Egypt and several Arab states. Jordanian opposition to the Camp David Accords has been basically a response to the *rapprochement*, temporary as it was, between Syria and Iraq, dependence on financial assistance from Saudi Arabia, and a special relationship with the Palestinians on the West Bank. Heavily dependent on the financial assistance of the oil states and military assistance from Syria, the PLO has perforce played a prominent role in the anti-Egyptian Arab front. However, until now, this front has had no real effect on Egyptian policy, nor has it affected Egypt's massive presence in the Arab world, for she continues to export thousands of workers, teachers, professionals and technicians to the Arab countries. At the same time, she continues to receive thousands of Arab students in her universities.

Another consequence of the treaty has been the change in the strategic position of the superpowers. Upon a careful reading of the text of the treaty and its appendices, some may argue that the USA has acquired the basis for a military presence in the region and a potential strategic capability resulting from its relationship with Egypt and Israel. This combination, however, may prove abrasive and uncomfortable, at least between Israel and the USA. Israel could become apprehensive over the massive rearming of Egypt by the USA and the likelihood of greater American pressure upon it to adopt a more accommodating policy over the West Bank.

But, in practical terms, the Sinai barrier between Egypt and Israel has been broken. The barrier between Israel on one side and the Palestinians and other Arab states on the other has yet to be breached. The possibility, slight as it may be, exists that the staged implementation of the treaty provisions may create new conditions favourable to change, regardless of how imperceptible they might be for the moment. For example, there could be a cumulative effect on the strategic and political thinking of all the parties involved in the conflict as these provisions are seen to be implemented. Under the treaty, Egypt is getting back the Sinai; recovery of this territory automatically improves Egypt's political posture and strategic position in the region. A stronger Egypt in the near future is perhaps one such development and a cause of apprehension among other Arab states. Then, the implementation of the treaty provisions may set in motion an irreversible process that may force others in the area to accommodate themselves to the newly created conditions. A formula of autonomy for the Palestinians, for example, may wean several groups and, possibly, one or two rulers away from the constellation of opposing forces, namely, the Arab Rejection Front.

Meanwhile, events in Iran and Afghanistan have shifted the regional centre of conflict away from its Arab core to the eastern peripheries of the Gulf and South-west Asia. This shift in itself directly affects the concerns of the Arab states within the region and the relations among them.

Egypt's Domestic Difficulties

There are, however, serious domestic threats and external dangers to Egypt's peace policy. At home, these are essentially economic (with their attendant social consequences) and political. In fact, the greatest threat to Egypt's peace policy may yet come from domestic difficulties, not from the opposition of the Arab states. The country's major problem for the foreseeable future will be that of feeding its rising population. It is staggering to think that the estimated population at the end

of the century will be 65-70 million, or an increase in twenty years of
fifty per cent. Forty per cent of the population now (estimated at the
end of 1977 at forty million) is under fifteen years of age. Only twenty-
five per cent of the total at the moment (9.5 million) constitutes the
working population. Despite the industrialisation programmes of the last
twenty-five years and the expansion of the service sector, nearly half
of this working population (44.7 per cent) is still engaged on the land,
35.9 per cent in services, and only 19.4 per cent in industry. In the
meantime, there has been a disproportionate exodus of the country's
trained and skilled human resources to neighbouring, prosperous Arab
countries and overseas. Egypt, therefore, will continue to depend on
outside assistance.

The new economic policy, inaugurated in 1974 and commonly referred to as the Open Door Policy (ODP), aims at tackling the country's
perilous economic conditions. The main features of this policy are a
shift to a free market economy in the hope of attracting foreign capital
investments, a greater determination to strike a more reasonable and
credible balance between industrial and agricultural development, a
decision to revitalise the existing public sector by promoting keener
competition from an enlarged private sector, and a conscious effort to
provide structures for the management of the economic and social problems that loom large on the horizon.

The ODP also intends to alleviate the employment problem by absorb-
ing the masses of Egyptian unemployed and underemployed secondary-
school students and university graduates in an expanding private sector
of the economy. With the greater attention to be paid to agriculture
and food production, the policy will, hopefully, slow down the movement of population from the countryside to the city.

It is too early to say whether the ODP will create the required new
economic structures. For the moment, it has established a parallel market for foreign exchange, reduced exchange restrictions, reformed banking laws, and, to some extent, decentralised the making of economic
decisions. More importantly, perhaps, it has increased the participation
of the private sector in the economy. But the ODP still faces great obstacles.

Although Egypt disposes of abundant cheap labour, most of it is
ill-fed, uneducated, or poorly educated and trained. There is, therefore,
a manpower problem. Municipal and other services, so crucial to the
success of the new policy, are poorly organised or have collapsed. Their
restoration can only be undertaken with massive outside assistance,
since technicians, craftsmen, artisans, and even managers of small-scale

businesses are in desperately short supply. Even more serious is the deplorable condition of the state administration, with its overmanned and wasteful bureaucracy.

The ODP, or *infitah*, must also be seen as going beyond economic considerations; it is the expression of a policy of openness, especially to the West. To this extent, it has been supported by the upper middle classes, elements of the small bourgeoisie as well as the new upwardly mobile segments of the population created by Nasser's old constituency, many of whom are now engaged in entrepreneurial activities.

Unfortunately, so far this policy has turned out to be a consumer, not a producer, and has led to bureaucratic corruption and parasitic capitalism. It has also adversely affected income distribution, widening the gap between the masses of the poor and the few rich. The new tax laws of 1978, for instance, favour higher income groups, foreign and mixed investment projects, construction companies and banks. The policy, on the whole, has led to inflation, the concentration of wealth in a few hands, flagrant consumerism and maldistribution of income. Foreign capital, so far, has invested in quick profit projects. Western capital, petro-dollars and big businesses are reluctant to invest in long-term projects because (1) they fear political instability; (2) anticipate wider regional instability; (3) are aware of a weak local infrastructure and bureaucratic red tape; and (4) observe the rampant inflation and the lack of technical and managerial skills in the country. The result has been that projects under the ODP (aside from tourism, hotels and construction) are not developmental. For example, foreign banks deal mainly in import finance. In short, a laissez-faire policy has led to the loss of government control, at least over the direction of investment. In the process, a new class of *nouveaux riches* has emerged, aggravating further the problem of social and political stability.

A reformulation of the country's political priorities in the 1980s, both at home and abroad, will depend to a great extent on the resolution of some of its most pressing economic problems. In fact, the very success of the regime's peace policy and its ability to withstand Arab opposition rests on its ability to cope effectively with the changing domestic scene. At this point, the few *loci* of alternative power to Sadat in the country — most notably in the armed forces, which, in any case, on the whole support the peace policy — will react primarily to the regime's failure to deal with domestic problems.

Significantly, it is the social consequences of these economic problems that constitute the covert threat to Egypt's peace policy. A galloping inflation (currently estimated at 40 per cent) has eroded living standards of the small post-1952 'middle class', the educated elements in it, the salaried bureaucracy and the army officer corps. Nor should the dangers of a psychologically-rooted national disaffection of the less well-off masses be minimised. Whereas the harsh economic conditions of the last thirty years were justified by the requirements of a war-time economy, the growing chasm between rich and poor, which is now of a magnitude never seen before, cannot be explained away so easily. This ever-widening gap between the few and the vast majority may create conditions reminiscent of, and parallel to, the period 1950-2. That many of the new rich have acquired their wealth as a result of access to influence and power only helps to fuel the resentment of the rest of society.

Although the response of the vast majority of Egyptians to President Sadat's policy has been one of welcome relief, opposition continues to be spearheaded by the stirring populist religio-political movements that had lain dormant for a long time. These are led by the resurrected Muslim Brethren, who have resumed their activities especially among students and in the press. Their *Da'wa* magazine provides a platform of steady opposition to the regime and its policy of peace with Israel. The experience in Iran also suggests that an ambitious economic policy could founder upon the rocks of a stubbornly authoritarian state system. Vast demographic change in the last decade in Egypt has also produced a mass of uprooted humanity that could provide militant, populist movements with political malcontents for whom Islam is the sole basis of political identity, solidarity and social cohesiveness.

The concern with opposition to President Sadat's policy is reflected in the difference between the establishment of formal diplomatic relations between Egypt and Israel on the one hand and the resistance to a wider normalisation of relations between the two countries on the other. It is not only Sadat himself and his establishment who are reluctant to open the floodgates of normalisation as long as Mr Begin's government remains intransigent, in their view, over the issue of Palestinian autonomy on the West Bank and Gaza. Equally significant is the rejection of such normalisation by groups of Egyptians, especially professionals, technicians and others, who fear their isolation from the rest of the Arab world where they have a vital interest in terms of jobs and influence. Similarly, the slow returns of the ODP in terms of a marked improvement in the economy erode the earlier expectation of the benefits of a closer relationship with Israel. One fears that President Sadat's apparent over-emphasis on the external factor for the resolution of Egypt's economic and social difficulties may be misplaced and, in the long term, disastrous. Solutions to some of these problems must be sought at home.

Another more serious threat to the regime's policy may come from the potential disaffection of the officer corps. Equally affected by inflation, officers observe their civilian relations enriching themselves in quick-return enterprises under the conditions of the new economic policy. They also view with great suspicion the better pay and conditions and the unnecessarily sophisticated weaponry of the police. They suspect the regime favours a strengthened police force as a makeweight to the army and as a means to control popular disturbances caused by economic hardship.

For the moment, in 1979, pressing economic problems at home and their social consequences have led to a deterioration of the domestic political situation. As a result, the so-called liberalisation policies of the years between 1975 and 1978 have been discarded if not, in fact, reversed, in 1979. There has been a tightening-up of internal security and a move towards greater autocracy. Thus, two very recent legislative steps taken by President Sadat are, in the view of some, ominous. Passed after a referendum, one requires that legislation be based on religious law (*shari'a*); the other decrees that the president can be elected for more than two terms. The first may be considered a way of countering extremist and militant religio-political opposition; the second, a way of amending the constitution in such a way as to allow Sadat to remain in office indefinitely.

The first of these legislative acts, however, has raised once again in Egypt the spectre of communal conflict between Muslims and Copts. In April 1980 there were serious clashes in Alexandria and parts of Upper Egypt. Milad Hanna's book, *Copts yes, but Egyptians*, appeared on the same day that President Sadat delivered his famous speech about a Coptic conspiracy to set up a Christian state in Upper Egypt. Coptic Patriarch Anba Shenouda's open letter in reply to the President's broadcast was not allowed to be published. Relations between the two communities remain strained, adding to the domestic turmoil and uncertainty. At a time when sectarian and ethnic conflicts are very much a part of the political landscape in other parts of the region, such a development in Egypt (historically the one country in the region least plagued by communal differences) contributes to the region's instability.

The Arab Rejection Front

The Arab Rejection Front also faces serious problems which can affect regional politics. Iraq and Syria have led the opposition to Egypt's peace policy. Although during the last decade both countries have been governed by Baathist regimes, their relations have been marred by mutual distrust. They came together briefly when their interest in opposing a peaceful accommodation with Israel converged. Syria's opposition to Egypt rested on military, strategic and political reasons, considering the Israeli occupation of the Golan since 1967, Syria's own military involvement in Lebanon, and its special relationship with the PLO. Iraq, on the other hand, saw its chance, with Egypt choosing to leave the wider inter-Arab political arena, to engage in the politics of Arab leadership. The alliance between the two countries, however, was short-lived, because it rested on unstable foundations. An attempt at union between them failed because of deep-seated enmities and traditional rivalries. Both countries suffered from internal weaknesses in their bodies politic, ranging from ethnic and sectarian conflict to narrow-based autocratic governing élites. Their domestic difficulties were such that no schemes of union between them could be implemented; nor could their joint leadership of the opposition against Egypt be made credible.

Ever since independence in 1946, every Syrian regime has been interested in carving out a major role for it in the Fertile Crescent. Equally, ever since independence, the rivalry between Syria and Iraq for the domination of the Fertile Crescent has also been a political fact of life, whether under *anciens régimes* or the military regimes that succeeded them after 1949; under the Baath regimes in Damascus since 1963; or even after 1968, when the Baath party came to power in both Baghdad and Damascus.

President Asad has been in power in Damascus for ten years. He is the leading member of the minority Alawite sect (11 per cent of the population), which, during the last ten to fifteen years, has come to control the two main centres of power in Syria, the military and the ruling Baath party. This situation in itself would not be significant were it not for the fact that, despite a great measure of cultural uniformity, Syria's population is characterised by strong religious and ethnic diversity. The Sunni (Orthodox) Muslims who constitute nearly 68 per cent of the population consider religious minorities such as the Alawites and the Druzes (3 per cent of the population) as heretical sects of Islam.

Furthermore, sectarian and ethnic diversity (exemplified by the presence of Kurds, Circassians, Armenians and Turkomans) has produced in Syria a fragmented political system. Political interference by European powers in the past has strengthened both the function of religious minorities as political units and their communal consciousness. Under the French Mandate (1920-46), sectarian loyalties were encouraged in order to counter the rise of Arab nationalism. This was particularly the case in the Latakia region, where most of the Alawites live, and the Jabal Druze region, where the Druzes are concentrated. As part of this policy, the French favoured the military recruitment of special detachments from among religious and ethnic minorities (Alawites, Druzes, Kurds, Circassians) to form the Troupes Spéciales du Levant. They used these troops to suppress local insurrections. The Sunni establishment in Damascus, Aleppo, and elsewhere in the main towns of Syria — who constituted the 'ruling class' of notables and merchants and who came to power after independence in 1946 resented this situation. In Syria, in addition to this basic sectarian and ethnic diversity, there are regional, local and tribal divisions between cities, localities and tribes, that further complicate the political fragmentation of the country.

Minorities such as the Alawites had been for a long time underprivileged agrarian communities, whose only hope for upward mobility had been to place their sons in military careers. Over the years, they attained a greater presence in the armed forces relative to their numerical strength in the population. When the Baath party was formed in the early 1940s, its secular ideology, including an element of socialism, attracted many members from the minorities, including the Alawites. For a long time, these minorities associated the traditional political parties of the Sunni establishment, including those with a platform of Arab nationalism, with Sunni Islam. They also resented their power. Within a period of twenty years, however, minorities came to dominate both the Baath party (in power since 1963) and its military organisation (in power since 1966), which military organisation, in turn, came to dominate the civilian wing of the party.

It is against this background that one must consider the manifestations of opposition and discontent in Syria in 1979-80, and the challenge these present to the Asad regime. Sunnis resent the regime's assistance of the Christians in Lebanon during the civil war there against the Lebanese Muslims and Palestinians. They also resent the monopoly of state power held by Alawites and their allies from among the other minorities. The older political formations of the Damascene establishment are opposed to the Baath party and its domination by the Alawites, whom they consider heretics. There is also a widespread grievance against corruption in the Asad regime, compounded by inflation and inequality. Finally, there are rivalries between Alawite officers and political aspirants, as was the case in the 1960s between Asad, Umran and Jadid.

In seeking to counter domestic instability, President Asad may seek greater assistance from the Soviet Union. While it is conceivable that such assistance could bolster his position in the Fertile Crescent and within Arab politics generally, it cannot resolve his domestic political difficulties. All the same, considering the crises in Iran and Afghanistan, a greater Syrian dependence on Soviet military support (including at some critical stage the transfer of Soviet troops to that country) would destabilise the Fertile Crescent and have serious repercussions in the region as a whole.

In addition to its rejectionist stand over peace with Israel, Iraq has recently embarked upon an aggressive Arab policy in the Gulf and South Arabia, and in view of developments in Iran and Afghanistan, it has moved toward some cooperation with Saudi Arabia. It opposes the involvement of the superpowers in the region and favours Arab regional security arrangements. Saudi Arabia's Crown Prince Fahd's most recent statement (13 August 1980) calling for a Holy War to establish a Palestinian state with Jerusalem as its capital, may well be, in part, a result of the recent talks between Baghdad and Riyadh. Given its domestic difficulties, however, it is unlikely that Iraq in the 1980s can provide, in any combination with other Arab states, a credible regional policy, including the kind of local gendarme force that dispenses with outside guarantors of regional security. Further afield in the meantime, it has strengthened its relations with some Western states, especially France and Greece.

In the 1980s, Iraq will continue to oppose potential Egyptian primacy in the Arab area and, to this extent, will collaborate with Saudi Arabia as long as the latter country's interests also demand its opposition to Egypt. For the moment, Iraq's relations with the PLO are as strained as those with Syria. These deteriorated in part because of the PLO's unqualified support of the Khomeini revolution in Iran to which Iraq is opposed for very good reasons. It remains one of the Arab countries that could most readily be affected by developments in Iran, not simply because of its contiguous border with that country but more significantly because of the Shia majority in its population and the possible effects of a wider Kurdish separatist movement in Iran spilling over to the Iraqi Kurds.

Saudi Arabia, an erstwhile ally of Egypt, shifted its position in order to oppose Camp David and Egypt's policy. It joined the Arab Rejection Front and provided financial assistance to Syria and Jordan. Events in Iran, Afghanistan and South Arabia, however, have prompted the Saudis to reconsider matters of domestic and external security.

Saudi Arabia in the 1980s will face the difficult problem of political stability. The major threats will come from two main sources. First, a rapid rate of economic development may have serious social consequences, ranging from demographic change to changes in life patterns; it will also at times heighten expectations that cannot be met. Second, the attendant political difficulties may result from the tension between the changed patterns of life produced by a new and different economy on the one hand and the desire to retain an essentially Islamic state and society on the other. These threats to the fabric of Saudi society and the nature of its polity are intertwined, not simply interconnected. Although, theoretically, these are domestic matters, they are inevitably affected by external factors to do with a wider Arab regional and international provenance. Of itself, the migration of Arab labour in the area, for instance, constitutes a powerful impetus for these projected changes.

There are those who argue that the Saudi Arabian ruling family will not be able to withstand for very long the pressure of demands for wider political participation and a more equitable distribution of wealth. To this extent, the prolonged intransigence of the family in the face of these pressures may create a condition of stasis in the country that may lead to sedition. Thus, there are those who have interpreted the storming of the Great Mosque in Mecca in 1979 as the first clear manifestation of political unrest in the country by religious militants, and as a protest against the ruling family's deviation from the principles of Islam. The case could be made, however, for the future ability of the ruling family to continue to successfully balance the emerging forces by slowing down a totally imported complex of economic development, by stringent immigration policies, and by a renewal of its arrangements with the religious brotherhood of the Wahhabis, the tribal groups, and its own members. Yet, with a population of barely five million Saudis, the country must continue to depend for its present policies on the importation of people and technology from the Middle East, Europe, the USA and Asia.

Saudi Arabia will remain concerned with preventing the Peninsula and the Gulf from falling under the influence of the radical Baathi regime of Iraq, the militant Iranians, or the Soviet Union through one of its satellites. At the same time, it must guard against militant, messianic religious movements at home by continually sustaining its own Wahhabi establishment. More concretely, it will seek to prevent the unification of the two Yemens (unless this takes place on its own conditions) since, in that event, Marxist South Yemen would dominate the North and allow its ally the Soviet Union greater political leverage over the Peninsula, thus threatening the sources of oil supply. Saudi Arabia will conduct its regional Arab policy in close cooperation with Kuwait, the independence of which is in Saudi interests. It will continue to placate the PLO by running political interference on its behalf with the Western world, using oil and capital as weapons, and will support Syria and Jordan in their opposition to Egypt's peace policy. As it cannot, even in the near future, dispose of a credible military force, Saudi Arabia will continue to depend on American assistance for its security. Further afield, it will continue to compete and cooperate with Egypt in East Africa, especially around the Horn, with a view to preventing the domination of the Red Sea area by the Soviet Union or any of its client states on the African continent.

Jordan, in a way, has had to walk the tightest rope of any Arab state in the last three years. In view of its earlier position in the West Bank, its sizeable settled Palestinian population, events in Lebanon and its partial dependence on Arab financial assistance, Jordan has had to shift its policy towards a closer cooperation with the Arab Rejection Front. Until 1979, it feared the consequences of a concerted Iraqi-Syrian policy and had to embark upon a *rapprochement* with both of these countries. But, following the estrangement of Baghdad and Damascus and the subsequent erosion of the Arab Rejection Front, Jordan has reassessed its position. In perceiving the weakness of the Asad regime in Syria, Jordan has renewed its interest in the fate of the West Bank, hoping that an eventual arrangement in association with it might yet be a compromise solution. There has thus been, in the last two years, a renewed collaboration between Jordan and the PLO, possibly with this end in mind. This is, however, a precarious and potentially dangerous relationship in view of what happened ten years ago. Nor is it possible for Jordan to ignore the old Palestinian constituency on the West Bank that must somehow be satisfied, whatever the final arrangements. And Jordan has to contend with the 1974 Arab decision that recognised the PLO as the sole representative of the Palestinian Arabs.

The PLO has been most active in the Arab Rejection Front. In 1979 it surfaced as a staunch supporter of the Khomeini revolution in Iran without, however, realising appreciable political returns. Its diplomatic offensive for recognition in Western Europe and the USA had a measure of success, at least in Western Europe, but has had no perceptible impact on the conflict itself on the ground. The PLO is still caught in its own dilemma, consisting of a difficult choice between a national covenant and the acceptance of a state on the West Bank. Constituent groups within it are sharply divided over this matter. Accepting a state on the West Bank would mean abandoning the central aim of its national covenant, namely, the recovery of all Palestine. Furthermore, it entails the risk of opposition from the local (ex-Jordanian) Palestinian leadership on the West Bank, and reaching an agreement with King Hussein.

It is interesting to note that the PLO in the 1980s will probably improve its diplomatic standing and find greater favour in the chanceries of some West European states at a time when its standing and popularity in the Middle East, especially in Jordan and Lebanon, are at a low ebb. Western European concern with energy supplies from the Middle East and a parallel dissatisfaction with American policy have been the principal factors in this development. The inconclusive negotiations between Egypt and Israel over Palestinian autonomy and the recent acts of the Begin government over East Jerusalem have contributed to it. On the other hand, the continued armed presence of the PLO in Lebanon, especially West Beirut and an enclave in south Lebanon, has alienated even the Muslim community in that country. This perhaps has been an inevitable consequence of the civil war. In Jordan, too, the events of 1968-70 have left feelings of resentment and distrust towards the PLO on the part of the long-established Palestinian community there, not to mention the East Jordanians themselves.

The role and fortunes of the PLO in the immediate future cannot be assessed separately from developments in Lebanon and, by extension, Syria and Jordan. Any future political compromise between the Muslim community of Lebanon and the recently strengthened Maronites may work to the disadvantage of the Palestinians. In order not to alienate the large Muslim community of Lebanon, the Syrians may well have to accept such a compromise or simply benevolently oversee, if not actually connive in, the PLO's eventual elimination from the Lebanese equation. For the moment, the Palestinians in Lebanon are surrounded by the Phalangists and the Syrian peace-keeping forces in the east and north and, in the south, they face Major Haddad's armed enclave, and the Israeli defence forces on the border.

A Composite Picture

The pattern of events in the coming decade will be marked by the continued instability of its regimes. The trend of developments will be one of shifting alignments among the states, with greater involvement of the superpowers. The close of the last decade saw the virtual dis-integration of Lebanon, the conclusion of the Egypt-Israel peace treaty, the overthrow of the Shah in Iran by an Islamic revolution, the Soviet invasion of Afghanistan, and the destabilisation of Turkey by unprecedented economic problems and social violence.

In the Arab Middle East, the competing *loci* of power and rivalry of regional interests will be centred in Arabia, Egypt, the Fertile Crescent and North Africa. Peripheral conflicts in Africa, the Red Sea area, the Eastern Mediterranean and South-west Asia will, naturally, affect this competition and rivalry. The pivots of conflict will be Egypt and the Arab states, Arabia and Iran, over the Gulf, Iraq and Iran, Syria and Iraq in the Fertile Crescent (the Palestinians and Jordan included), Algeria and Morocco in North Africa, and with Libya fomenting peripheral conflict in Tunisia, Egypt and the Sudan.

Four trends now dominate the Arab regimes' perception of regional politics in the Middle East. One is the outcome of the Egyptian-Israeli peace treaty. Another is the long-term impact of events in Iran and the spread of militant religious-populist sedition. A third is apprehension over the Soviet incursion into Afghanistan. Compounding this is the overall fear that the USA will not or cannot protect the region from the growing Soviet threat.

For a long time now, power in the states of the region has rested in the hands of older, traditional élites and 'class' minorities. Vast demographic changes in the last decade now threaten these arrangements. With readier access to money and arms, the transformation of discontented masses into holy warriors or revolutionary forces becomes easier. They can be led not only against their own respective state political establishments, but also against those who they presume have undermined their cultural autonomy, invariably some foreign power.

In my opinion, it is more useful to view the resurgence of Islamic militancy as a socio-political phenomenon than as a manifestation of a religious revival. It is a response to certain economic and social problems created by several decades of modernisation, economic development, and social change. Its political thrust is directed against the governing classes, their élites at home, and foreign connections abroad. Having said this, it is important to realise that Islamic resurgence remains in the main a protest movement, and is still negative in character. Yet, even as a negative movement, it will clearly influence politics in the region, at least to the extent that a condition of stasis tends to destabilise regimes.

If the experience in Iran so far is any indication, this movement will not succeed in making Islam a workable principle for political organisation or the sole basis of a political order. It will nevertheless sharpen the dichotomy between things perceived as Islamic and those considered to be non- or anti-Islamic. To this extent, it will use this dichotomy — perilously, one might add — in the relations between states. Also, to this extent, as a challenge to the status quo or as the agent of sedition, Islamic militancy will be a threat to foreign powers with vital interests in the region.

Closely connected with Islamic resurgence is the problem of minorities, which will plague regional politics, particularly in Iran and in the Fertile Crescent, but also in Turkey and the Gulf States, which have sizeable Shia, Persian and other non-Arab communities. It is felt even in Egypt. Apart from its adverse effect on the cohesion and, therefore, the stability of states, it can also have extra-regional and international repercussions. The greater or more frequent the incidence of militant Islamic movements, the more critical the minorities problem will become. In the past, peaceful coexistence of minorities with majorities, and therefore their survival, was guaranteed by imperial orders and, more recently, by secular political arrangements. The longer the problem remains unsolved, the harsher the internal security arrangements of the states in the region will be.

A source of regional problems in the 1980s may be the extensive migration of labour within the Arab countries. Some view it as a factor of greater integration. Without going into the impact of this migration on labour-exporting and labour-importing countries, there is an assumption that its greater regularisation via bilateral and multilateral Arab state agreements can promote its integration and also a financial market's. The constraints on such a development are not only economic but political, as has been the case, say, between Egypt and Libya, Egypt and the Sudan, and Egypt and Iraq.

The disparity between oil-rich states and poor ones, all of which must of course feed their populations, could conceivably inaugurate a new dimension of regional conflict. Libya and Iraq, for example, have already engaged in aggressive regional policies that are made possible by their comparatively richer conditions. The type of periodic clashes between Egypt and Libya in the past may become more common in the future.

Given these conditions, how credible are suggestions by some Middle Eastern states of a return to a policy of neutralism? Similarly, how credible are suggestions of regional defence arrangements that eschew ties with either of the superpowers? Is the reassertion of an Islamic identity enough? On the other hand, given the conflicting interests and rivalries between the states of the region, how effective or stable would be, say, any alliances between a superpower, especially the USA, and a Middle Eastern state?

The Superpowers

General Sir John Hackett has argued that the experience of the Second World War has shown that the Middle East is not the key to winning a war, but that its control is absolutely essential to not losing it. For the West, it is a much-needed fulcrum. The Soviet Union seems to have grasped the geo-political importance of this fulcrum and, in the last decade, has established its military presence astride the Red Sea, southern Africa, and, now, South-west Asia. In this way it can block the operation of this fulcrum. Otherwise, it is difficult to explain the Soviet presence in South Yemen, Libya, Syria and Africa in the 1970s and, now, in Afghanistan. If this presence is to be extended to a politically-fragmented region like the Middle East, the possibilities of new centres of regional power emerging with Soviet support or under Soviet control are greater.

In the 1950s and 1960s, the Soviet presence in the Middle East polarised regional politics. Now, the Egyptian-Israeli peace treaty, the Soviet invasion of Afghanistan, the Islamic resurgence in Iran and elsewhere, are all new causes of another, and perhaps different, polarisation of the region's politics.

The argument is often put forward that if the priorities of the two superpowers in the region are different, they can be accommodated. In the current confrontation, it is clear that the USA has sought to exclude the Soviet Union from peacemaking at the western end of the region. The Soviet Union, in turn, has embarked upon a more adventurous policy at the eastern and southern ends, constituting a threat to the West's vital energy supplies from the Gulf. This new situation may well force Western leaders in the 1980s to consider more urgently alternative overland means of oil transport, which may be easier to defend and protect than the sea lanes from the Gulf. In the meantime, the United States is seeking to consolidate its military presence in the Gulf (Oman) and the Indian Ocean, a development which in itself could provide a new rallying point for militant opposition in the region. Nevertheless, these developments have introduced a new kind of superpower rivalry over the friendship of the 'Islamic world'. Thus, while their respective interests demand a more direct involvement in the region in the 1980s, the consequences of their confrontation have introduced a new constraint on this involvement, namely, the sensibilities of Islam.

In the most recent of the confrontations between the superpowers in the Middle East, the United States faces a serious difficulty that the Soviet Union, for the moment, does not, namely, disagreements with allies over Middle Eastern policy. Events in the region have strained the Western Alliance, whose roots lie in Europe. The dissatisfaction of the EEC with American leadership of the Alliance is expressed in a policy of appeasement toward the Middle East. Concerned as they are with oil supplies from the region, West Europeans believe in placating Arab oil suppliers with a more pro-Arab stance over the Arab-Israel conflict. Some of them have also actively tried to appease the Soviet Union over Afghanistan. In fact, they fear that a greater American military involvement in the Middle East will reduce the American contribution to the defence of Western Europe and, therefore, place a heavier defence burden on them.

In conclusion, regional politics will be affected by the recent major change in the Middle Eastern regional balance. The two main events responsible for this change are the Egyptian–Israeli peace treaty and the Islamic revolution in Iran. The first has had a destabilising effect on the region to the extent that it has polarised the Arab states. There is now – no-one can say for how long – an Iraqi attempt at a regional policy, in collaboration with Saudi Arabia, aimed simultaneously against Egypt and at bringing her back to the Arab fold. In the meantime, Egypt's inter-Arab role has diminished. The second event has eliminated a staunch ally of the West, rendering the 'Nixon Doctrine' inapplicable and undermining the role of the USA in the area and fostering insecurity among its client states, chief among them Saudi Arabia.

The priority strategic interest of the USA and its allies is oil. In view of the recent change in the regional balance, the USA now intends to guarantee directly its military presence in the region. This it hopes to achieve with bases in Oman and the Indian Ocean, and related facilities in Egypt, Israel and perhaps Somalia. Such a policy in itself, however, may prove problematic.

The Soviet Union, in contrast, has embarked upon a more dynamic and, therefore, threatening policy in the region. Whether its long-term strategic interest is to endanger Western supplies of oil or access to the oil reserves themselves is immaterial. It could be both. Equally important may be the acquisition of regional influence through an attempt to secure its communications from the Dardanelles, Suez and Bab el-Mandeb to the Malacca Straits, Indo-China and Vladivostok. The route is vital. Geo-politically, concern with security along southern borders may have prompted the Soviet Union to gain a more pervasive presence in South-west Asia, the Middle East and the Horn of Africa. In this way, it is in a better position to project power, influence events and challenge the West.

If this is a fair depiction of recent changes, we may be entering a period of renewed imperial-type rivalry between superpowers in the Middle East. The rivalry will probably be conducted less by proxy and more by direct involvement, and regional politics will become proportionately more dangerous.

7 AUTHORITARIANISM AND AUTOCRACY IN THE MIDDLE EAST

Democracy has been such a popular term since the Second World War that it has acquired new and varied applications. It has become the supreme legitimating category for states, regimes and political orders, universally invoked by all rulers and governments to designate their rule. Before the Second World War, there were parliamentary democracies, constitutional monarchies and republics; now there are social democracies, people's democracies and republics, workers' democracies and mass democracies. In the face of such application of the term, it is difficult to define its essence, or assess its social and political significance. Its denotation has expanded to cover a variety of political arrangements, but its connotation has been blurred and eroded. Before the application of the term to describe political systems became berserk, and its invocation by rulers became indiscriminate and widespread, democracy existed where the leaders of a political system were selected by competitive elections in which the population over a certain age, and with certain qualifications, had the opportunity to participate freely.

Historically, democracy arose in the Western world. Its institutional origins may be traced back to feudal Europe, but its philosophical-ethical premises and foundations have been associated with classical Greece, republican Rome, the English and American revolutions, the European Enlightenment and the French Revolution. The ideas of democracy, however, spread eastwards to other parts of the globe and acquired a momentum under the impact of European colonialism and imperialism.

Clearly no modern political system is perfectly democratic, since all political order has to reconcile and justify authority with obedience and obedience with dissent; in short, it must demarcate the limits of authority. At the heart of every political system, including a democratic one, is authority, and to this extent inherent in all political organisation is an authoritarian element or dimension. How this is organised and exercised is of the utmost importance, because it is in its exercise or use that one can distinguish between the authority inherent in, and necessary

Source: This chapter was originally published in French in *Le Debat* (Paris), no. 14 (July-August 1981).

for, political order on the one hand, and authoritarianism on the other. That, too, depends on the institutions and procedures devised for its exercise and for defining its limits. Important also is a clear designation of the purposes for which authority is exercised. Equally important are the foundations, bases and perceptions of authority in any political system by both rulers and ruled: the basis of legitimate power. If, for example, authority is seen to be derived from, or based upon, super-human (e.g., divine) sources, there is little or no room for its limitation by human standards or action.[1]

A political condition of authoritarianism exists in practice when those in power leave little or no freedom of choice to those over whom they govern, either because they believe that the governed have no such right to free choice or because they assume they know best what is good for the people. This paternalistic-directive attitude may derive from the belief that their power is not publicly accountable, and should be exercised without constraints or limitations upon it.

Islam and Political Authority

After these preliminary elementary observations, I can now proceed to examine patterns of authoritarianism in the Middle East. We ought first to consider the traditional and religious bases of power and authority, and the extent to which these have influenced attitudes, perceptions and institutional arrangements of power in the region; how these evolved or developed, and their relevance to the political arrangements of Middle Eastern societies today.

If we take for granted that in the Middle East we are dealing with overwhelmingly Islamic societies, we must recognise that supreme authority, that is sovereignty, in Islam, rests with God. The exercise of authority by the Prophet Muhammad over the earliest seventh century Islamic community was divinely legitimated as the execution of God's will, and expressed in the revealed Holy Koran which constitutes the fundamental basis of the sacred law. All authority in Islamic society after that rested on this holy text, the purpose of which was the regulation of the life of the believers. To this extent, Islam remained a source of legitimacy for all power; other man-made institutions were secondary. Political procedures and institutions to determine, define and regulate its exercise and limits were, therefore, difficult to create. And the dialectic of individual freedom versus state coercion remained a serious problem.

In assessing the impact of this initial stamp on the nature of authority in the Middle East, it is important to consider other sources of the legacy of a strong autocratic tradition in the region, and to distinguish between older, more traditional forms of authoritarianism on the one hand and more recent ones on the other, including the contemporary forms seen in mass societies, influenced as these are by vast demographic change, economic development and access to modern technology.

Despite a uniform faith and common Islamic sentiment, the social structures in which this traditional legacy prevailed differed from one society to the other and from one country to another. In practice, that is, there has been no single or uniform Islamic understanding or explanation of phenomena. The differences have been observed historically and existentially between, say, Mesopotamia, the Arabian Peninsula, the Nile Valley and North Africa, not to mention the Indian sub-continent, Africa south of the Sahara and South-east Asia. Islam, therefore, and its legacy of political authority − even its political arrangements − cannot be viewed merely as scripture or doctrine, but as the complex religious-cultural ethos of a civilisation associated with a vast political dominion. Within that dominion there was huge variety. Ethos and tradition were accompanied and influenced by different political experiences, ranging in recent times from the Ottoman state and empire to the impact of the West, the reformist attempts of Muslims themselves, and the more recent activist or radical integrative ideologies, such as nationalism, revolution and socialism, these last mixed with the effect of wealth from petroleum.

The fact remains that Muslims have always faced a difficult dilemma regarding political authority, for they inherited a rigid, static political ideology, characterised by the acceptance of what is. Their order had been consecrated in orthodoxy many centuries before; any change or innovative political thought and action have remained problematic. Rejecting what is, means subversion or rebellion and, worse, heresy and apostasy. The Islamic obligation to observe the sacred law and obey those in authority encouraged passive politics and later discouraged the active notion of politics as participation. This tradition was maintained by modernising autocrats in the nineteenth century and even by more radical rulers today. The idea of politics and the state was never a dynamic one. Moreover, the difficulty of positive legislation hindered institutional development and obstructed change. Instead of constituting creative acts for the political integration of the community, subsequent legislation tended to be mechanical and opportunistic. In fact, given the divine source of legitimacy and the religious basis of authority, the whole issue of political integration in the Middle East remained intractable. The special *dhimma* (People of the Book) category of toleration regarding non-Muslims, under the modern conditions of the nation-state, contributed to the further fragmentation of the body politic. Sharper dichotomies were created by the need of modernising rulers to introduce military, administrative and other reforms and changes which were totally divorced from the Islamic sources of authority, without however integrating them in it.

Given the rigid and static concept of authority in Islam, the earliest crisis of legitimacy in its history had to be met by force, through civil war. Because Islam, or the profession of faith by its believers, became early on the basis of political behaviour, because it affected martial overtones as it acquired vast territories by war and conquest, and because as a religion it did not arise in a state, the militarisation of the Islamic temporal realm was an early development. The rather rapid weakening of its major, central political institution, the caliphate, representing Islamic authority, permitted its usurpation by force and thus the rise of autocratic rulers, especially military satraps. This development, in turn, contributed to the permanent contradiction between authority as perceived by Islam the faith and tradition on the one hand, and the reality of power on the other.

The duality of power was a fact in Islam by the tenth century. Actual power had accrued to military castes, élites and groups which rendered the caliph, the supreme spiritual and temporal leader of the community, almost powerless. As the Islamic realm was transformed into a 'natural kingdom' or empire, he became merely a source of legitimacy for sultans and dynastic rulers, and a guarantor of orthodoxy. The religious teachers and interpreters of the sacred law, the *ulema*, became the guardians of Islamic law, ethics and morality, but were equally powerless in limiting the power of the actual ruler, the sultan. The interests of the latter or his state's were expressed in, and served by, his own edicts and decrees.

Duality of power gave rise to a duality in the sources of legitimacy and legislation. In taking on the mantle of the caliphate, the Ottoman sultans, for example, based their legitimacy not on the revival of the caliphate but on the divine right of those who had established effective power and used it for the protection of Islam against infidels, and in the interests of the *umma*, the Islamic community. They became the new 'Commanders of the Faithful'. The two sources of their legitimacy therefore consisted of the assumption of the spiritual leadership of the Islamic community and their ability to protect it. As for the duality of law and legislation, the *sharia* soon came to coexist with the decrees, edicts, administrative and other power acts of the sultan or ruler.

The Mamluk caste of slave warriors in Egypt also developed this duality. In both cases the traditional social structure was barely affected, since there prevailed a dynastic-religious division, and a sharp demarcation of functions between the state and the religious institutions. The former were concerned with war, taxation and administration; the latter focused on doctrine, social relations and the social order. In both cases, by the nineteenth century there had developed parallel institutional frameworks, one administrative-legal, the other religious; that is, a dual hierarchy. The cohesiveness and solidarity of society was looked after by the religious institutions, and any loyalty remained to Islam, not the state. This was particularly so in the Ottoman case, where the observance of the *millet* system contributed further to this division.

Political obligation in Islam had, in any case, been conditional upon the observance by the ruler, caliph or imam of the tenets and limits of the *sharia*. With the decline of caliphal power and the emergence of the duality, legitimacy and legislation, the obligation became absolute. The control of those who interpret the religious law by the power holders facilitated this transformation. Political obedience became an absolute duty, for it was assumed that an unjust ruler, who nonetheless defended and protected the Islamic realm and community, was better than none. The concept of conditional political obligation was, however, revived under alien rule, finding expression in the secular nationalist movements of this century and the more militant Islamic movements of today.

Much of the difficulty in resolving these dualities and the problem of political obligation has been due to the Islamic theory and conception of knowledge. For centuries this has, in effect, consisted of the mechanical acquisition of learning, the amassing of the known corpus of Islamic wisdom and tradition which is eternally true, not the discovery of the unknown. Islamic learning has usually concerned itself with seeking the recognised authority or source which determines what is and is not acceptable to Islam. It constitutes part of what was noted earlier, namely, the acceptance of what is, a received ideology. If change is required, it must be one that seeks to restore eternal truths, the verities and values of Islam. To this extent all Islamic revolution tends to be restorative rather than innovative.

Having sharply divided the world into that of Islam (Peace) and that of non-Islam (War), another source of tension and conflict was provided. Most serious was the fact that very early in Islamic history the theoretical Islamic sacred tradition was superseded by force which determined the relations between authority, the holder of power, and the ruled. It became clear very early on that Islam would face great difficulties in truly being, both in theory and practise, the organising principle, the

foundation of political order. The organisation and exercise of temporal
power moved further and further away from the ends or goals of political authority as conceived by Islam's revealed message.

Inevitably,
Muslims developed an intricate social order based mainly on a web of
personal relations, regulated by the ethos and conventions of the faith
and supervised by religious teachers, the interpreters of the sacred law.
It was an effective social order. The arrangements for state or political
power were left to the ruler and ultimately came to be viewed by the
faithful as remote, alien and hostile. If all authority is alienating, the
absence of *any* participation by the public meant that the state remained
wholly alien and alienating. But this social order satisfied most of the
needs of Muslims, especially when the ruler, or political authority, was
concerned mainly with war and taxation, and did not, for a long time,
touch too many aspects of the life of the believers. Equally inevitably,
the concept of loyalty to political or temporal authority remained in
direct opposition to that of loyalty to the faith and the religious community.

In these circumstances there was really no strong impetus or incentive
to develop political institutions, regularise political processes, or promote the rule of positive law for the integration of a common citizenry.
Unfortunately, later on, especially in the last two hundred years, this
intricate and, until then, effective, social order could not adapt in order
to cope with change, the network of political institutions being underdeveloped. So long as there was no loss of power for the Islamic dominion, this disequilibrium between a highly-developed social order and
a weak political institutional base was not serious or problematic, because it was not apparent. The moment, however, that Islamic dominion
disintegrated it fell prey to imperial autocratic or other authoritarian
rule. Its demise at the hands of non-Muslim powers led to the disintegration of the perceived, largely theoretical, unity of the Islamic world,
and when the foreign powers retreated from this world, the problem of
political authority again returned to plague Muslims.

By 1920, the spiritual and political unity of the Islamic world was
irretrievable; it became an ideal to be realised. After 1920, successor
states to empires and foreign, infidel European power arrangements
had emerged, aspiring to a secularly-defined economic and social modernity. The problem of the relationship between religion and political
authority, Islam and the nation-state, had been inadequately dealt with;
if anything, until very recently, it had been ignored. What is significant
is that after a tolerably less autocratic/authoritarian political experience
during their apprenticeship for independent statehood under foreign

power tutelage, during the inter-war period, most of these states, once completely free or independent of foreign control, very quickly moved towards highly autocratic-authoritarian patterns of rule.

Patterns of Authoritarianism and Autocracy in the Middle East

The increase in state executive power everywhere since the First World War at the expense of the other branches of government, especially the legislature, has been widely and frequently noted by observers, scholars and politicians. Under the impact of radical ideologies and movements, including that of national liberation, the strengthening of state executive power has been even more rapid. Its main arm or instrument, that of administrative organisation, became ever more ubiquitous, insidious and omnipotent. The problem of its limitation and accountability is widely and readily recognised in the few remaining liberal pluralist political systems in the world. To the extent that a greater official class is created, the curbing of the authoritarian tendencies of its essentially, and naturally, hierarchical structure becomes urgent. It requires ever more vigilant legislatures, independent judiciaries, a free press and a free private economic sector. Above all, it requires a citizenry that is free to participate in politics, one, that is, that enjoys free political choice.

The virtual disappearance by 1958 of even emulative pluralist political systems in the Middle East, the proliferation of ruling military oligarchies and autocracies, the adoption, in some cases, of single or one-party organisation, not as a party but as a vehicle for mass mobilisation and an adjunct of central government control, all contributed to the prevalence of authoritarian regimes. Organised political opposition virtually disappeared; it could only survive underground in the form of secret groups. The two main features of political opposition in the Middle East in the last twenty to twenty-five years have in fact been secrecy and conspiracy. No government or regime in power believes in, or allows for, the idea of an alternative government. It holds power until it is overthrown by a successful conspiracy, by subversion. Often, in order to be heard, opposition must be articulated from the safety of voluntary or forced exile. Interestingly, however, the devaluation of radical ideologies in the last decade, possibly even since the Arab-Israel War in June 1967 in which radical regimes were routed, has enabled many autocratic regimes to survive. These include Libya, the Sudan, Syria, Iraq and the two Yemens. In some of them it has facilitated the orderly, peaceful succession of power (e.g., Egypt, Saudi Arabia and

Algeria). It may be that autocracy and authoritarianism are culturally more suited to the Middle East; that the experience of an emulative pluralist system during the inter-war period was a transient phenomenon made possible only by the influence and sanction of the European power in the background. Moreover, the economic and social conditions for its growth, proper functioning and survival were too weak and, in many cases, entirely absent. Whether one considers, for example, rule under the Umayyad and Abbasid caliphates or their successors Seljuk, Mamluk, Ottoman and other Turkish sultans, princes and governors from Asia to North Africa, power was mainly autocratic. Foreign observers of the Egyptian political condition in the second half of the nineteenth century, for instance, were struck by this feature of rule. Writing about the Khedive Ismail, one of them stated:[2]

> But in the hands of the present sovereign as in those of his grandfather [Muhammad Ali], councils and ministers are the mere agents of his personal will, without responsibility — except to himself — as without power . . . The only checks on his otherwise absolute power consisted of foreign revenue controllers [the dual control of foreign powers, England and France] and the international tribunals [more widely known as the Mixed Tribunals].

Another described government in Egypt as follows:[3]

> The pyramid exemplifies the type of government to which Egyptians are used, and had been used for many centuries.

Such observations suggest that authoritarianism is part of the native cultural idiom; that it can be mitigated, undermined, controlled or diminished only by the infusion of a powerful external element or force; and, unrealistically, no doubt, by the abandonment of the native tradition and legacy. On the other hand, it is clear that a hundred years ago, Egypt, and possibly Turkey, seemed the only countries between Europe and Africa or India which had effected the beginnings of a break with conservative Islam and become inclined to Western civilization. On closer examination, though, much of this development was due to and based upon the personal choice of the ruler — the autocrat — and could not therefore be viewed as a more widely relevant public or popular choice. Nevertheless, personal or not, the choice led to the creation of a new official class committed to carry it on. What has been disappointing to many, however, has been the tendency of even these towards authoritarian rule.

Patterns of authority since 1920 have been influenced, then, by religious, social and political factors as well as by custom and tradition. The family structure, the tribal ethos which left its imprint on the settled peasant and urban communities, the ethic of honour and shame, the predomination of status determined by a communal or familial identity over contract and individual identity, together with widespread poverty, militated against an integrated society characterised by trust among its members. Public endeavour and public political life have been neither attractive pursuits nor common features of the polity. Religious law has largely continued to regulate matters of personal status; those relating to the individual *vis-à-vis* the state had become regulated by imported, alien legal norms and codes. As a result, there were standards of official legality but hardly a more widely or commonly understood rule of law.

The authoritarian tendencies of rule in the Middle East were inherent in the different types of leadership that emerged after the First World War. One was the traditional-religious type, best exemplified by Sherif Hussein of Mecca and his family. His leadership of the Arab Revolt, encouraged and financed by Britain in 1916-18, was based on his claim to descent from the Prophet's family, his belonging to the notability of *sayyids*, his position as guardian of Islam's holy shrines, and on his tribal Hashemite antecedents. Moreover, he put himself forward as the restorer of the Arab kingdom and, by implication, the Arab caliphate. Nearby, to the east, Ibn Saud from Najd, had carved out a desert kingdom, by the sword and with an alliance with the puritanical Wahhabi revivalist religious movement. The Sherif Hussein's son, Faisal, briefly king of an Arab kingdom in Damascus (1918-20) and subsequently king of Iraq (1921-33), invoked the same sources of legitimacy, and governed with the assistance of an élite of Arab ex-Ottoman officers, local notables and rich landowners and tribal leaders, with the blessings of the British mandatory authorities. The membership of the Iraqi parliament and administration until 1958, for example, consisted of men drawn largely from the upper reaches of traditional society and its establishment, that is, religious teachers, tribal chiefs, leading merchants, landowners and communal, ethnic or sectarian leaders. The same was true of his brother Abdullah's principality in Jordan until 1950.

In Syria, Lebanon, Egypt and Turkey one encounters a second pattern, a transitional one, but one that, with the exception of Turkey, was sanctioned by foreign powers. It is characterised in various degrees by the superimposition of a new form of government on a traditional social structure. Parties and other political groups in Syria and Lebanon in particular coalesced around a mixture of economic, sectarian and regional interests. In Egypt, the oldest and possibly the only genuine state among the Arabic-speaking countries, parties emerged from a longer gestation period under the gradually eroding autocracy of the Muhammad Ali dynasty, from the mid-nineteenth century. In the relatively homogeneous society on the Nile, they had a better chance of being more representative and meaningful. Senior government officials, palace courtiers, landowners, religious dignitaries and, in Middle Eastern terms, a relatively sizeable professional class, comprised the new political forces. A territorially-defined Turkish nation-state was the product of a war of national independence led by a charismatic autocrat who established the first literally one-party state in the region. Egypt, too, had its charismatic, though very popular, autocrat, Saad Zaghlul, leader of the Wafd, the only mass electoral party in the Middle East. He was pitted against an equally autocratic monarch, King Fuad, in keen competition for political supremacy. A dynasty of oriental despots in Iran was overthrown and soon followed by a more modernising despotism of a soldier, Reza Shah Pahlavi, who founded his own dynasty.

Most of these instances may be described as transitional because they represent semi-autocratic systems that were constrained by a minimum of rules and foreign powers on the sidelines. They were not democratic, nor yet quite authoritarian. With the exception of the Wafd in Egypt, political parties had no grass roots; patron-client relations based on kinship, tribal, sectarian and other personal considerations constituted the basis of political relationships and behaviour. At the same time, the functions of highly centralised government had not yet expanded to the point where they greatly affected the bulk of the rural population. Politics was confined to the official and moneyed classes, as well as to the rising new generation of the intelligentsia in the capital cities. The traditional social order was still central and meaningful to the life of the masses.

The third and last pattern could be described as modern. Its features are the military control of the state or state power, the further bureaucratisation of its organisation and the abolition of a plural or multi-party system. It is more concerned with national liberation and less particular about individual freedom and civil liberty. The nation-state is seen as an organic whole, a moral and spiritual personality that is greater and more important than the individuals who make it up. The development of the collectivity that is the national community, and loyalty to it, take precedence as an ideal over more secular notions of individual and group interests.

One could suggest a hiatus of roughly three years between the departure or removal of European influence and power and the overthrow of the rickety plural political systems they left behind in Syria, Egypt, Iraq and the Sudan by military *coups d'état*. Thus the British military mission wound up its duties in Egypt by 1949, and the Free Officer coup took place in July 1952. The direct British military connection with Iraq was replaced in 1955 by the Baghdad Pact; the Kassem-led coup which overthrew the monarchy occurred in July 1958. The Sudan became independent in 1956 and the first coup led by General Abboud was carried out in November 1958. The French presence in Syria finally came to an end in 1946 and Colonel Husni Zaim carried out his coup which overthrew the newly independent Syrian Republic in March 1949. Even in Jordan the effects of Nasser's radical Arab policy in 1954-6, the dismissal of General Glubb in March 1956 and the virtual supercession of the Anglo-Jordanian Treaty by Jordan's signing of the Arab Solidarity Pact in January 1957, leading to its abrogation in March of that year, became a prelude to the abortive military coup headed by General Ali Abu Nuwar against the monarch.

It may be inferred that the foreign military missions responsible for training and equipping the armed forces of these countries exercised a measure of restraint over their political activities. This is not to ignore, of course, the complex economic, social and political factors that contributed to the overthrow by the soldiers of *ancien régimes*, about which there is a vast literature. What can be postulated is that the *ancien régimes* which maintained at least a façade of constitutional government and a plural political system were able to do so largely because of their links with an outside power. Once the links were severed, these regimes could not withstand the cumulative pressures from several radical movements seeking to undermine their authority, and the effects of sedition and conspiracy in the army officer corps for a return to more autocratic forms of rule.

In Libya a religiously-based monarchy, after feeling compelled to take up radical stands in its inter-Arab and foreign relations in the mid-1960s, succumbed to a military coup led by Colonel Qaddhafi in 1969. Even in countries which attained independence in the 1960s, such as Algeria and South Yemen, the departure of the colonial power was followed by one-party regimes and partly-militarised autocracies. These radical military regimes affected near-medieval regimes in the area. After a brief and brutal coup, the Yemen was transformed overnight into a republic, and the country was plunged into a five-year long civil war.

It can be argued that regimes in the inter-war period had simply grafted the trappings of pluralist forms of government onto societies lacking the economic, social and cultural prerequisites. Furthermore, with the exception of Egypt and Turkey, none of the successor states to the Ottoman empire possessed the minimum characteristics of a nation-state; they were not homogeneous or even integrated societies, but conglomerations of ethnic and sectarian communities. They suffered the additional disability of a sharp division between rural and urban societies and tribal and peasant cultures. The fact remains that foreign power control gave rise to new political élites which led the various independence movements under the banner of transplanted ideas of nationalism, constitutionalism and parliamentary government. These, however, were pitted against a different cumulative political experience, a traditional social and cultural ethos.

The New Trend of Authoritarianism

There has been a process of progressive authoritarianism in the Middle East since the First World War. The process was only briefly arrested, or slowed down, during the British and French mandates over some of these countries. Yet even as early as the 1930s, the appearance of radical, militant religious and other extremist youth organisations throughout the region, which rejected the transplanted political ideas and institutions of Western liberal democracy, was an indication of things to come. Thus the Muslim Brethren and the Young Egypt Society in Egypt, the League for National Action in Syria (precursor of the Baath party), the League of Arab Nationalist Youth and the Muthanna Club in Iraq and the Syrian Popular party (later renamed the Syrian National Social party) of Antoun Saadeh in Lebanon and Syria, came into being.

Calling for direct, violent action against the secularised establishments of the old governing classes and for a revival of a more native culture, these movements were influenced by the mass militarist, charismatically-led Fascist and Nazi movements in Europe and their pale imitations in parts of the Mediterranean. Discipline, leadership and paramilitary activity outside the existing formal institutions of the state were the ideals to be emulated. They soon became involved in extra-parliamentary mass agitational politics in their respective countries, and engaged in conspiracies and sedition in collaboration with members of the political establishment and the armed forces. In this way some of them also became instruments of leading establishment politicians in their internecine struggles for power. What is significant, nonetheless, is that they influenced the political formation, perceptions and attitudes of a whole new generation, some of whose members, especially the soldiers among them, emerged as rulers in the 1950s and 1960s. The search ever since has been not only for a neat political formula of national liberation, but also, significantly, for a strong leader or ruler, the so-called strong man in politics.

At the same time, the nature and behaviour of the ruling élite, the governing classes of these countries, were not too far removed from the autocratic or authoritarian mould. Thus the Hashemite monarchs in Iraq and Jordan, King Fuad and his son, Faruq, after him in Egypt, the Saudi dynasty in Arabia, and the Imam ruler of the Yemen. Plural systems entail discussion, debate, conflict and compromise. They are therefore relatively slow in providing answers or solutions to problems. The new generation, since the 1930s, has sought quick and simple answers — even salvation — readily promised by the new action-faith oriented radical movements. Meanwhile, the weakened power of the European democratic powers in the Middle East under the weight of the challenge from totalitarian regimes on the Continent further encouraged this proclivity. Absolute monarchies, however, dressed up in a panoply of constitutional and parliamentary institutions and procedures, maintained themselves in power with the help of foreign patrons. In Turkey and Iran, soldiers turned republican president and emperor respectively ran tightly centralised, near-corporatist, states.

It was inevitable that when the *ancien régimes* were overthrown by the soldiers, in the absence of any foreign power protection or support, the resulting authoritarianism or autocracy would be unfettered, exclusive and revolutionary. Earlier autocracy, including that of the inter-war period, was at least limited or circumscribed by traditional religious, tribal and other constraints. The mere scaffolding or façade of constitutional checks and parliamentary institutions, not to mention the ultimate sanction of foreign power in the background, tended to temper the indiscriminate use of power. Elections, when they occurred, may have been imperfect, but were not as yet mere plebiscites. Parties may have represented small clusters of the wealthy, the influential and the powerful in society, but the existence of several of them allowed a measure of competition. In short, some political activity, even open politics, was possible. Courts functioned with reasonable expectations of an impartial interpretation and application of the laws of the land.

What is significant about the more recent forms of authoritarianism is the abolition of politics, at least public political activity, and its replacement by a single state-controlled political organisation; the replacement of elections by plebiscites; the concentration of power in the hands of an oligarchy or one man, and his personification of national goals. This type of personal autocracy may be more suited to a contemporary mass society with which, given today's technology, the single leader-ruler can easily communicate directly, without the intermediary of other institutions. Or, as has been observed, it makes it easier to lead a government and control a state 'by monologue', to which there is a simple mass response, that of acclamation. The use of intimidation and terror, and the difficulty of recourse to judicial agencies for the redress of public wrong became, however, the ugly face of this new autocracy.

If one considers the thrust of the revolutions in Egypt in 1952, in Iraq in 1958, as well as the accession to power of the fairly militarised Baath parties in Syria and Iraq in 1966 and 1968 respectively, all of them serving in one way or another as models for radical movements in other Middle Eastern countries, one is struck by several common features which contributed to the new trend of authoritarianism. One is the extension of state control over virtually the whole spectrum of economic and political activity and social organisation. A new, presumably socialist, economy, but in fact another version of state capitalism, is presided over by a ruler or oligarchy assisted by a troika of power consisting of the army, the bureaucracy and the security services. Its vehicles for the monopoly of political activity, the mobilisation and regimentation of the masses are 'national' or 'socialist' unions, national or popular militias, state-controlled trade unions, professional and other syndicates, a nationalised press and media, and an emphasis on the near-corporativist ideal of national solidarity and consensus by the prohibition of all other competing political parties, organisations and groups. At some point, political and administrative activities became the monopoly of the military establishment, a new state official and privileged class. In the case of Baath rule in Iraq and Syria, membership in the party became a requirement for advancement in the hierarchy of state offices. More often than not, party membership is a prerequisite for the holding of any state or public office. Politics as a public activity diminished to the point where the only politics practised became confined to the 'palace' variety of competing cliques. The cult of personality – Nasser, Kassem, the Shah, Ben Bella, Ayatollah Khomeini, Saddam Hussein – became rampant and the norm.

Conclusion

Authoritarianism and autocracy in the Middle East may be unstable in the sense that autocracies may follow one another in frequent succession. Yet the ethos of authoritarianism may be lasting, even permanent, for, among others, the reasons discussed in this chapter. One could venture into a more ambitious philosophical etiology by pointing out the absence of a concept of 'natural law' or 'law of reason' in the intellectual-cultural heritage of Middle Eastern societies. After all, everything before Islam, before God revealed His message to Muhammad, constitutes *jahiliyya*, or the dark age of ignorance. Similarly, anything that deviates from the eternal truth or verities of Islamic teaching is equally degenerative, and therefore unacceptable. That is why, by definition, any Islamic movement which seeks to make Islam the basic principle of the polity does not aim at innovation but at the restoration of the ideal that has been abandoned or lost. The missing of an experience similar, or parallel, to the Renaissance, freeing the Muslim individual from external constraints of, say, religious authority in order to engage in a creative course measured and judged by rational and existential human standards, may also be a relevant consideration. The individual in the Middle East has yet to attain his independence from the wider collectivity, or to accept the proposition that he can create a political order.

Is this rather persistent, if not fluctuating and intermittent, authoritarianism an ideological preference of Middle Easterners, or is it endemic for other quite objective reasons? Analysing politics in the Middle East on ideological bases is a hazardous and misleading exercise, since it fails to explain the *behaviour* and *policies* of regimes in most of these countries, especially Syria and Iraq. With the exception of Turkey, Egypt and Arabia (even in the Arabian Peninsula this is now changing), most countries are fragmented. Moreover, they do not have the proper institutions which could safeguard the cultural, ethnic and religious diversity of their societies while at the same time promoting national integration. In these circumstances, citizenship is not a clear concept, and ideological approaches are the least suited to explain behaviour and policy.

Authoritarian tendencies therefore may be due more to historical-political experience, the environment in which the contest for political power occurs, their economic arrangements, and the until recently comfortable traditional social order, and the corresponding weakness of political institutions. There are, however, differences between one country and the other. Egypt, for example, the most secularised of the Islamic countries and one of the poorest, is socially and educationally the most advanced. It has also had a relatively more meaningful and sustained experience with alternative political forms, namely, constitutional government. Public participation in politics under this constitutional framework had not been, alas, allowed to mature or become extensive and more inclusive. No-one can therefore say with any certainty how successful it may have been had its further development not been arrested in 1952.

A contributing factor to the climate of authoritarianism and autocracy today are the various militant Islamic movements. By their very nature and that of their fundamental ideology, they cannot accommodate politically the 'other', that is, the non-Muslim. Toleration is possible only on condition that the tolerated accept a subservient political status, not that of a full participating citizen. The matter of free choice associated with a plural political order is limited to the *homoioi*, that is members of the community of believers, the Muslims.

The continued concentration of power, moreover, in the hands of exclusive ideological parties or movements such as the Baath in Syria and Iraq, the Marxist ruling party in South Yemen, the FLN in Algeria, the neo-Destour party in Tunisia, dynastic monarchies and principalities in Saudi Arabia, Morocco, Jordan and the Gulf states, or in the hands of military oligarchies and/or charismatic rulers, will sustain authoritarianism and, in some cases, even further promote it.

There is no law of nature, however, which condemns these societies to a permanent condition of political autocracy. So far, political power has been in the hands of small groups or élites which have been loath to share it with wider sectors of their public. Rapid economic change, with its incalculable social consequences, militant and radical movements, however, may produce fundamental political changes in the *locus* and distribution of power in the future. With demographic and economic change, the involvement of an ever greater number of the disaffected and disoriented masses in politics may prove too great a strain on the lingering fabric of tradition and oligarchic rule. On the other hand, they may bring about even greater autocracy under the leadership of 'national saviour' demagogues.

In the last twenty years, at least, the tendency towards authoritarianism and autocracy has been marked by the regimentation of the dominant economic and political institutions of a country under the supreme control of the oligarchic state and, in some cases, the single party. In the latter cases, the situation could verge on totalitarianism if a controlling single party completely overwhelms the state and fuses itself with the nation, and if its militia acquires a certain supremacy over the regular armed forces of the state. A totalitarian condition, though, has not prevailed, perhaps being avoided because there remain, in all instances of Middle Eastern autocracy, some competing agencies and contradictory sources of authority beneath the leaders and the oligarchies. These include the religious establishment, the mosaic of ethnic and cultural diversity, the extended family, clan and tribe. A monolithic situation has been, and is, difficult to achieve. Instead, what has predominated in the Middle East over the last twenty years is a political system of populist autocracy. It is quite possible that economic needs, the fragmentation of several of these countries along ethnic, sectarian and regional lines, and the major splits or dichotomies these produce, dictate authoritarian political orders.

Elsewhere in the modern world strong one-party systems have been the principal forms of authoritarian politics, but not in the Middle East, with its military and dynastic oligarchies and plain one-man rule. If a plural system is defined as a multi- or two-party political order, then authoritarianism in the Middle East has not been the opposite of a plural system, since the tendency toward a one-party system has been limited, and is often a dimension of a more oligarchic or personal control of state power. Authoritarianism found its organisational expression in a tightly controlled bureaucratic, almost corporativist, system, under which the will of the leader-ruler prevails, and politics and policies are highly personal and personalised.

Notes

1. Ancient Near Eastern rulers in Egypt and Mesopotamia were also chief soldiers and chief judges. In imposing their authority and seeking the obedience of their subjects they usually invoked sanctions in the name of a god, and a panoply of other religious sanctions, or constraints.

2. J.C. McCoan, *Egypt as it is* (London, 1877), pp. 87, 119.

3. Baron De Kusel (Bey), *An Englishman's Recollections of Egypt, 1863 to 1887* (London and New York, 1915), p. 137.

8 CONFLICT IN THE MIDDLE EAST RECONSIDERED

When my book, *Conflict in the Middle East*,[1] appeared in 1971, it was considered by some critics as being too pessimistic an analysis of the sources and nature of conflict in the region. It was the result of a series of seminars held between 1967 and 1969, in which I tried to characterise in a more general way the nature of politics and political conflict in the Middle East by considering the history of the region since 1920, and the patterns of its evolution since that time. I essayed some general propositions not peculiar to any time, but rather expressing constant features of the political morphology of the region. I also ventured certain projections based on my analysis. The following are random excerpts from the book, written thirteen years ago:

> It must be clear to the Great Powers involved in the Middle East that the supreme characteristic of the region is its conflict-generating quality and condition. It is an unstable area, not necessarily because of the so-called power vacuum created by the departure of Britain and France after the Second World War, but because many of the problems which stimulate conflict are indigenous and susceptible to only partial control from the outside. (p. 117)

This statement was followed by a comparison between the crucial strategic position of Turkey and Iran on the periphery, and how, from the 1940s to the 1970s these two countries became closely associated with American-dominated Western security arrangements (CENTO, NATO). But I added:

> It does not however preclude change in the future, especially if some of the conflict-generating issues erupt in the seventies, such as Turkey's involvement with Greece over Cyprus, its domestic difficulties, and Iran's involvement with Saudi Arabia and Iraq over the Gulf. (p. 120)

Source: This chapter was originally a paper prepared for a seminar at the Leonard Davis Institute for International Relations, Hebrew University, Jerusalem (June, 1983).

152

By contrast, I argued that the conflict generated by the domestic politics of Arab states and the relations between them, as well as their long-standing dispute with Israel over Palestine 'precluded the same . . . benign bilateral relations between either of the superpowers and the Arab states'. (p. 120) I still contend that normal bilateral state relations between the superpowers and the Arab countries — possibly all the countries in the Middle East — are as difficult to maintain now as they were in the 1950s and 1960s, because of a situation created largely by conflicts peculiar to the nature of these states or their regimes and indigenous to the region. Perennial instability of the core Arab area makes it impossible for an outside power to thoroughly manipulate it. Thus, ever since the Second World War, the USA, for example, has experienced a general disability when it has tried to maintain friendly relations with all the Arab states.

In 1971, I thought that

> . . . only now, and more so in the seventies as Britain withdraws completely from its last Middle Eastern outposts in the Gulf, will Iran . . . re-enter the Middle Eastern purview of political conflict . . .

> Both on the wider Arab and Great Power scale, strategic, oil and communications interests will remain the fundamental elements (and sources) of conflict . . . Conflict may be either exacerbated or contained by the introduction of the non-Arab Persian element into the situation . . . the inter-Arab as well as the Power conflict in the area (will) move . . . to the peripheries (Arabia and the Gulf).

In connection with the last thought, I stressed the view that

> One can only speculate at this time about the course of events in the seventies when (i) the superpowers will have made their intentions and interests in the area clearer, and (ii) when a non-Arab — in fact, traditionally anti-Arab — local power, Iran, may come into confrontation with Arab interests in the Gulf.

But I asserted then, and I still contend today, that the Middle East is only important to the two superpowers for their European strategic interests. As for Russian objectives in the area, I underlined,

> . . . access to the Mediterranean and the prevention or containment of hostile forces emerging south of the Russian border, i e , in Afghanistan, Iran and Turkey.

Having called the clash between the Palestinians and the Jordanian state in 1970 a civil war, I suggested the 'extension of civil war in the Lebanon'. In fact, I argued that the clash between the Palestinians and Arab governments, as evidenced in Jordan and Lebanon, was inevitable. I singled out Jordan and Lebanon as the two obvious states in which this collision would occur (pp. 178-9), mainly because these two states were, relatively speaking, militarily weak, and their respective regimes depended on the goodwill of both their internal political forces and their foreign power patrons (p. 180). Much of this prognosis was based on an assessment of the October 1969 crisis in Lebanon: I added that 'The spectre of another civil war, only a few years after the last one (1958), hung over the country. For whatever the immediate causes or pretexts of internal conflict in Lebanon, these, if not contained or checked in time, always develop − deteriorate − into one between the two major religious communities in the country.' (p. 183)

Touching upon the changes resulting from the oil industry, foreign aid and other economic development, I concluded, in 1969, that

> . . . there is the prospect of continued conflict in the Middle East . . . Conflict in the seventies will extend to the regional peripheries, especially the eastern extremities of the Arabian peninsula. The territorial nation-state . . . in the Middle East will continue to clash with wider militant Muslim revivalism. (p. 208)

After drawing what I thought was a false analogy between the permanently conflict-ridden Middle East now and the Balkans in the period 1908-14, I described what I thought was the crucial difference:

> . . . unlike the case of the Balkans, one observes in much of the Arab Middle East the weakness of a local basis and foundation of a state nationalism that is compounded − if not in fact paralysed − by an abstract formula of greater integration, that of Arab Nationalism. One is confronted by the artificiality of the nation state as a political unit in the Arab Middle East; yet one is impressed by its tenacity. Moreover, international conditions of disorder and conflict, especially local wars, are such that the fate of the Middle East seems inexorably linked to the rival strategic and security interests of the Great Powers.

Such political aridity, I described as follows:

Radical change has occurred largely in the area of the economic activities and aspirations of Middle Eastern states: it is the result of a fantastic oil industry, improved communications, the massive infusion of arms into the region by external powers, and the extensive economic and technical aid received from them. Yet the ambivalence of the Middle Easterners regarding an organizing principle of political and social life essentially continues as one between an ethos inherited from the cultural and political experience under varieties of Islamic domination on the one hand, and several imported varieties on the other. (p. 199)

I suggested that:

. . . the conflict generated by indigenous local and regional sources and conditions has . . . become internationalized under the circumstances of the Cold War, or the continued rivalry between the Great Powers. The very framework of Arab Nationalism itself, or the Arab-Israel confrontation, do not merely permit inter-Arab propaganda and subversion but invite external interference too. Moreover, the disparity in conditions of economic and social life and development between Middle Eastern states will always present a source and area of conflict between them.

Writing about inter-Arab relations later, in 1976, I argued as follows:

Inherent in the Arab alignments and realignments of the October War and its aftermath are the seeds of new, perhaps different, inter-Arab discord and conflict. Since the October War the tendency in inter-Arab relations has been one of eschewing the old objective and ideology of Arab unity in favour of solidarity, based on the convergence of the interests of individual Arab states. This was manifested in the use of the oil weapon . . . the most likely development in the immediate future will be one of the consolidation of several *loci* of Arab power . . . To this extent the whole area of inter-Arab relations and relations between Arab and non-Arab states in the Middle East, as well as with Europe and the superpowers will remain dangerously problematic . . . The controversy over oil supplies, oil prices, the confrontation between Iran and the Arab states in the Gulf, all of these matters constitute sources of tension and potential conflict.
  The centre of wealth, if not economic power strictly speaking, in the Arab Middle East, has shifted from its core to its peripheries: Arabia and the Gulf in the East, Libya and Algeria in the West.

The Arab-Israel conflict is only one of several conflicts . . . in the
region. Developments in the Gulf may entail some conflict between
Arabs locally, and regionally between Arabs and Iranians.[2]

It was along these lines that I saw the prospect of continued conflict
and greater disruption in the Middle East.

As for the respective policies of the superpowers in the region in the
seventies, I thought they would be dictated in large measure by their
positions in Europe, the Mediterranean and the Indian Ocean; and these
positions 'will be further affected by developments in the Gulf'. Given
the more or less global deployment of Soviet naval forces, I also speculated on a shifting balance of power affecting the whole region. I even
went so far, foolishly perhaps, as to say that 'These changes indicate a
kind of reversal to early twentieth-century imperial diplomacy, backed
by strategically distributed naval and air power.' (p. 195)

What perhaps I was not hopelessly wrong about was my speculation
about how the first steps towards peace, or the resolution of the Arab-
Israel conflict will come about. In this connection, I argued that

> The two major clients of the superpowers in the Middle Eastern con-
> flict are Egypt and Israel [they were in 1970]. Therefore the shape
> of any peaceful settlement reached in the next few years will be de-
> termined by Egypt and Israel, which in turn will reflect the decision
> of their patrons to solidify their respective positions in the area. By
> the summer of 1970 it was clear that this pattern of accommodation
> was a distinct possibility . . . If this process is followed to its conclu-
> sion, and provided King Hussein and his regime survive in Jordan and
> Lebanon does not disintegrate, both of these countries may follow
> suit. Although it is certain that other Arab states and the Palestinian
> Liberation Movement will resist this process, it will not be possible
> to arrest it. (p. 195)

I was right about the process and the main partners in it. But I was
wrong about one of the superpowers (the Soviet Union); Lebanon did
disintegrate, and Jordan did not follow suit. Given the latest developments in Lebanon, however, there are new and different conditions
which may yet expand the peace process. In any case, such was the
general direction of my analysis between 1967 and 1976.

The salient feature of politics in the Middle East so far has been
its endemic instability generated by local, regional and international
conflict. The use of violence in the resolution of conflict has been a

recurrent phenomenon. Despite efforts at modernisation over several decades, the expected peaceful conduct of public affairs has not materialised. Recent rapid economic change has led to vast social dislocation and even more violence. The most glaring example has been Iran. Other examples may soon follow.

Disputes over territory, as in the Arab-Israel conflict since 1948, or the civil war in Lebanon, or the more recent Gulf War between Iraq and Iran, have occasioned widespread violence and instability in the region. These in turn have affected the economic and political relations between the states in the region and between them and other world states, especially over oil supplies, international trade and financial investments, ideological orientations and political alignments. But they have also brought to the fore new or old, though recurrent, sources of conflict, which directly challenge legitimate rule, the presently-constituted state structures and their institutions; in fact, the map of the region itself. Such are the sharpened divisions of national identity and political loyalty among ethnic, religious and sectarian communities in several parts of the region, including Lebanon, Syria, Iraq and even Egypt. These are exacerbated further by the wave of militant Islamic movements. The more active and forceful the latter become, the more determined the search for autonomy by disaffected, terrified minorities, and the more real the threat to the integrity of existing states. Stated differently, autocratic regimes which rely for their survival on sectional or communal interests have enhanced the alienation of other groups, leading them to sedition and conspiracy and, more recently, to consider challenging the state and seeking their own territorial autonomy. Among the means they resort to is the organisation of communal para-military forces. Even the militarily most successful state in the region, Israel, is succumbing to the dangerously fissiparous effects of recurrent violent conflict. Its body politic is being polarised, and the national unity of the state is being undermined.

The sectarian/communal problem is of course not new. Periodically it becomes exacerbated, depending on the nature of regimes, political orientation currents in the region and respectively perceived threats. But it continues basically because of unresolved problems, such as the basis of legitimacy and the patterns of authority in the Middle East, the absence of abstract conceptions such as that of the corporation and the corporate personality (in Islamic 'political culture' only physical persons have an existence, a persona) as it applies to 'public', 'nation' and the 'state'. If the essence of political activity is the search for security and advantage, in the Middle East it goes on mainly outside an institutional or other corporate framework. And since religion as politics (or vice versa: equally the Inquisition) is common in the region, it generates greater insecurity among minorities as well as among governments and opposition. The only corporate notions may well be those of the Community of the Faithful, the Islamic *Umma*, the ethnic and sectarian community, the *milla*, and the tribe, clan and family.

In the past, outside powers manipulated these groups for their own purposes. This may not be as possible to do now, when the strategic importance of the region is so sensitive. Another difficulty is that foreign powers must deal with whoever is in power, i.e., the regime, or the ruling authority of the state, that is being challenged domestically or even regionally. The corollary of this may be that any arrangements or alliances made by foreign powers with these regimes are problematic, dangerous, transient and even meaningless. What does it mean, for example, to be the ruler of one of these countries? Something drastic happens, as in Iran or Afghanistan, and one is ruler no more.

Such conflicts tend to spill over state boundaries, divide and factionalise national communities, and threaten to change the map of some areas. Thus Israel has been engaged in map redrawing since 1948; Syria and Israel, as well as other interested parties, have been similarly engaged in Lebanon. Iraq tried, unsuccessfully, to do the same at the head of the Gulf. Libya may aspire to do the same in north-east Africa. Saudi Arabia is an old hand at map-making, and may be tempted to do so again in the Peninsula some time in the future, especially in the southwest (Yemen) and in the Gulf Emirates.

The impact of wealth from oil has produced changes in inter-Arab relations over the last fifteen years. It altered the balance of power in favour of oil-rich states that subsidise the poorer ones and attract their trained manpower. For example, ever since 1967 Saudi Arabia was perceived by others as influential in Arab affairs and now perceives herself as such. She performs the role of financier, power broker and guardian of Arab co-operation and solidarity. Oil wealth also came to exercise a moderating influence on Arab ideological cleavages, emphasising pragmatic policies to the point where by 1971 Arab unity came to be perceived in terms of solidarity and cooperation rather than in constitutional, political terms. At the same time, however, oil wealth made the Arab world more susceptible to foreign penetration, since the region contains the most important strategic commodity of this century. At the beginning of the 1980s, the struggle for it is reflected in superpower moves in Afghanistan and the Gulf.

In short, it would appear that geopolitical priorities have changed:

the centre of political gravity in the Arab world has moved from its traditional sites in the Fertile Crescent and Egypt to the Arabian Peninsula and the Gulf. The control of oil and the waters of the Gulf, especially the Straits of Hormuz, have become important. Energy and typical turn-of-the-century geopolitics are the main issues now.

What are the sources and patterns of this change? In the past, I risked the controversial formulation that inter-Arab politics cannot be understood only in terms of ideological differences in orientation and sympathies between regimes or states. There are also personal and situational variables to be considered, because of the personalised style of policymaking, and domestic pressures of economic and social provenance, involving various groups and interests. Witness the conflicts between regimes of similar ideological orientation such as Iraq and Syria. Other variables are the different states of economic and social development among Arab states, what I described thirteen years ago as constituting a source, level and area of conflict between them.[3]

In the 1950s and 1960s, inter-Arab relations oscillated from consensus to disagreement, especially under Nasser's Pan-Arab or radical Arab leadership. Except for the ideologically polarised period 1961-7, inter-Arab politics were also characterised by a flexible system of short-lived alliances. These shifted in the context of weak or unstable regimes, personalised foreign policies, and the influence of external factors. Nevertheless, there was consensus over a number of core Pan-Arab issues and concerns in the struggle for Arab leadership, such as Arab unity and Palestine. These constituted sources of legitimacy for Arab leaders, and they all invariably invoked them. There was also a general acceptance of Egypt's central position and crucial role in Arab politics. Both her traditional position in culture, religion, the arts and institutions, and her radical Arab policy of the 1950s and 1960s gave her that centrality. None the less, this position was frequently challenged by Iraq and Saudi Arabia. Equally significant was the penetration of inter-Arab politics by external influences, whether because of oil, the protection of minorities, or Israel (e.g., the Baghdad Pact, the Soviet presence in Egypt, the Eisenhower Doctrine) leading to a sharp rivalry and keen competition between the superpowers.

The Six-Day War of June 1967 undermined the radical leadership of Nasser in Egypt and the Baath in the Fertile Crescent, both of them representing the mainstream of revolutionary Arab politics. The Khartoum Arab Summit Conference of that year signalled the historic compromise between radicals and conservatives (Egypt and Saudi Arabia) and the beginning of Egypt's partial, if not massive, dependence on the ιducing states. Simultaneously, the Islamic overtones of the late Feisal's regional policy (which began in 1962, but especially after the burning of al-Aqsa Mosque in Jerusalem in 1969), and the Rabat Summit Meeting of that year, gave Feisal and other conservative Arab regimes the chance to increase their influence at the expense of the radicals.

The death of Nasser in 1970 left a leadership vacuum and deprived Egypt of a source of regional prestige, leading to a rivalry for leadership between other Arabs. At the same time, between 1968 and 1970, Egyptians themselves, including Nasser, were gradually disengaging from their active, aggressive Arab policy, looking inward and externally to a balance in their relations with East and West, even including a *rapprochement* with the West.

The October 1973 War marked the emergence of the oil-producing states as the new variable in the dynamics of inter-Arab politics, and rendered the Gulf the new centre of political gravity, regional influence and international rivalry. It also highlighted a potentially explosive source of Arab disunity: the rich versus the poor Arab states. Equally significant is the fact that this new variable affected the institutions of the Arab system, its balance of power and the norms governing relations between its members. It also changed relations with the outside world, making inter-Arab relations even more open to external penetration.

What are some of the developments brought about by these changes? There has been a growth of inter-Arab institutions, and an increasing role for economic organisations, such as joint economic ventures and Arab development and monetary funds, reflecting the new weight of the oil countries and more pragmatic considerations in inter-Arab politics. Moreover, the location of these institutions has moved away from Egypt and the Fertile Crescent to the Gulf and the Peninsula or other peripheries where Arab League meetings are concerned. Venues now include Algeria, Tunisia, Iraq, Libya, Kuwait, Saudi Arabia and the Gulf Emirates.

A fundamental change is reflected in the devaluation of ideological Arabism and the promotion of state interest. The tension between the old ideological cry of Arab unity and the interests of individual Arab states has come to the fore. In Egypt, as already noted, there has been a more inward-looking orientation since 1973; in other Arab countries the goal has become Arab solidarity and cooperation rather than unity. Thus the new Arabism under the influence of oil wealth tends to emphasise Arab solidarity in preference to unity, economic cooperation based on mutual interest and the maintenance of the political status quo as opposed to radical nationalism, non-alignment, republicanism and socialism. The main weapons of the new Arabism have become diplomatic and financial, rendering it openly élitist, technocratic and status quo-oriented. It operated at governmental level, not in the streets via mass demonstrations.

Pragmatic Arabism has led to the relaxation of the so-called Arab Cold War and the de-ideologisation of inter-Arab relations.[4] They put forward the politics of consensus and compromise, not of confrontation, allowing a relatively high degree of stability of Arab regimes, e.g., Iraq (1968), Syria (1970), Algeria (1965), Sudan (1969), Libya (1969). Furthermore, in this climate, the regimes of Egypt, Saudi Arabia and Algeria survived peaceful political successions after the death of strong charismatic leaders (Nasser, Feisal, Boumedienne). But this survival was also very much due to these governments' efficient use of the instruments of repression and manipulation, the exhaustion of the forces of the opposition, and the use of oil wealth. It was Muhammad Heikal, the prominent Egyptian journalist and confidant of President Nasser, who suggested that *tharwa* (wealth) has taken over from *thawra* (revolution). Radical army officers and ideologues of the 1950s and 1960s were replaced by power brokers, influence peddlars and money middlemen and arms dealers. Wealth cut across conservative and radical regimes, creating new areas of common interest such as oil prices and foreign aid. It was also in this climate that Iraq, for example, achieved an accommodation with the Shah of Iran in 1975 and Saudi Arabia in 1978-80.

Oil may have moderated ideological differences, but has not made them wholly irrelevant. Suffice to point out here that the impact of oil on the social structure of conservative states has been one of dangerous, albeit paradoxical, radicalisation. The Saudi policy of Arab solidarity through the de-ideologisation of Arab relations since 1967 has ironically involved the country in the complex web of Arab politics which has often forced it to take radical stands. This has been called the 'Saudi dilemma'. It may also be described as the 'revolutionary conundrum'. At the same time, the receding ideological thrust of inter-Arab politics has been replaced by a growing interdependence of Arab regimes, including Saudi Arabia, in certain economic matters. The best illustrations of this interdependence are to be found in the demographic revolution, comprising the migration of labour to the Peninsula and the Gulf which, until now at least, has not been subject to the vagaries or conflicts of inter-Arab politics.

The new Arabism also lacked an obvious single, charismatic leader of the Nasser type or variety. Instead, there have been several influential aspirants to its leadership (what I described thirteen years ago as '*loci* of regional power'). Thus the centrality of Egypt in the Arab world may have been weakened, but not quite negated. In fact, it remains crucial by virtue of its massive presence, its relative human and military capability, technical and other expertise.

There is a paradoxical situation in the changing balance of power since 1967. The oil-rich states which have moved to centre stage in the politics of the region are also the weakest in all other respects. Thus, despite its enormous wealth, Saudi Arabia feels vulnerable demographically and strategically in relation to other states in the region. This feeling of vulnerability and uncertainty explains, in part, the tendency of the Saudis to ally themselves with one or another of the traditional — and rival — regional powers, Egypt and Iraq, and their extreme caution. They are also aware of the fact that if the era of oil is transient, they must somehow in the meantime translate their wealth into more durable sources of power.

For the time being, the fact remains that as Egypt partly disengaged from the inter-Arab political arena, the late King Feisal translated wealth into political influence through a policy of mediation and intervention, as in the Egypt-Syria feud over the disengagement agreements with Israel, in the Lebanese civil war, in the Algeria-Morocco dispute, in the Iraq-Syria dispute over the Euphrates waters, and in the Israel-Palestinian ceasefire and Israel-Syria missile crisis in Lebanon in 1981-2. Wealth, that is, was converted into an effective instrument of policy, as for example, in the General Organisation for the Development of Egypt, the problem of the two Yemens in 1972, the Iraq-Kuwait dispute in 1973, the PLO, and the two Yemens again in 1979. However, after the Mecca *haram* episode of November 1979, the Saudis became more cautious and circumspect in their regional role. This is very much due to the awareness on their part of certain discrepancies, for instance, between wealth and the ability to protect it, or between wealth and social development. There is also the problem of digesting fast development (e.g., a new five-year plan, 1981-5 of $225 billion), not to speak of the spectre of declining oil revenues. Some of the domestic problems generated by wealth are accelerated social change and its consequences, regional cleavages between Najd and Hejaz, over which the Najdis currently hold a monopoly of political power, the army, and a potential professional-technocratic class. In short, wealth has brought with it tensions and conflicts, and the Saudi élite remains uncertain of its new role. It is trapped in an influential one whose maintenance is not always happy.

From 1973 to November 1977, the Arab world was under the umbrella of a Cairo-Riyadh axis which represented an alliance of Saudi money and Egyptian military power and other expertise. It was an axis encouraged and supported by the USA. There was also a brief triangular relationship between Egypt, Saudi Arabia and Algeria which ended with the failure of Egypt and Arabia to support Algeria against Morocco. Another triangular arrangement between Egypt, Saudi Arabia and Syria ended when Sadat went to Jerusalem. In 1979, a new arrangement in the shifting Arab alliances between Iraq and Saudi Arabia was occasioned by their common interest in the security of the Gulf and the threat from the Iranian revolution. This was also a reflection of a changing policy on the part of Iraq, which seemed to have all the elements of a potential regional power: a population base of some twelve million, a diversified economic base, oil (second-largest exporter), a sizeable educated élite and an increasing military capability. Yet its prospects for Arab leadership remain problematic: geographically it is on the periphery; it also suffers from national fragmentation and from a poor political image because of the regime's excessive use of violent repression. It became bogged down in the quagmire of a stalemated war with Iran over the control and possession of Shatt al-Arab at the head of the Gulf. Nevertheless, in 1975 Iraq embarked upon a simultaneously aggressive and accommodating policy in the region: Iran in 1975, Kuwait in 1976, Syria in 1977; the centre of radical Arab conferences in 1978 and 1979, as the coordinator of anti-Sadat forces and as the leader of the Conference of Non-Aligned Countries; and in 1980, the leader of Arab defence against the encroachments of the heretical Islamic regime in Iran.

Amidst these changes, Egypt remained ambivalent about her Arab role; in fact the politically articulate Egyptians have been divided over this issue. Then, throughout the 1970s, there was a greater involvement of non-Arab states, namely, Israel and Iran, in inter-Arab politics.[5] Iran became involved in Dhofar (1971), the strategic islands of Tumb and Abu Musa, and generally affected to police the Gulf. Her relations with Arabia were ambivalent. The Khomeini revolution posed new problems, especially for the Saudis, much of whose labour force is non-Saudi, at a time when the PLO turned pro-Iranian and militant Islamic movements spread throughout the region. These are now intensified by the Gulf War against Iraq. Israel, for her part, achieved a peace treaty with Egypt, constituting a new variable in the patterns of conflict and, among other things, limiting the options of Syria and Jordan.

There has also been an intensification of superpower rivalry, prompted to some extent by the disengagement of Egypt from an active military role in the Arab-Israel conflict and the fall of the Shah in Iran: in Afghanistan, the Horn of Africa, the Yemen, and highlighted by the American search for military facilities in the region. If in the 1970s the defunct Nixon Doctrine envisaged the protection of American and Western interests by local policemen (e.g., Iran), the subsequent Carter Doctrine (and probably any future Reagan Doctrine) envisaged a more direct American involvement in the region, because oil and the recycling of petro-dollars remain paramount American interests. Having lost its influence in Egypt and even Iraq, the Soviet Union has turned its attention to the Gulf and the peripheries of the Middle East: Ethiopia, Afghanistan, South Yemen, Libya and Syria. Its effect, however, on the region has been the disarray of the Arab states and their divisions, and the rearrangement of various *loci* of regional power. Bearing in mind that relations with the superpowers are influenced mainly by the threat or danger to power perceived by its holder, as well as by his opportunities and effectiveness in regional politics (e.g., Nasser and the Russians; Sadat and the Russians; the Shah and the USA; Iraq and the Soviet Union; Saudi Arabia and the USA), this may become an interesting dialectical — if one can use this term — relationship.

In inter-Arab politics today political Islam is overshadowing Arabism. The new power map is blurred; the leadership vacuum left by Egypt has not been filled, and it is an open question whether either Iraq or Saudi Arabia can fill it. For a while, it appeared as if new non-Arab influences were being nurtured in the arena of inter-Arab politics and the Arab system: Sadat with Israel, the PLO with Iran. What is certain is a growing penetration of the region by the superpowers and a growing dependence on the West by some Middle Eastern states at a time when political Islam seeks the cultural and spiritual reassertion of the Muslim community by the vehement rejection of not only the West, but all alien power and influence. A less apparent but none the less real source of instability in the 1980s and 1990s could be that of potential internal upheavals in Arab regimes, growing from the fact that the new power map sketched by Arab governments since 1967 and supported by outsiders could well be challenged and undermined by social forces within Arab societies. In the meantime, Israel has already challenged, if not yet changed, the power map in the Levant and the Fertile Crescent.

There will probably be more ethnic, sectarian and territorial disputes and conflict in the region (Lebanon, the Gulf, South Arabia, North Africa, the Red Sea). A muted struggle between rich and poor states could also erupt in the future. The current realignment of the Arab world as a result of two epochal events in the last decade, the Egypt-

Israel treaty and the fall of the Shah in Iran, looks roughly as follows: in search of Arab leadership and objectives against neighbouring Iran for the control of the Gulf, Iraq has moved closer to the conservative Arab camp, and toward maintaining a balance in its relations with the superpowers. Given its hostility to Syria, it has forged closer ties with Jordan. Receiving sizeable financial assistance from Iraq, and with a poor relationship with Syria, Jordan has responded. Troubled by domestic upheavals, bogged down in Lebanon, and opposed to Camp David, Syria feels isolated. She has moved closer to Libya and turned to the Soviet Union for help, signing a Treaty of Friendship and Cooperation with it. More dangerously, perhaps, it has jeopardised its standing in the Arab system by declaring its support for Iran against Iraq in the Gulf War.[6] The Gulf states are in a delicate quandary. They have sizeable Iranian populations and fear Iraqi ambitions in the Gulf. Kuwait sticks to the Saudi lifeline. The Palestinians are also in some difficulty between Syria, Iraq, Jordan and Iran.

Against this state of Arab disarray, Israel's confrontationist Begin regime embarked on a policy of 'pacification by force' in the Levant. Its invasion of Lebanon and the brutal siege of its capital dispersed the PLO's military forces and, in a way, exacerbated sectarian conflict. But it also exposed the immediate region to a more direct involvement by foreign powers, the future consequences of which cannot as yet be clearly foreseen.

For a fleeting moment the likely rise of Iraq as a regional power was perceived by Israel as a serious threat to its regional hegemony. The PLO as another serious threat has been greatly weakened, if not wholly eradicated by its expulsion from Lebanon and the dispersal of its forces to several Arab states. Peripherally, the Islamic revolution in Iran, the Soviet invasion of Afghanistan, the military coup in Turkey and the Gulf War, all suggest turmoil, shifting alliances and an evolving new pattern of power relations. Will these trends alter the face of the Middle East? Will there be a redrawing of maps as I termed it over a decade ago, and has it begun with Lebanon, the West Bank and the Shatt al-Arab at the head of the Gulf?

The Gulf War, in the meantime, has placed all Arab alignments in difficulty (e.g., the qualified Arab support for Baghdad amidst fears of its potential domination). Internationally, we may see two broad Arab camps: the so-called moderate pro-Western one, and that which is pro-Soviet. In fact, regionally, the new division seems to be in three camps. Egypt, representing Western influence in the Middle East; Iraq-Jordan (with the qualified support of Saudi Arabia and the Gulf states) in the middle; and Syria-Libya backed by the Soviet Union at the other extreme. However, none of these alignments possesses any quality of permanence. Economic difficulties and disparities between Arab states may lead to conflict between them. This conflict could also become domestic. Even though the economic factor on the whole is not yet prominent in these conflicts, it will acquire greater significance and urgency in the next twenty years. With the exception of the oil-rich states in the region, they face difficult economic problems and will continue to depend on massive assistance from their richer neighbours, the outside world, or both. One must consider the agricultural or industrial sector of their economies, the problems of feeding their rapidly-increasing populations, and generating enough foreign exchange with which to buy essential commodities and goods. For the moment, they face crippling foreign debts. Despite the proliferation of inter-Arab economic and financial institutions and the availability of huge surpluses of capital from oil, there is no evidence, so far, that a rational scheme for their use for a balanced regional development has been, or is likely to be, devised for the near future. On the contrary, the oil-rich states seem bent on schemes of rapid and massive development within their own respective borders, even when most of them lack the human resources and social conditions for their lasting success. Thus trade between states in the region remains minimal, attempts at a common market in the past twenty years have been unsuccessful, and continuing political divisions seem to preclude further advance in regional economic development. The danger in all of this is that the poorer states will sink further into debt trying to feed their populations and struggling to increase their domestic output, and the richer ones will be stuck with mammoth industrial and other installations, operated by imported skills and technology which, if these stop, decay into heaps of rubble once the 'black gold' is depleted. In the meantime, disparities in income between the countries of the region, between individuals and groups within each country, the classes of society and the monstrous bureaucracies which result from poor management, and the unequal distribution of income, will all contribute to the further exacerbation of social and political conflict in the region.

Even if the haves, with their astronomical surpluses of capital, were to share their good fortune with the have-nots of the region in a rational scheme of regional development, this presupposes certain minimal — if not ideal — political conditions. One of these is stability in the sense that several outstanding conflicts in the region are settled, namely, the Arab-Israeli, the Lebanese, the Iraqi-Iranian one over the Gulf, and, further afield, the Algerian-Moroccan. The settlement of the conflicts may relieve many of these countries of the burden of spending some twenty per cent of their gross national products on defence. But this applies only to regional and international stability. Another kind of stability that is required will be domestic.

Another essential requirement is the attempt to reduce the rate of population growth, one of the highest in the world outside Latin America. No less important is the improvement of economic and social management in agriculture, industry, social and educational services.

The attempt to meet all of these conditions could be undermined in the meantime if external powers were to make further incursions into the region, or if in the event of some regional or international conflict the sources of immense wealth — the oil fields — their infrastructure and supply routes were destroyed.

For the West the implications of these developments are important. The Nixon Doctrine died with the fall of the Shah. The surrogate policeman of the Gulf disappeared and there followed a contest for the post between Iraq and Iran. The Soviet presence in Afghanistan has been perceived by many ever since as constituting a threat to the Gulf. All local powers, especially Turkey, Iraq and Iran, seem to be defying the superpowers, suggesting that it is no longer possible, if it ever were, for superpowers to control client states.

Because of the change in the strategic map of confrontation between the superpower blocs, there was, perhaps only briefly, talk about an extension of NATO functions, in tandem with an already more direct involvement of the USA, to the region. These changes and recent developments have generated their own difficulties and problems within the Western alliance, the most immediate of which arise from the divergent perceptions of the Middle East held by the USA's European allies. The extension of NATO functions to such peripheries as the Middle East is a cultural and political absurdity. In the same sense, American 'strategic consensus' for the defence of the Middle East is problematic.

It is, I think, true to say that the West lost political control of the Middle East after Suez in 1956. This also marks the dawn of the oil age and the economic boom in the region. Until the 1990s, the West will certainly remain heavily dependent on Middle East oil, i.e., dependent on a group of states that are underdeveloped in a paradoxical way: they have too much money, and their wealth leads to instability, as in Iran. The absence of financial limitations encourages bad development. The conundrum of the revolutionary trap in which countries like Saudi Arabia and the Gulf states are caught, is one of too much or too little economic growth, of too much or too little cultural borrowing and innovation.

Islamic resurgence or militancy and nationalism also create problems for the superpowers. Will Turkey, for example, be the next crisis point in this contest? And will all this turmoil and regional fractiousness tempt one or other or both of the superpowers to intervene? Would it be done jointly if, as I believe, the Soviet Union has a very high stake in a healthy Western economy for its own well-being? Or would it be conducted as a struggle?

It is also true to say that neither militant Islamic nor radical revolutionary regimes in the oil-bearing regions makes the West or the Soviet Union happy. The difference is perhaps that the Soviet Union is nearby, whereas the USA is far away. The USA and its Western allies suffer further disabilities: the traditional ties of Arab and/or Middle Eastern states with them have been loosened, firstly, because the West has lost political will and military power, and secondly, because many of them are in some way closely associated with Israel. To this extent, the resolution of the Arab-Israel conflict has a long-term significance.

It is thus clear that the strategic situation in the region remains precarious, even after the Egypt-Israel Treaty. It will remain so unless other Arab states, Jordan and Syria especially, are prepared to negotiate on the basis of the Camp David peace negotiations, and the Israelis are prepared to compromise over the West Bank in talks with Jordan regarding the Palestinians, or even with the Palestinians themselves.

The disengagement agreements between Egypt and Israel in the Sinai and between Israel and Syria on the Golan negotiated by the American Secretary of State Dr Kissinger between 1974 and 1976 suggested at the time, as it turned out, prematurely, that the USA at last had a clear Middle Eastern policy. These were followed under President Carter by the Camp David Accords in 1978 and the Egypt-Israel peace treaty in 1979. Yet despite these real achievements, American policy remained piecemeal, and the Arab-Israel conflict is still very much with us. Israel's policy over the West Bank and the continued occupation of Lebanon by its forces, Syrian troops and PLO guerrillas, do not promote a speedy settlement of that conflict. In fact, a survey of the Middle Eastern scene from the Gulf war in the east to the turmoil in the Levant in the West suggests a 'witches' brew'. The notorious intransigence of international politics persists.

Israel for one is determined to change the power structure in the Levant and the balance of power in the wider surrounding area. Its stubborn, rapid and massive settlement (at present 25,000; by 1985,

100,000) of the West Bank clearly indicates its intention to annex, and, if necessary, de-Arabise, it by slowly pushing its Palestinian population across to Jordan. Only a small number of Israelis and diaspora Jews, so far, settle on the West Bank for religious and/or ideological reasons. Most settlers are attracted by relatively cheap housing that is heavily subsidised by the government. This way they escape the hardships of a difficult economic situation in Israel proper. At the same time, Israel is loath to forgo the opportunity created by force of its arms of establishing a new and different political relationship with Lebanon which would pacify and secure its northern frontier. At the moment the consequences of its policies and actions are complex and, in the long term, could be incalculable. They have put a terrific strain on its relations with its patron power, the USA. While the latter appears to be the only peacemaker in the region (the Soviet Union does not seem willing or able to try this role, and Western Europe, which has, does not carry credibility), Israel insists upon an imperial role in the region, backed, as such a role historically is, by force. The superpower patron is not willing to restrain its client's actions by imposing meaningful sanctions, such as the withholding of military and other assistance.

The military defeat and dispersion of the PLO, as well as the erosion, if not disintegration, of its political power, can have serious consequences for the Arab regimes. Its leader, Yasser Arafat, momentarily moved closer to King Hussein of Jordan with the aim of securing a negotiated settlement over what may remain of the West Bank, on the basis of a marriage between the Arab League (Fahad) and Reagan's peace plans. But as this new move threatened to split the PLO and fragment it into several splinter groups which would have reflected once again the rivalry between Arab regimes, the several meetings between Arafat and Hussein came to naught. More significantly, the Palestinians are still divided among themselves over negotiating with Israel, through whatever intermediary, and ignoring the ultimate objective, enshrined in their national covenant, of retrieving the whole of Palestine. All this makes it difficult for anyone to act for the Palestinians, to 'give them anything', so long as they cling to their ultimate aim of replacing Israel with a 'secular democratic state of Palestine', i.e., a predominantly Arab one. Their tragedy is of course that within three to ten years there may not be much of an Arab Palestine to reclaim or negotiate about. In the meantime, a kind of *condominium* over the existing Arab population on the West Bank may be the best outcome of any negotiations, say, between Israel and Jordan. But, for the moment, even such negotiations are not desired by the Israelis, who believe they can annex and settle

the West Bank and get away with it. Nor is King Hussein's important
East Jordanian constituency keen on involving themselves again in the
affairs of the West Bank.

Israel's invasion of the Lebanon in the summer of 1982 and its intransigent policy regarding the West Bank placed a great strain on its
relations with Egypt. The normalisation of relations between the two
countries, as envisaged in the 1979 treaty, was completely arrested.
Egypt recalled her ambassador to Israel for an indefinite period of con-
sultations. Negotiations over the disputed territory of Taba in the Sinai
foundered and were abandoned. More significantly, Egypt is being
pressed to re-engage herself in the Arab political arena. She is, however,
circumscribed in this by two main constraints: her peace treaty with
Israel, and her own domestic difficulties. The pressure is nonetheless
there. The Saudis look to Egypt to provide a regional balance against
the more radical Arab states. The Iraqis, who are otherwise rival aspirants to Arab leadership, now seek Egyptian military and other assistance
in their long war against Iran.

In effect, Israel's policy in Lebanon and the West Bank has forced
Egypt to freeze her relations with it under the treaty. A strong chorus
of Egyptian critics is now heard arguing that even without Lebanon or
the West Bank, Egypt must not allow the further development of trade,
commercial and cultural relations with Israel. They believe Israel desperately needs the Egyptian market, and they are apprehensive of its dynamic and technologically advanced industrial complex and élite. Some
of these critics assert that the normalisation of relations with Israel,
allowing its commercial, industrial and cultural concerns free access
to Egypt, would overwhelm the weak, and in many respects stagnant,
native economic structures and institutions. The Egyptian economy
would become subservient to a dominant Israeli one; Egyptians would
become consumers of Israeli products. Culturally, they fear Egyptians
will be thoroughly secularised, overwhelmed by foreign education and
values. Here there is, of course, a more fundamental rejection of a normal
state-to-state relationship. It is an essentially cultural-religious moral
denial of any advantage or benefit to be derived from normal relations
with Israel.[7] In a sense, this school of thought in Egypt expresses a wider
fear among Arabs generally about Israel's potential for dominance, if
not domination, in the region. Yet Egypt, Israel's most credible rival for
the strategic control of the core area of the Middle East, having fought
three wars for the control of straits, strategic passages and territory, and
potential oil transport routes, is fated for the moment to remain in a
treaty relationship with the country. She needs at least a generation to

cope with her pressing domestic problems. What may force her back into Arab regional politics is the recent division in Islam between Arab and non-Arab, highlighted by the Islamic revolution in Iran, and the threat many Arab regimes believe it poses for them.

A more lasting consideration is whether Egypt and Israel will inevitably contest the control of regional politics in the core area of the Middle East. Can, in other words, the relationship between them ever be a complementary one? More specifically, can Egypt and Israel allow one another to dominate the Levant and/or the Fertile Crescent at the expense of the other?

A further complication arises from America's strategic interest in the Middle East. The overriding consideration here is the perceived Soviet threat to the region. The loss of Iran forced America back into the complexities of Arab politics. Similarly, the crisis in Iran and the Gulf has propelled America's European allies into the same cockpit. At the end of 1982, that is, the further evolution of the treaty relationship between Egypt and Israel was bedevilled by the intricacies and complexities of a series of regional conflicts, ranging from the Gulf to Lebanon, and by the rivalries of the superpowers. Yet the hard reality remains that whatever the complexities, and however wary or cautious relations between them may be today, Egypt and Israel are fated, for the foreseeable future, to be the first partners of peace on the rocky road to the resolution of the Arab-Israel conflict. Egypt may require a generation of peace, or at least the absence of war, if she is to treat, let alone overcome, some of her economic and social ills. Israel may soon discover that it shares this need. In the meantime, each will try to check the other over the exclusive strategic control of the Fertile Crescent and the Levant.

There is, however, no reason why relations between Egypt and Israel since the Treaty of 1979 should not be viewed with hope and optimism. Equally though, there is no reason why they should not be subject to the ambiguity and uncertainty that strongly characterise relations between states.

Another imponderable derives from the already noted oscillation of political orientation in the region. Thus, during the period from 1956 to 1967, there was a phase of Left radicalisation which polarised the politics of the region between the local states, and in their relations with external powers. In the last decade a new phase of political orientation has been inaugurated, characterised by a swing to the Right throughout the region. Its main features are religious militancy: Islamic, Jewish in Israel, and sectarian in many states; the impact of oil money in the region and the world economic order, and the stubborn recession in the industrial states of the West; and local wars, civil ones in Lebanon and Iran, and the Gulf War between Iraq and Iran. It is these developments which lead one to suggest the revival of older problems, such as that of minorities, of state boundaries and the integrity of states, all reminiscent of the immediate post-First World War period.

For the moment, the crisis in the Middle East consists of, or encompasses, at least three major categories of conflict and potential conflict. The first, regional conflict, has several prominent features. Among these are irredentist disputes/wars and potential disputes. Such are the inconclusive Gulf War between Iraq and Iran, which is also an Arab versus non-Arab contest, and a sectarian conflict between a Sunni ruling class in Baghdad against a militant Shiite revolutionary regime in Tehran; the contest between Israel and the Arabs over the West Bank and Gaza; the Polisario separatist rebellion and claim over the Western Sahara against Morocco; Iranian claims over Bahrain (or Iraqi claims over Kuwait); and the claims and counter-claims involving Saudi Arabia and the Yemen in South Arabia, and Saudi Arabia and some of the Emirates in the Gulf. At the same time, Israel's policy of confrontation in the Levant and the Fertile Crescent of the last few years, with its attempt to re-structure the strategic and power arrangements to its advantage, by force, has had its first application in Lebanon — with as yet indeterminate results. What is so far clear is Israel's determination to retain a presence in south Lebanon and to incorporate the state of Lebanon itself in its sphere of influence. The repercussions of this are numerous, varied and unsettling. The Arab states, and especially Saudi Arabia and the Gulf Emirates, fear the wider extension of Israeli influence, while remaining keenly apprehensive of Iran. They consider Syria and Jordan useful buffer states which they must support against the extension of Israeli influence, and look to the Western powers for a containment of, and protection against, these threats.

Yet a serious constraint on the confrontation policy of the Begin regime — or the Right as a whole in Israel — may not simply be American pressure, but the deep division in the Israeli body politic. This could be significant in the long term. For the first time in its history, Israel went to war without consensus, or at least the agreement of most Israelis. The invasion of Lebanon and the subsequent Kahan Judicial Inquiry Report on the Phalangist-perpetrated massacres of Palestinians in the Sabra and Chatila camps in West Beirut have brought to the surface the deep division between government and opposition, as well as among the wider body politic over a perception of national security. For the opposition in the Knesset, and many Israelis, national security means the defence and protection of the *Jewish* state of Israel. It does not envisage, nor can it accommodate, a concept of national security which leads Israel to occupy and control by force densely populated Arab land, bringing into its jurisdiction diverse linguistic, ethnic and sectarian societies. In order to administer and control such areas, the Jewish state of Israel would have to transform itself into an empire. Furthermore, such extension of power through conquest in order to acquire strategic depth for defence, or zones of strategic security, can have, as it has, repercussions for the political system in Israel. These include the erosion of the pluralist democratic system, cabinet government and electoral process.

In the meantime, inter-Arab politics will remain volatile, especially over the control of the remnants of the PLO. Syria, for example, will try to prevent its control by Jordan, as well as any accommodation between Lebanon and Israel. In short, Syria will try desperately to remain a credible rival of Israel for the control of the Levant. Israel's bid for strategic pre-eminence, that is, exacerbates the tensions between Arab regimes and has, as already noted, serious consequences for its relations with Egypt, as well as Egypt's relations with other Arab states.

Another feature of this first category is the widespread challenge to the authority of states and the legitimacy of regimes by militant Islamic groups and by sectarian unrest. These generate violence, tax the state security arrangements, invite greater coercion and repression, and detract regimes from dealing with pressing domestic social and economic issues. The Muslim militants, in particular, are seeking to attain power by appealing for the allegiance of the public at large.

Some of the above features are linked, if not due in part, to a second category of regional conflict, one generated by economic problems. Demographic change, or at least shifts in the demographic morphology of the region, including internal migration from country to town and the movement of migrant labour from one country to another present serious, often insurmountable, economic and social problems for many of the population-exporting countries. Their gain in remittances is balanced by their loss of skilled human resources. For the importing countries, it adds to their dependence and aggravates their political-security concerns. Domestic economic difficulties of individual countries are no less grave. Egypt, in particular, suffers from a relatively stagnant industrial sector, an imbalance in capital investment, inflation, a still highly inequitable distribution of income, overpopulation and a gradual depopulation of the countryside. Consumerism raises the import bill without a parallel appreciable rise in production, and the size of the external debt grows. For many of these countries (e.g. Iraq), expenditure for arms and war threatens the once healthy prospects of their economy. Even the very rich among them may, as a result of the prolonged world recession, experience political difficulties, since a great deal of their ability to play a political role and conduct policy has depended on the size of their purse.

The third category is that of the role of external powers. So far, the USA has been the only power to undertake the role of peacemaker in the area. It is not yet clear whether the Soviet Union is willing or able to fulfil such a role. Furthermore, most Arab regimes do not, for the moment, wish it to take it on. On the evidence of the war in Lebanon, one could fairly assert the Soviet Union's ineffectiveness and possibly lack of interest. The difficulty with American policy, however, is that it is, under the Reagan administration – although this may change in the future – hampered by a rigid ideological dichotomy regarding the East-West global struggle. It also has a special relationship with a stridently powerful state in the region, Israel. Any role the EEC countries may fancy for themselves in the Middle East remains, so far, limited and ineffectual. Moreover, it tends to generate difficulties for the Western alliance.

It is, incidentally, unlikely that the USA, as peacemaker, can implement its peace plans or schemes such as the Reagan Plan when these are rejected outright by the Israelis and effectively opposed by the PLO. The most it can do is reassure several Arab states by means of economic and military assistance of the protection of their respective regimes. What remains true, as it was for the 1960s and 1970s, is that external powers are unable to effectively control or completely contain indigenous or regionally generated forces of conflict within their externally devised frameworks, whatever these may be. To this extent, neither the USA, in conjunction with Western Europe, nor the Soviet Union, can seriously entertain the 'imposition' of a general peace on the Middle East. Such 'peace' usually gets sabotaged by one or other of the regional antagonists, or, as is often the case, by some of the externally uncontrollable indigenous forces already referred to.

Finally, 'because largely traditional societies in the Middle East are caught in the vagaries of the twentieth century, their accustomed comfortable view of man and the universe is up against the bleak picture afforded by modernity. Consequently, we may witness in the region more violent acts of passionate traditionalism that are indifferent to their consequences, but are supported by the consolation of martyrdom.

At the same time, the repercussions of modernity applied to traditional societies will remain massive and endless, whether economic, social or political. And this may invite autocracies, if not tyrannies. The newly found wealth in the Arabian Peninsula and the Gulf will ironically only exacerbate the situation. The victims of this turmoil are not only those of the region, but also outsiders. But who will dare to plunge into the witches' brew, and stir it by military intervention? Whoever does can only make it more potent.'[8]

Notes

1. London, Allen and Unwin, 1971.
2. 'Inter-Arab Relations', in A.L. Udovitch (ed.), *The Middle East, Oil, Conflict and Hope* (Lexington, Mass., 1976), pp. 172, 173, 175, 176.
3. See *Conflict in the Middle East*.
4. See Malcolm Kerr, *The Arab Cold War*, 3rd edn. (New York, 1971).
5. Cf. the projection in the 1971 *Conflict in the Middle East*, regarding the greater involvement of non-Arab states in the politics of the region.
6. There are those who believe that Saudi Arabia and the Gulf States are not averse to this Syrian stand, since they think it could serve to restrain Iran against them.
7. An example of this criticism is Galal Ahmad Amin, *Mihnat al-iqtisad wa'l-thaqafa fi Misr* (*The Crisis of the Economy and Culture in Egypt*) (Cairo, 1982).
8. Private communication about the Middle East crisis from Professor E.H. Buehrig.

PART THREE: HISTORY AND POLITICS OF MODERN
EGYPT

9 SOME POLITICAL CONSEQUENCES OF THE 1952 REVOLUTION IN EGYPT

One necessarily approaches the task of describing the political consequences of the revolution of 1952 with trepidation.[1] Thirteen years is too short a period of time for an accurate assessment of these consequences. Mere observation by the student suggests trends in the political orientation of the rulers of Egypt, perhaps traces the barest outline of their policy aims and the ways in which they try to achieve them. Yet vital information about the detailed political transactions and the motives of rulers for making them is not available to the student of politics in the short period of time since the leaders of a military conspiracy seized power on 23 July 1952. Compared with the historian who studies the less recent past, the student of politics is at a disadvantage.

In addition to the difficulty of time and information, there is the more complex problem of determining the extent to which far-reaching revolutionary change has in fact occurred in Egypt since 1952. Without necessarily subscribing to Pareto's theory of 'the circulation of élites', one still needs to ask the question: Did the displacement of one ruling group by another — even though the latter may be different in social composition, professional identity and political outlook — constitute a revolution? To deal with this question adequately one must be able to study and analyse changes in the structure and functions of social, economic and political institutions. The latter, after all, reflect in great measure the arrangements of authority for the maintenance of a political system and order.[2] The change that has occurred in these institutions reflects in part the desire of man for exceptionally new conditions of social life and organisation, in short, for a new order. It also indicates action taken to fulfil this desire. Despite the progress being made, for example, by students of economic development in describing and analysing the economic policy of the Egyptian government since July 1952, they find it is still too early to assess its total impact upon, and consequences for, the country.[3]

Revolution, commonly understood, implies the overthrow of an existing order, a status quo, by a new group of leaders (or by a single

Source: P.M. Holt (ed.), *Political and Social Change in Modern Egypt* (Oxford University Press, 1968).

activist) purporting to establish a new order. The modern Greek term for revolution, *epanástasis*, is instructive in this connection, for it denotes simultaneous action in two directions: an *insurrection* against a ruler or a regime, and the resurrection of a society towards new achievement.[4] The Free Officers, led by Jamal 'Abd al-Nasir, embraced both these goals. The first was attained fairly quickly after their successful coup. The second, namely to effect a revolution in Egyptian society of economic advancement, of political modernisation and development, is the current major task of the regime. Meantime, a new dimension has been added to the revolution in Egypt since 1955 which extends to all the Arab states in the Middle East.

Recent studies of the regime in Egypt fall into two distinct categories. First, there are those who, employing a socio-economic analysis of Egyptian society, argue that there is no evidence that the traditional relationship between ruler and subject has changed. They support their contention by documenting the fact that the social and economic condition of 80 per cent of the rural population comprising some 15 million out of a total 27 million inhabitants has not improved materially, whether one measures this condition in terms of land-ownership, per capita income and share in total national wealth, or in terms of wage-earning employment in agriculture. They try to show moreover that the swelling of population in the urban centres of Egypt, the result of emigration from country to town and city, has produced a mass of abjectly poor and disinherited young Egyptians, amounting to 50 per cent of the total 8-9 million urban population of the country.[5] Given such conditions, these observers conclude, among other things, that the revolution of 1952 has meant nothing more than the replacement of a monarchy (which was assisted in governing by a propertied group of landowners, financiers and administrators, as well as by a foreign power), with a new state bureaucratic élite of soldiers, technocrats and petty officials.[6]

There are those, on the other hand, who by an emphasis on ideological trends in the Afro-Asian world, especially the movement against imperialism and colonialism, view the Egyptian Free Officers' coup of July 1952 as the fountainhead of a profound revolution against a decadent order, on behalf of a popular demand for social, economic and political emancipation. They discount the absence of a popular, or mass, uprising in July 1952, or of the involvement of any organised civilian groups associated with the Free Officer conspirators, in the overthrow of the monarchy and the *ancien régime* politicians.[7] In a sense, one may consider the holocaust of 26 January 1952 in Cairo as a desperate, and therefore futile, protest of the downtrodden against opulence, the veneer of European civilisation, and authority associated with the status quo. The fact remains that a new rule and order were imposed six months later by a military junta, consolidated over a period of ten years with the aid of an autocratic policy. This, however, is no departure from the behaviour of revolutionary groups that have come to power elsewhere. The Free Officers who overthrew the monarchy were anxious to stabilise their position by creating a new and unchallenged power structure.

Having suggested that it is premature to discuss revolutionary consequences for the Egyptian *nation*, I should like to confine my discussion of these consequences to the Egyptian *state* in terms of the concentration of power and personal rule.[8] Moreover, having to deal with such a short time-span in historical terms, my discussion is perforce suggestive of propositions which cannot be historically documented until much later. I may justify a departure from a closely documented historical treatment by the simple observation that the rise of executive power is today almost a universal phenomenon. In many of the states of Asia and Africa, the emergence of supreme national leader-rulers, often in the form of Knights on Horseback, indicates an even greater concentration of power in the hands of one man.[9]

I am not interested, for the purposes of this paper, in arguing the virtues or shortcomings of military rule. Studies of the involvement of the military in politics, and their relationship to society, especially to civilian authority, abound.[10] Like Ibn al-Tiqtaqa, who wrote in the fourteenth century, one may for the moment postpone judgement in this matter:[11]

The realm is guarded by the Sword and administered by the Pen. There has been disagreement of opinion as to which is more important among them, and which one should dominate the other. Some think the Pen should dominate the Sword because the latter upholds the former as a guardian and servant. Others have argued the contrary relationship between Sword and Pen on the grounds that the Men of the Pen provide those who wield the Sword with their wealth and livelihood and must be servile to them. Yet a third view upholds that Sword and Pen are equal in importance, and neither can do without the other.

Nor do I intend here to describe in detail why and how the Free Officers came to power in Egypt in July 1952.[12] It is only necessary to remark briefly that the impasse reached in the relations between King Faruq on the one hand, and party politicians, especially the Wafd, on the other, produced deadlock in the processes of government, and rendered the political élite unable to rule. Internal political chaos, accompanied naturally by frequent breakdowns of public order, reflected the disarray of the ruling classes. When the latter augmented their difficulties by a breakdown in their relations with Britain in October 1951, they undermined their position even further. A combination of disorderly conditions at home and propitious circumstances abroad gave the military — the only organised institution remaining in the state with access to the use of force and, therefore, to the exercise of power — their first political victory: the overthrow of a dynasty which had reigned in Egypt since 1805.

Whereas in 1801-11 Muhammad 'Ali the Great established his authority and imposed his rule over an Egypt which the factious Mamluk princes could not agree to govern by a similar access to force, it nonetheless took him at least four years of negotiation and manoeuvre to secure the necessary support of notables, religious leaders and others who mattered politically in the country, for his plans. The ruling élite he ousted from power did not relinquish it without fierce opposition. Only a cold-blooded and carefully planned massacre of Mamluk leaders in the Citadel in 1811 assured Muhammad 'Ali of his undisputed domination over the country. In the case of the Free Officers, their coup was swift, the resistance of the political élite itself divided, over-confident, and therefore, ineffective. There was no need for a massacre, because the monopoly of the means of violence rested with the military establishment of a modern state.

The Modernising Leader and the New Elite

It is difficult to assert a cause and effect relationship between the achievement of real political independence since 1954 and the revolution led by the Free Officers. Political independence, undiluted by the special relationship with Britain, might have come about without revolution. For Egyptians, however, there is a causal relationship between political independence and the revolution. They consider it, that is, a major consequence of the 1952 revolution. They add to this a series of other consequences which they view as real achievements of the new élite: a radical and inspired programme of economic and social reform and development which has infused a sense of hope and purpose. They see their new leaders as the first group of native Egyptians to govern their country in many centuries. Moreover, they believe that the new leadership is sincerely concerned with their welfare. Generally, Egyptians have experienced in the last ten years a psychological uplift (sometimes to the degree of dangerous euphoria) directly related to the inter-Arab and international prestige of their leader.

While these, and many other developments, have been consequences of the 1952 revolution, they do not explain the transformation of the structure of power in the state, its use and purposes as exercised by the new leadership. And I have assumed that the question of authority is central to the study of politics — in this instance, to the study of a revolution. What arrangements, then, appear to have been made so far for authority, and for the use and exercise of public power by the new revolutionary leadership? Despite the repeated generalisation that this is the era of 'mass participation' in politics (and participation is not synonymous with active involvement in the making and implementation of policy), one must still cope with the problem of leadership and élites who lead ever-greater masses. The ideal revolutionary polity in which the masses truly govern has yet to appear anywhere in the world. It remains not only a myth, but also an unfulfilled prophecy. The leadership element, however, is very much with us, especially in societies where:

1. the adequacy of previous institutional arrangements and procedures — actually political orders — has been seriously challenged and, in the case of Egypt, overthrown;

2. there is a rapid transformation of governmental functions to embrace a wide spectrum of public affairs;

3. a radical revolutionary ideology regards individual and group political freedoms as obstacles to political and economic modernisation and development — in short, to progress; and suggests that the new leadership, supported by a carefully selected political cadre and related to the masses via a single state organisation, is the only one that can bring about progress.

The question is, then, how this power structure in the state has been transformed. How is it limited and controlled? Is there an effective check against its rather narrow organisation?

To deal with these questions one must consider two major consequences of the 1952 coup which lay at the heart of the revolution. One was the abolition of the monarchy less than a year after the coup, and its replacement by a republic. The other was the suspension of political life by the suppression of all organised political groups. This process, initiated almost immediately after the coup and carried out throughout 1953-4, was not merely directed at the known political parties and their leaders of the *ancien régime*, but also at all other groups and associations whose leadership had not participated in the formation of a government, and at those who were not represented in parliament.

Neither of these consequences is in itself significant. They must be viewed within the context of the struggle for power among the Free Officers' group which went on between July 1952 and March 1954. The abolition of an unpopular monarchy was a relatively simple matter, accomplished by decree in July 1953. More difficult was the replacement, for purposes of government, of the ousted cadres provided by the old political groups. Although many members of the old political organisations found no difficulty in switching their allegiance to the new rulers, the military junta was anxious to mobilise public support for its new rule. A Liberation Rally was launched to associate the masses with the new regime which now proclaimed a sweeping revolution in Egypt. The destruction of the old order was to be followed by a revolution in the social, economic and political life of the country, aiming at greater material well-being, justice and freedom within a democratic polity. Economically, the emphasis was placed on the redistribution of land through agrarian reform, together with intensive industrialisation which would raise the standard of living for every Egyptian by the more equitable distribution of national wealth. Socially, the revolution implied a levelling process which would bridge gaping disparities between the very few haves and the masses of have-nots. Politically, the revolution promised an elevated status for Egypt of sovereign independence, prestige in terms of a modern industrialised economy and modern military force and power, both at home and abroad.

While it is easy for soldiers to seize power, it is not easy for them to govern effectively under conditions of induced massive change. The centralisation of power in Egypt is not a surprising phenomenon; it has a long history that needs no elaboration here. The accession to power of a radical officer group, which aimed at the establishment of a new revolutionary order, tended to increase the centralisation of both political and economic power. The formulation of an all-embracing revolutionary policy for the modernisation of Egyptian society was thus incompatible with notions of diffused power. Yet the persistent inability of the military regime to organise the masses into an effective political force is reflected in, and documented by, the consecutive failure of the Liberation Rally (abolished in 1956), and its successor, the National Union (dissolved in 1961 upon the secession of Syria from the United Arab Republic). The Arab Socialist Union organisation formulated and announced in President 'Abd al-Nasir's Charter (May 1962) represents the latest attempt in the continuous, but frustrating, search by the regime for a formula of organised mass support, and a basis for a permanent institutionalised political structure. Its prospects cannot be fairly assessed at the present time. I will discuss the general outline of its organisation in the next section.

If the efforts of the military regime to organise popular support for their revolution proved difficult, the question of a new political apparatus for the control of government was more crucial once the old élite had been destroyed. It is in this essential feature of any rule that the revolution has been most successful. In the absence of wide participation by the citizens in the conduct of public affairs, at the local, provincial or national level, a new state apparatus became necessary. Unwilling to risk their newly acquired power, the Free Officers had to consolidate their gains. Anxious to impose a new order of revolutionary achievement as outlined in their proclamations between 1952 and 1956, the military junta sought at first to recruit the cadres of their new power structure from their most obvious ally: the armed forces.

President 'Abd al-Nasir has consistently reminded the armed forces that they constitute the vanguard and base of the revolution in Egypt. They have been in effect the major source of his active support, as well as his hungriest clients for power. Army officers were quickly given watch-dog duties over civilian administrative organisations. Soon thereafter they acquired permanent bureaucratic functions. When in 1957 the serious nationalisation of foreign commercial interests and capital began, culminating in the July 1961 'socialist' measures, military personnel found themselves in key positions, responsible for the planning of economic and social policy. Diplomatic posts, provincial governorships, and all conceivable appointments in the higher echelons of the state administrative services were opened to them.

Just as rapid development of agriculture, irrigation and other public works related to the Egyptian economy in the nineteenth century led to the concentration of great power in the hands of Muhammad 'Ali, so also the desire for the rapid development of an industrial economy today leads to a similar, though greater, concentration of power in the hands of the revolutionary leader. The political power which economics affords the state and the ruler today as a result of the extension of governmental functions and services, including an enlarged bureaucracy, is far greater than any in the past. The resulting prestige of the executive, who is associated with radical and prompt action, enhances the chances for personal rule. The state in Egypt today is the greatest industrialist, economic and financial entrepreneur and the biggest employer. The expanded power of state over society is immense. Whereas in nineteenth-century Egypt such power was frequently mitigated by the organised political and financial intercession of such groups as the *ulama*, the merchants, the guilds of artisans and craftsmen, and the notables, today the prohibition of the existence, let alone independent activity, of intermediate groups has practically eliminated similar mitigating intercession.

In declaring itself against 'politics', i.e., against the existence of political groups in society which at least purport an alternative to power, the military regime had, by 1956, pre-empted all political activity in Egypt. But as political activity is never usefully confined to crass demagoguery and ideological excursions which lack any substantial intellectual and programmatic content, the military junta had to man an administration which would not only permit them to govern, but would also enable them to maintain effective political power over society. It is in meeting this requirement by recruiting their cadres from the armed forces that the junta gradually transformed its regime for the first five years into what I shall call here a *stratiotocracy*.

By *stratiotocracy*[13] I mean a regime which, in contrast to a 'military oligarchy' involves the total military institution as a new political élite. It would be erroneous to refer to this élite as a new ruling class. Before the 1952 revolution, there was a ruling class in Egypt to the extent that its members were recruited from (1) members of the royal house and (2) the rich landowners, high-ranking state administrators, liberal professions, the few industrialists and financiers most of whom were related either by blood, marriage or common economic interests to the rich landowning families. The *stratiotocracy*, however, can only be designated an élite because its members have varied social and economic backgrounds, or origins, even though one assumes that in terms of training, perhaps even education, they share a common, if not uniform, experience. In the Egyptian army, perhaps more than in the armies of other Arab states, expertise in the disciplined use of violence is more developed, permitting a greater sense of professionalism among officers. It is doubtful at the moment, pending further study, if members of the *stratiotocracy* also share a strong sense of corporateness. To refer to them merely as New Men, as some Western observers have, without more precise information about them, is to suggest a misleading typology.

The modernising leader can recruit widely from the ranks of this institution for the various services of the state. This élite, therefore, is not only the privileged group of the revolutionary regime, but should by definition be able to check, as well as to assist, the leader (the *strategós*) at its head. Moreover the body politic is vested in this élite as the best representative of its revolutionary aims. It cannot derive its authority from any constitutional provision or arrangement, for it already possesses it as the maker of the revolution. The modernising leader in turn embodies the vitality and goals of the revolutionary body politic and expresses its will. In this capacity he consolidates his power in the first instance via the *stratiotocracy*. But the basis of his legitimate authority, too, is the revolution, not any intricate legal or other formula for sovereign power. Later, as we shall see, he moves from the position of a *strategós*, leader of the *stratiotocracy*, to that of a popular modernising leader.[14] His leadership becomes temporarily a plebiscitary one, when the myth of power reposing exclusively upon the masses, instead of a legislative body and its attending associational groups, is articulated. Soon this popular sovereignty permits the modernising leader greater personalised power in accordance with new constitutional rules, and this becomes the supreme organ of popular sovereignty. He embodies the general will to lead the struggle against economic exploitation at home, imperialism abroad and, along with the élite, is entrusted with the task of achieving the goals of the revolution.

In the tenth and eleventh centuries, sultans and princes who had established powerful realms in various parts of the Islamic empire, legitimated their authority and dominion by resorting to a nice agreement with the almost powerless caliph: recognition of supreme, though nominal, caliphal authority by mention of his name in Friday prayers in exchange for his recognition of a sultanate or principality. Today, however, resort to such a convenient arrangement is not possible. How, then, does the popular innovator and moderniser at the head of a revolution justify the immense concentration of power in his hands and the personalisation of his rule?

One can argue that action on any level of human activity is more readily associated with executive power. And the latter, in turn, is usually associated with a single person, not with deliberative bodies. Action was the strength of Muhammad 'Ali as the 'founder' of a modern state in Egypt. Action presumably impressed the Egyptians when they accepted Sa'd Zaghlul as the 'father' of an independent Egyptian nation-state. Similarly, revolutionary action in the economic, social and political development of the country renders the head of a *stratiotocracy* a moderniser. It is not unfair to suggest that long before the coup of July 1952, the military in Egypt were popularly associated with efficient action, whether in quelling disturbances when all other measures available to civilian authority had failed, or in accelerating the execution of large public works. Moreover, reform in Egypt has been traditionally associated with personal power.

But there is a more significant reason for the political success of the new élite and the concentration of power in the personal rule of its leader. The suppression of religious and other communal social units, and the proscription of associations and other organised groups from urban Egyptian society — except as part of a state-decreed national organisation — have contributed to this power concentration. Such units and organisations which, in addition to their local community functions and services, performed political functions recognised by the ruler, are no longer officially permitted to do so.[15] The disbanding of both secular and religious political associations since 1953, accelerated the total control of the new élite over society, and increased the personal power of its leader. Traditional social units and modern political groups could conceivably have defended society from the excesses of personal rule. The 'people' (*al-sha'b*) are never able to do this for themselves. The 'sovereignty of the people' divorced from any intermediate institutional devices and mechanisms to check ultimate power, has always presented the best chance for the concentration of that power in a single ruler or ruling élite.[16]

To argue that the old political élite of pre-1952 Egypt, which also represented a ruling class, has been eliminated, is to state the obvious. It began to collapse some time before the coup of July 1952. Although it was generally able for a period of thirty years to check the concentration of power in the hands of any single leader, king, Wafdist Nahhas, or other, it soon ceased to respond to, or even represent, public needs. Nor was it able to promote policies that would have met these needs. In these circumstances, not only did this élite dissipate its power, but also lost its legitimacy. The latter condition was inevitable because it had anchored its authority in a constitutional formula which it ceased to respect. The crisis in its relations with an alienated, but articulate, minority of politically conscious young Egyptians produced, as in other instances in the history of revolutions, a liberator, who was easily, and in many respects justifiably, considered a saviour.

One must therefore examine the new political élite that has arisen with the revolution, if one assumes that such are best equipped to check personal rule. The consolidation of its power was determined by the outcome of the 'Abd al-Nasir–Nagib struggle for power in 1952-4. A strong leader emerged from this. In 1954 he was still the recognised head of a functional élite, consisting of military officers, whose task it was to lead the revolution and 'to mobilise the masses' for the achievement of its goals. Strangely enough, only with the expansion of the composition of this élite since 1955 did the concentration of power in the hands of the modernising leader occur. It is worthwhile to observe this development.

The mass exodus of foreigners, long resident in Egypt, from 1956 to date represented a minor drain of human resources trained in certain tasks essential to the maintenance of a modern state, especially in the fields of trade, commerce, industry and ancillary services ranging from insurance and the liberal professions to skilled crafts. The military could not provide adequate replacements for all these categories. The need to recruit native civilians from a variety of social strata into top technical and administrative state posts became urgent. Economic planners, development engineers, statisticians and experts in a wide range of technical fields were brought into the various national organisations, many of which were directly controlled by the government, while others enjoyed quasi-independent status, to cope with the emergence of the state as the largest single entrepreneur and social services agency in Egypt.

The expansion of the public sector economy   its almost total control of the national economy — was organised into such bodies as planning commissions, economic councils, various boards dealing with trade and public services. Both military officers and civilian technologists were appointed to head many of these agencies. The expropriation of foreign and native capitalist property, the nationalisation of commercial enterprises, public utilities, the Suez Canal, and the socialist laws of 1961-2 made it impossible for the new élite to remain confined to the military institution. Its expansion to embrace an ever-widening civilian element became necessary.

A new state technocracy came into existence which was not a consulting one, but an integral part of the state bureaucracy. It did not belong to a fully formed professional community; it had no corporate ethos with all the independent attributes that this implies. Its members simply became state employees: a state technocracy, that is, which, when bureaucratised because the state required its skills and services, did not constitute a separate élite with serious political potential. Even though the economic and social interests of this new technocracy seem to converge with those of the ruling military élite, it cannot, so far, act as a check upon the power of the modernising leader, because it has no alternative to state employment. Moreover, it cannot find refuge, or room to manoeuvre, in a civilian political force.

One must note that the revolution has emphasised action in the economic and technological fields of national development. The premium placed on the old liberal professions which were closely allied with the *ancien régime* ruling élite is therefore today at a minimum. It is partly for this reason that the intellectuals have been denied their essential role of critics of the regime and society. One may argue, of course, that, like many intellectuals the world over, those in Egypt are attracted by a radical notion of a resplendent future. The appeal of a revolutionary ideology which promises a 'democratic socialist' society is indeed great.[17] Even though during the struggle for national independence the traditional ruling élite partly recruited its cadres from the class of intellectuals, or from an intelligentsia which they produced, the latter unfortunately never acquired a proper political function in society. Today, all intellectuals and members of the liberal professions are 'integrated' within a state-decreed Arab Socialist Union organisation. Whereas in the inter-War period a privileged élite ruled with the help of these liberal professions, today an alliance (perhaps no more than an association) between politically (for the moment at least) unequal partners, soldiers and technocrats, governs. The soldiers are often loath to permit the political ascendancy of the civilian professional man. Together they constitute the *khassa*, or élitist group, of Islamic terminology; while the masses, or *al-sha'b*, retain their qualification as the *'amma, hoi polloi*.

Because the chief executive can, as he needs, recruit scientists and experts (soldiers presumably being lacking in similar qualifications), his prestige and power are enhanced. He can retain his powerful position by maintaining a delicate balance between those two groups in the new composite élite. He is thus not just a bureaucratic lord, assisted in his task of governing and in his plan for national modernisation by committees of technocrats, but remains a commander at the head of a military institution. So long as no real civilian political force is organised on a mass scale, soldiers can influence his authority and check his power. The technocrats in the élite, just as the intellectuals at large in society, cannot claim the same privileged role. As members of a bureaucratised technocracy, they find that their rights and privileges derive from the state. In this sense, it is difficult for them to curb the power of the modernising leader so long as his *stratiotocracy* sustains him.

An important consequence of the revolution which is not, however, peculiar to Egypt, is the question of the control and limitation of public power. The capitalists were eliminated between 1957 and 1962. Divested of their economic wealth they are now without power or influence. Legislatures, whatever their virtues or vices, have no place in a radical autocracy. The beneficiary of these purges has been public authority, wielded by the new élite headed by the modernising leader, the chief. Theoretically, those who now limit public power are the technocrat-bureaucrats, alongside the military, since the modernising leader as a *civilian chief* depends on them for the attainment of his economic and technological goals, and must delegate some authority to them for the fulfilment of their tasks. In these circumstances, again theoretically, the technocrats acquire interests they must defend. But the *civilian chief* is also a *military chief* who so far depends for his coercive power upon his soldiers. Consequently, he is well-placed between these two heterogeneous groups in the élite to maintain the continued personal authority of his *za'ama*, or popular leadership, *vis-à-vis* the masses.

The Leader and the Masses: the Search for Political Organisation and Institutions

If one considers the Charter of National Action presented to the Congress of Popular Forces in May 1962 as the official ideological handbook of the Egyptian revolution, it is clear that the regime has sought to achieve social and economic reform by revolutionary means. Ever since 1956-7, at least, it has assumed that the sharp economic and social divisions in Egyptian society derived mainly from the exploitation of the many by the privileged few. Forceful state action was therefore necessary to end this exploitation by the economic and political liquidation of the privileged class and the improvement of the condition of the masses. The state in this revolutionary ideology is to act as the dynamic liberating force of the masses. The containment, if not destruction, of the privileged classes will in turn lead to the eradication of social conflict. As their power was derived in great measure from their control over the economy, a programme of nationalisation was begun in 1957 which lasted until the spring of 1964.

Land reform instituted in August 1952, and extended in 1961, abolished extensive landholdings, and distributed land to peasant farmers. Egyptianisation of foreign companies in 1957 (the beginnings of which can be traced back to the Companies Law of 1947), following the nationalisation of the Suez Canal, put into Egyptian hands certain enterprises owned and operated by foreigners. The nationalisation of banks and the press in 1960 placed financial and banking transactions as well as mass media and the publishing industry under state control. The nationalisation of commercial and industrial enterprises in July 1961 (completed in August 1963) was soon followed by a sequestration order against certain local capitalists in November 1961. The latter measure was, to some extent, a political act during the crisis engendered by the secession of Syria from the United Arab Republic in September. A 50 per cent nationalisation of shipping companies followed a year later in October 1962. Cotton-exporting and flour mills came next, in April-May 1963, petroleum in March 1964, and contracting companies in April 1964. The programme of agrarian reform and nationalisation of all sorts of enterprises was accompanied by the institution of planning for the state-controlled economy with a view to increasing both agricultural and industrial production, the doubling of national income within a period of ten years, the achievement of full employment, and the institution and implementation of successful social legislation for the benefit of the masses.

While forceful state action under a revolutionary regime finally eliminated the old privileged class and élite from the economic and political arenas of national activity, it also widened the periphery of the new élite of soldiers and technocrats, with an expanded bureaucracy. Lately, therefore, two major political problems have confronted the Egyptian leadership, namely: (1) the improvement of bureaucratic performance in coping with a state-controlled and run economy, and (2) the mobilisation of the masses into a single state-devised political organisation to assist the leadership in the achievement of its revolutionary goals.

A revolution in the ownership, management and developmental planning of the economy has indeed occurred in Egypt. What has proved to be a more difficult task so far has been the organisation of a mass political structure, whose members will accept the responsibilities and the price of the ideological requirements of the revolution as these are identified and formulated by the modernising leader and his élite.

The persistent search by the regime for a civilian formula for legitimate authority betrays its awareness of the danger inherent in an indefinite dependence upon a *stratiotocracy*, and the new élite of technocrats. The relentless efforts of the regime since 1953 to mobilise and integrate the masses into a single state organisation have been expensive and unsatisfactory.

The secession of Syria from the UAR in September 1961 constituted a watershed in the short history of the regime in Egypt. While it hardly elicited regret on the part of the general public, it moved the rulers to seek measures to safeguard themselves against all eventualities. Public self-criticism of Egyptian policy in Syria under the union was led by the president himself, especially in his famous speech of 16 October. Further isolation of elements in the country presumed to be inimical to the regime was effected by the expropriation measures taken in November. Now that the UAR comprised only Egypt, the old National Union

organisation became obsolete. President 'Abd al-Nasir declared that reactionaries had infiltrated the old National Union. He insisted that the
most important task facing Egypt in the autumn of 1961 was the reorganisation of the National Union in such a way as to make it 'a revolutionary instrument for the masses'. On a different level, the regime
now recognised the urgent need to devise a scheme by which the leaders
could associate selected sections of the public with the policies of the
government. Towards the end of 1961, the government were exploring
the possibility of launching a new mass state organisation into which
would be recruited the so-called popular forces of the country. This
was formally announced in 1962 as the Arab Socialist Union (ASU).[18]

After the announcement of a new government on 18 October, a
Preparatory Committee of Popular Forces met in Cairo in November.
It was charged by the President to prepare for a National Congress
which would produce a Charter of National Action. Consisting of 1,750
members elected by labour, professional syndicates, farmers and other
groups, the National Congress met in May 1962 to hear the president
present his draft National Charter. A nation-wide debate followed and
the Charter was quickly approved unamended. The National Congress, it
turned out, did not lay down the Charter; they discussed and approved
the draft submitted by the president.

The ASU was declared in the National Charter to be the nation's
single political organisation. It did not differ drastically from its predecessor, the National Union, in so far as its pyramidal structure and
organisation, from the village and the basic units to those at the district,
provincial or governorate levels, were concerned. There were, however,
two innovations. One consists of a provision that 50 per cent of the seats
in all selected ASU structures shall be filled by farmers and workers as
these two categories are defined in the National Charter. The other is a
provision for elected ASU basic units in factories, business firms, min-
istries and state-controlled industrial enterprises. The latter extension is
a logical outcome of the vast nationalisation policy and industrialisation
programme since 1957.

Elections from the basic to the higher level units, culminating in a
National Conference, began in May 1963. It is difficult to discuss them
here for, at the time of writing, they were not yet completed.

The ASU is designed to meet the ideological premise that there must
be popular participation and representation on both the local and
national levels of the revolution. The ASU must represent the interests
of all popular forces. These have been identified in the Charter as consisting of farmers (*fallahin*), workers (not just labourers, but anyone who

works for his living), intellectuals, 'national capitalists' (independent shopkeepers, etc.), members of organised professions (lawyers, doctors, teachers, journalists, engineers and others) and soldiers. Participation by these forces in revolutionary activity must be in a single mass organisation of the state in order to avoid social conflict. The latter was, according to the ideology of the revolution, the result of political party activity, when parties represented social classes. The revolution must prevent the emergence of political groups by mobilising the popular forces in the ASU.

It is estimated that there are 5,000,000 members of the ASU. Theoretically, these are the militants of the revolution. Their task, as well as that of the government, is to spread and inculcate in the masses a sense of participation in the leader's implementation of the revolutionary programme. Although not designated a party, the ASU so far is organised in a hierarchical framework. It was noted that there are to be elected local committees, regional and provincial councils, a general conference or Congress, an organisational Secretariat and an elected Higher Executive Committee. For the moment, the president of the ASU is President 'Abd al-Nasir. He has appointed the members of the present Higher Executive Committee consisting of the vice-presidents of the Republic, some of his old Free Officer colleagues. The eighteen to twenty members of the General Secretariat represent army officers, technicians, intellectuals, Marxists and experts.

From the deliberations between the president, his Executive Committee and the General Secretariat, it is clear that the political mobilisation of the popular forces under a single state mass organisation remains a difficult undertaking. It involves a series of crucial questions: What is the best means of committing the public to enthusiastic participation in the regime's revolutionary programmes and policies, ranging from socialism to Arabism? How can an organisation devised, and controlled, by the state, elicit the active support of the public for planned industrialisation and other policies at home and abroad? Most difficult, however, is the problem of a mass state organisation in which the public can actively participate by criticising technical matters of state administration, planning and efficiency, but cannot oppose the established regime or its structure of power.

As there are also other so-called popular democratic organisations, such as farmers' cooperatives, trade unions and professional syndicates, the problem has arisen of linking these to the ASU. The president has complained about its organisation in that it has not so far been able to allocate responsibility in the various committees and on different levels of its structure; in short, that it has not been able to create a political cadre of leadership on any level. Another difficulty that has faced its organisers has been one of communication between local, provincial and national leaders. This apparently has been a major obstacle in the formation of an initial political cadre.

The official view of the ASU as expressed by the president reflects his desire for a public commitment to his programme. He considers its basic objective to be twofold: first, as a popular organisation, it must explain to the public the aims and policies of the regime, and second, it must establish within its organisation a political cadre structure. What this implies is that a core political party, consisting of militant elements unreservedly loyal to the regime, should exist within the ASU in order to give the mass organisation direction and control. It would also ensure that organised groups within the ASU structures, especially in trade unions, cooperatives and syndicates, will not permit the rise of politically unfaithful leaders and cliques. Thus, what is envisaged is a mass organisation, supervised by a group of select militants approaching a party within it, both ultimately controlled by the regime.

Some confusion has arisen because of the existence of organised trade unions, professional syndicates and other groups alongside the wider ASU organisation. Presumably, members of these groups and their leaders are also members of the ASU. President 'Abd al-Nasir has suggested that this duplication be avoided by posing the question of whether to retain these secondary and parallel groups, or to amalgamate them into a single ASU structure. While certain members of the General Secretariat representing various interests – labour, agriculture and the professions – have expressed scepticism over the amalgamation of all organised groups into the ASU, the president appears anxious to do exactly that.[19]

On 10 March 1964 a general election was held for a 350-member National Assembly. About 1,750 candidates stood, all of whom had to be literate, over thirty years old and members of the ASU. One hundred and seventy-five constituencies were to be represented by two deputies, at least one of whom had to be a worker or a farmer as defined in the National Charter. About 1,000 of these candidates were workers or farmers and some twenty-eight or thirty were women. Voting was compulsory with a fine of £E1 for failure to do so. The absence of party affiliation for candidates led many electors to vote for their traditional local leaders

A day before the Assembly convened on 26 March 1964, the president reorganised the government. A new Cabinet headed by 'Ali Sabri replaced the old Executive Council of Ministers, operating since September 1962. The Presidential Council which was also formed in September 1962 was abolished. Instead, the president appointed his most trusted Free Officer colleagues to vice-presidencies. One, Marshal 'Abd al-Hakim 'Amir, was appointed to the new office of first vice-president, the other three to plain vice-presidencies. At the same time, a provisional constitution was proclaimed. Although it describes the National Assembly as the executive power of the state which controls the acts of the president and the Cabinet, the provisional constitution also states in Article 113 that the president 'in collaboration with the government lays down the general policy of the state in all political, economic, social and administrative fields, and supervises its execution'.

Charged with the task of drafting a permanent constitution, the present National Assembly is theoretically a constituent assembly. Also, theoretically, the Assembly is an organ of the ASU, that is, of the popular forces. When it meets as a National Congress, it will have the primary responsibility of laying down the broad principles of the country's policies, and will be expected to supervise their implementation by the National Assembly, the president and his Cabinet.

There is confusion and difficulty in these relationships between, on the one hand, the framework, which is still in the making, and the National Assembly, the president and the Cabinet on the other. It should be noted, moreover, that the 1963 and 1964 elections were only two in a series of periodical elections, constitutional and administrative organisations under the regime of the revolution, since its inception. Despite the transformation of the structure of power by the Free Officers, and the stability and popularity of the leader, there were, between 1956 and March 1965, nine elections and referendums and three constitutions. Over the same period, President 'Abd al-Nasir has effected eight major administrative reshufflings and changes at Cabinet level. While retaining most of his early colleagues of 1952, he has continuously co-opted new aides from the military and from professional civilian groups. To some extent, changes in administrative and executive personnel were essential to the economic revolution the president was instituting. What is politically significant is that these changes reflect unequal progress in the evolution of stable institutions.

For the first time in the recent history of Egypt, representation in the National Assembly extends to workers and small farmers. It is also no longer confined to urban professionals, lawyers, landowners and men of affairs. In the sessions of the Assembly, moreover, there have been lively and dexterous deliberations of government policies, as well as uncomfortably close questioning of ministers. What has been signally lacking in both the Assembly and the ASU so far has been initiative in legislative and other policy matters. The latter are still the exclusive function, if not prerogative, of the president, assisted by a Cabinet and a Higher Executive Committee of the ASU, both of which bodies he heads.

The attempts at decentralisation initiated by the 1960 local government legislation continue to be hampered by the pyramidal structure envisaged in both the old National Union and the new ASU, and its ultimate control from the top. Events also play a part in this situation. Involvement in inter-Arab affairs, especially in south-west Arabia, with dubious results for Egypt, has diverted the attention and energies of the president and his government from sustained action in this direction at home. Moreover, like other measures of the revolutionary leadership in the past, the currently attempted political structure is blatantly a creation from the top. It is not the result of a gradual grass roots development in the country at large. It is not too reckless to assert that the National Charter which declared the ASU to be the kingpin of the proposed new political system is the president's own idea. He must therefore depend upon his loyal and trusted aides for its implementation.

The major difficulty he faces in this whole matter of a new political structure for Egypt arises partly from the nature of his rule and authority. He came to power at the head of a military conspiracy which effected a coup that was phenomenally successful in the post-war world. He was not the theoretician, or leader, of a revolutionary party. With the exception of a few extremists on the Right and even fewer on the Left, neither were any of his junta colleagues in this category. In the country at large, such revolutionary militants as were to be found in the small and fragmented Communist Party were immediately rejected and incarcerated by the regime. Recently, most of them have been rehabilitated in the ASU organisation, the nationalised press and other state services. Judging from the recent mass arrests of fanatical Muslim brethren in July-August 1965, it is unlikely that the regime will readily delegate real powers to any of the institutions envisaged in the proclaimed political system.

The Quest for Leadership in the Arab Middle East and Africa

The most significant consequence of the Anglo-Egyptian Agreement in

June 1954 for the evacuation of British troops from the country, was the fact that the Egyptians had to shoulder alone the difficult task of governing themselves. The Agreement was, moreover, concluded by the new leadership of native Egyptian officers. The contemporaneous withdrawal of effective British influence from other states in the Middle East had further consequences for the new regime in Egypt. It ushered into inter-Arab state relations an era of conflict and instability. Within this, Egypt, under the military regime, became the foremost contender for power.

Although one can carefully document the past infrequent involvement of Egypt in the affairs of traditional Arab political struggles in the Fertile Crescent and the Arabian peninsula until the Second World War, one cannot claim the total dissociation of Egyptian society from an Arab-Islamic orientation since the ninth century. But this was religiously based, and not often free of political power conflict with other Arabs. The newly acquired and widely articulated Arabism of revolutionary Egypt since 1955 was not strictly a consequence of a revolution in the attitude or the cultural-political identity of Egyptians. It represents rather a response to power political realities. Without commenting on the Arab-Israeli issue, one may practically associate the intensity of Arabism as an adopted Egyptian policy in the last ten years with the new realities of inter-Arab politics in an area practically shorn of direct great power influence.

The revolution proclaimed by the Free Officers in 1952 for the benefit of the Egyptian people soon moved from its platform of Egyptian independence achieved in 1954-6 to that of independence from foreign control for all Arab states. By Arab independence, Egyptian leaders meant the severance of even those treaty relations between Arab states and foreign powers which were based on mutual sovereign status. To be sure, success in imposing total control at home through a state dirigistic system produced a basis for active policy abroad.

This new Arab orientation of Egypt was buttressed by encouragement from the East, whether this came from the Soviet bloc in Europe or from the new Afro-Asian bloc founded in Bandung in 1955. Egypt soon came to lead the Arab states in the ability to escape once and for all the political captivity of Western influence. The great power rivalry of the 1950s further aided this orientation and development of Egyptian Arab policy.

By May 1962, President 'Abd al-Nasir was ready to inscribe the wider ramifications of his revolution in Egypt for the rest of the Arab world in his Charter to the Egyptian nation. Radical revolution, based on scientific socialism and pragmatic endeavour for the creation of a powerful realm, was linked to the renascence of an essentially strong but long submerged cultural entity: the Arab-Islamic dominion. In this form, not only did the Egyptian revolutionary model have great appeal for other Arabs, but in some cases led also to the taking of active steps for its realisation. Attempted coups in Jordan (1956-7), the bloody communal conflict in Lebanon (1958), the Iraqi rebellion of July 1958 and the civil war in the Yemen which began in September 1962 are all responsive echoes to the Egyptian cry of revolution.[20]

To a great extent the revolution in Egypt did not simply produce a confrontation with foreign powers in the area; such confrontation preceded the revolution. It accelerated an inter-Arab confrontation which some have described as a struggle between the new forces of radical revolution, led by Egypt on one side, and the old forces of conservatism and reaction on the other.

Egypt's attempts to extend her revolutionary leadership in Syria (1958-61), in Iraq in 1959 and again in 1964-5, and in the Yemen since 1962, have so far proved expensive and not satisfactory. Failure in certain instances was due to lack of the necessary power and resources. But, more significantly, it was due to the late adoption by Egypt of an Arab policy, which was, to a great extent, dictated by the requirements of national interest. Radical revolutionary nationalism, however, is integrative. Given the Free Officers' coup in 1952 and the revolution it inaugurated, there was no reason why its nationalism — whether one calls it Egyptian or Arab — should not be just as integrative. In short, Egypt has, since 1955 at least, been anxious to fill a power vacuum in the Arab world.

The serious confrontations between leaders of the Egyptian revolution on the one hand, and the Ba'athists in Syria,[21] King Husayn in Jordan, 'Abd al-Karim Qasim as well as 'Abd al-Salam 'Arif in Iraq, the *imam* in the Yemen and King Faysal in Saudi Arabia proved to be serious obstacles in the realisation of their aspirations in the Arab Middle East. Organic union schemes were abandoned in 1961-2 in favour of a policy of socialist revolution within each Arab state, to precede closer unity. The latter, in turn, was diluted in the spring of 1963 by a new policy of cooperation between Egypt and the other Arab states in what was recognised as a politically pluralistic Arab world.[22] Direct Egyptian military involvement in the Yemen is also about to be abandoned. It appears that sovereignty and the interests of various ruling élites in the Arab states are too solid and tenacious realities to permit, for the moment at least, voluntary state liquidations in the name of wider Arab unions.

The problem of leadership here too appears to be at the heart of the matter.

Similar difficulties and obstacles have faced the active African policy of the regime since 1958. An intensive Islamic and anti-imperialist (mostly anti-Western) Egyptian campaign in Africa from 1958 to 1962 sought to extend Egypt's revolutionary influence and leadership over the newly independent black African states. At the same time, it sought to undermine, and hoped to end, the increasing relations between many of these new states and Israel. The latter entered the African scene as a supplier of technical assistance with fair success.

Active Egyptian interest in Africa was shown by members of the Muhammad 'Ali dynasty in the last century. Both Muhammad 'Ali the Great and his grandson, Khedive Isma'il, conquered African territories south of the First Cataract. The Sudan itself has been a constant policy preoccupation of Egyptian rulers for an obvious and vital reason; namely, the control and distribution of Nile waters. With the revolution, however, and the active espousal of the anti-colonial cause of national independence in Africa and Asia, Egyptian leadership has sought to make Cairo the political, intellectual and cultural capital of emancipated Africa. A series of African and Afro-Asian conferences to discuss all sorts of matters (non-alignment, youth, writers and intellectuals, neo-colonialism, the combating of the European Common Market) have been held in Cairo since the end of 1957. Also, since that time, Cairo Radio has been broadcasting a daily twelve- to fifteen-hour programme under the general title 'Cairo Speaks to Africa' in Swahili, Hausa, Somali, Amharic, Arabic, English, French and Portuguese. These broadcasts presumably reach over 100 million Africans.

Financial and military assistance to rebel groups and organisations as in the Congo have been another facet of the regime's African policy. Support for the territorial claims of independent African states, such as Somalia, against lingering European enclaves and other older African states, has been given liberally and readily. Denunciation of white supremacist policies as appear in South Africa, and, more recently, in Southern Rhodesia, has been vociferous.

Alongside these aspects of Egypt's African policy, an extensive Islamic campaign of religious education and cultural infiltration (executed primarily by the Islamic Congress founded in 1954, and the institutions of al-Azhar) has been especially marked in northern Nigeria and certain parts of Muslim West and East Africa. Cultural counsellors, who are Azhar-trained, have been attached to embassies and legations in Africa as missionaries. In 1964, a religious institute for the training of Muslim missionaries from Africa was opened in Cairo. Moreover, some seven to eight hundred Azhar teachers have been sent to African countries.

A combined political-religious campaign has sought since 1958 to extend Egyptian influence in Africa by identifying the leaders of the Egyptian revolution as the international spokesman for independent Africa. The regime has been anxious to elevate Egypt, astride the Arab Middle East and the African continent, to the position of the leader of an Africa in the process of political emancipation. It has also suggested that Egypt would be the country best qualified to act as its liaison with the Mediterranean and European world.

The difficulties Egypt faced with her policy of Arab unity and of a socialist revolution for all Arabs since that time, as well as the independent tendencies of new African leaders, have proved serious obstacles to the success of her African policy. More specifically, black Africans do not feel close to Muslim Arabs. The memory of Arab slave-traders in their continent is only too fresh in their minds. What has been even more shattering has been the harbouring and support by Egypt of rebel groups living in exile in Cairo, such as those grouped in the African Association, who work to subvert existing African regimes. Africans suspect that Egypt is over-anxious in its desire for domination, and are naturally reluctant, now that they have escaped European colonial rule, to accept another hegemony. Even though Muslim black Africans may readily accept instruction and cultural training in Arabic — the sacred language of their faith — they have so far resisted the advances of political Arabism as professed by Cairo.

Considering the limited financial and technical resources Egypt can offer Africans, a number of African states have resisted Egyptian pressure upon them to sever their relations with Israel. By 1963, at the Addis Ababa Conference, President 'Abd al Nasir had recognised the limited impact his African policy was having upon leaders of independent African states. His campaign of African unity was consequently diluted with the same alacrity which accompanied Egypt's reconsideration of Arab unity after the Arab Summit Conference in March-April 1963.

The conflict of economic and political interests between black Africa and the Arab Middle East, particularly Arab North Africa (Egypt, Libya and the Maghreb) cannot be underestimated. An overpopulated Egypt, anxious to industrialise rapidly, would naturally seek to establish markets for its products in Africa through political influence which could succeed in keeping others out.[23]

For the Egyptian perhaps the sharpest consequence of the July 1952 revolution has been his rapid projection into the wider Arab world and certain parts of Africa in the service of his state. His age-old, proverbial isolation has been, at least outwardly, shattered in search of national prestige and power. Yet, historians must note that the rulers of Egypt, whoever they are, respect the precedent set by the traditional policy of their predecessors of avoiding isolation, especially from the Arab East, at all costs.

Despite the continuing Western influence of technology, industry and science, the 'Egyptianity' of the UAR in terms of a rural community whose life is still greatly affected by the flow of the Nile and threatened by demographic profusion, has hardly been shaken. The massive public works project begun in 1960 with Soviet aid to construct a dam at Aswan, desert reclamation projects and active campaigns to introduce effective birth control are only some of the measures which currently occupy the authorities in Egypt in dealing with this permanent feature of their country. Attempts to erode this 'Egyptianity' began with Bonaparte; Muhammad 'Ali and his successors tried to undermine it further. The first nationalists of this century thought they could modernise their political life by the adoption of European liberal ideas and institutions. Having had to do this in collaboration with a foreign power, and in a relationship of tutelage to it, these liberal nationalists were swept away as soon as the collaboration ended. Now, the radical revolution continues to adopt, emulate and seek ways and means devised mostly by Europe for the attainment of modernity and power; but it insists upon the rejection of Europe's intellectual, cultural and political legacy. Instead, the momentum of the attempted radical revolutionary change derives from a new combination: the political revival of the Islamic-Arab legacy and culture on the one hand, and a state socialism devised and applied in an autocratic political scheme on the other. The modernising leader embodies the force and spirit of the former, and plans the latter. In doing so, he remains the sole nexus of political loyalty and allegiance, aided both by modern techniques of control available to him for the concentration of power, and by the more traditional meaning of Islam with its implications for personalised rule.

There is no doubt that the modernising leader and his new élite have succeeded in projecting an independent Egypt into the prominence of Arab and international affairs. They have successfully and without bloodshed dismantled an old privileged class that dragged its feet over social and economic reform. Significantly though, and in a characteristically Egyptian way, they have replaced it with a new establishment of soldiers, technocrats and bureaucrats, constituting a new and relatively prosperous group which make up the state apparatus. They may be the new political cadre of the Egyptian revolution. They are recruited from a variety of social strata, no longer confined to the old landed and administrative aristocracy. Among them are some 1,500 to 2,000 ex-military officers, lawyers, journalists and technical experts (professors, engineers, economists and administrators). To this extent revolution has widened the participation of certain categories of Egyptians in the conduct of the affairs of the state. Nonetheless they function as part of the state apparatus, the revolutionary decisions of which continue to be largely the responsibility of the modernising leader, assisted by aides who are personally loyal to him.

The revolutionary desire of Egyptians, as articulated by this leader and his élite, to attain respectable membership in industrial civilisation, must be predicated upon political activism. It is this activism on a wider public scale that so far has eluded the leaders of the revolution and now constitutes a fundamental and urgent problem. Only institutionalised political activity can provide adequately for permanent and effective change. The leader, with an immense concentration of power in his hands, and its use for the achievement of both socio-economic and political aims, has shown the way. His invitation to a public that has traditionally been politically apathetic to become actively engaged in the revolution has so far been qualified by his reluctance to relinquish any real power from the centre in favour of other levels in society. He has repeatedly invited criticism, disagreement and debate. But his invitations have always been prefaced with the warning that the system will not countenance rivals. The political activism of the dynamic modernising leader is thus only faintly buttressed by an accompanying public political activity.

Perhaps accelerating the rate of economic growth and attaining a more equitable social system in Egypt do not require organised popular support: the state apparatus alone may be capable of bringing it about. The question however remains: how effective and lasting a change would this constitute without the active commitment of at least the majority of the population to the state scheme? The fact that the world has come to refer to Nasserism as a political phenomenon of the 1950s and 1960s attests to the central importance of the modernising leader, and to the relative success of his political activism. His insistence upon a radical programme of social and economic reform and his uncompromising nationalism are indications of 'Abd al-Nasir's achievement beyond the average Asian, African or Latin American personal ruler, or ephemeral dictator.

Yet even Nasserism, committed as its leader has consistently been to the realisation of a strong and prosperous socialist Egypt, and to an Arab world free of all outside influence and united under Egyptian leadership, has not so far been able to escape an autocratic political form in which to attain its revolutionary aims. The revolution of 1952 seems unable to escape this rather Egyptian legacy. Until it can successfully do so, one is left with historical contrasts and comparisons. An ambitious autocrat, Muhammad 'Ali the Great, succeeded, in the true Islamic-Ottoman style of the nineteenth century, in transforming Egypt into a modern state. In doing so, he permitted some of his subjects to acquaint themselves with the civilization and culture of Europe. The intellectual, cultural and political descendants of those subjects later overthrew Muhammad 'Ali's dynasty. Today, an autocrat of the technological age — some have called him a Muhammad 'Ali of the twentieth century — nurtures wider revolutionary ambitions for his country, with power at his disposal far greater than any of his predecessors ever dreamt of possessing. He is, moreover, using the immense power concentrated in his hands for the realisation of revolutionary goals which will produce a modern society and polity in Egypt. What is even more significant is that Egyptians have responded with both loyalty and acquiescence, and deferred to this leader. They consider him both an efficient administrator, and a protector who has provided them so far with a way of overcoming their anxieties.[24] This may be the major consequence of the revolution of 1952. What it portends for the long-range evolution of Egyptian society cannot be speculated upon at this early date.[25]

Notes

1. The more general remarks about revolution and ideology derive from work I am pursuing on intellectuals and radical revolution in the Arab states, and I wish to acknowledge the assistance of the Carnegie Seminar in Comparative Politics and the International Development Center, Indiana University, in the early stages of this work. A general examination of Arab politics upon which some of these remarks are based was partly supported by the Programme in Legal and Political Philosophy of the Rockefeller Foundation 1959-60.

2. At this stage, one can only assume that new institutions are in the making. Until they can be clearly identified as such and their functions observed, one must avoid their premature assessment. This chapter was written in April-October 1965.

In a recent article, 'Political development and political decay', *World Politics*, vol. xvii, 3, (April 1965), pp. 386-430, Samuel P. Huntington distinguishes between 'political development' and modernisation. The latter, especially in the new states of Africa and Asia, he finds, rests upon mass mobilisation. He argues, however, that it is dangerously misleading to assume that modernisation of this sort also constitutes political development. The latter he forcefully suggests rests primarily and fundamentally upon the institutionalisation of political organisations and procedures. He further questions 'some tendencies frequently encompassed in the concept of political development as characteristic of the 'developing areas'', and with this the 'underlying commitment to the theory of progress'. He finds that there is a tendency towards simple political systems which depend on one individual and which are therefore neither stable nor capable of producing peaceful change. He suggests emphatically that 'Institutional decay has become a common phenomenon of the modernising countries'. The decline of institutions is reflected in the rise of charismatic leaders, or what I call here the modernising leader; these men personalise power and weaken institutions which might limit it. 'Institutionalisation of power means the limitation of power which might otherwise be wielded personally and arbitrarily.'

3. See C. Issawi, *Egypt in Revolution, an Economic Analysis* (London, 1963); P.K. O'Brien, 'An economic appraisal of the Egyptian revolution', *The Journal of Development Studies*, vol. i, 1 (October 1964), pp. 93-113. See also P.K. O'Brien, *The Revolution in Egypt's Economic System* (London, 1966) for the first systematic assessment of the regime's economic policy.

4. There is in the Egyptian revolution led by the Free Officers just as potent a myth in terms of a faith in a future that is resplendent with modernity and power as in all other revolutionary movements. Its ideology may not be couched in the articulate and uncompromising terms of a dogma. Yet, its leader and élite contend that they reflect a popular will oriented towards such a future. It is in the name of, and for the sake of, this future that revolutionary leadership can exercise immense power to suppress all adversaries in order to act for the fulfilment of its aims. A near-Mazzinian conception of the people and the nation surrounded by political messianism tends to produce an autocracy (the Bonapartist parallel is tempting but dangerous) that is not in serious conflict with local and cultural tradition.

Talmon, *The Origins of Totalitarian Democracy* (New York, 1960) and *Political Messianism* (London, 1960) and Raymond Aron, *The Opium of the Intellectuals* (New York, 1962) are instructive in this connection but not quite freely applicable to an Islamic-Arab or Egyptian setting. On the question of ideology and culture, see the article by Clifford Geertz, 'Ideology as a cultural system' in David E. Apter (ed.), *Ideology and Discontent* (New York, 1964), pp. 47-76. See also the suggestive monograph by Chalmers Johnson, *Revolution and the Social System* (Stanford, 1964).

5. The United Nations, for instance, has recently reported that the UAR has the smallest number of working inhabitants anywhere in the world – barely 30 per cent of the total population of the country.

6. These are essentially the conclusions of two recent studies by Egyptian Marxists in exile in Paris. See Anouar Abdel Malek, *Égypte, société militaire* (Paris, 1962), and Hasan Riad (pseudonym), *L'Égypte nassérienne* (Paris, 1964). See also 'Nasserism and Socialism', *The Socialist Register*, Ralph Miliband and John Saville (eds.) (London, 1964), pp. 38-55.

7. A few examples of such studies are Wilton Wynn, *Nasser of Egypt* (Cambridge, Mass., 1959), Tom Little, *Egypt* (London, 1958), Jean and Simone Lacouture, *Egypt in Transition* (New York, 1958), Charles Cremeans, *The Arabs and the World* (New York, 1963). A recent book by Leonard Binder, *The Ideological Revolution in the Middle East* (New York, 1964), attempts rather unsuccessfully to link such 'movements' as Arabism and socialism to earlier systems of Muslim philosophy. More cautious are the two articles by Malcolm Kerr, 'The Emergence of a Socialist Ideology in Egypt', *The Middle East Journal*, vol. xvi, 2 (1962), pp. 127-44, and 'Arab Radical Notions of Democracy', *St. Antony's Papers*, no. xvi (Middle Eastern Affairs, no. 3), Albert Hourani (ed.) (London, 1963), pp. 9-40. In my book *The Egyptian Army in Politics* (Bloomington, Indiana, 1961), I primarily

emphasised the way the military junta consolidated its power and rule; see especially Chapters 3-4.

8. Besides the observable developments in new states, I have been led to this approach by a few more classic discussions of revolutions and their consequences for state power. Among these, Ortega y Gasset, *Revolt of the Masses* (London, 1930), is still relevant. Bertrand de Jouvenel's work since 1945 has also been concerned with this question. See his *On Power* (London, 1945), and his more recent essay 'The Principate', *Political Quarterly*, (January-March 1965). See also a similar suggestion in my 'The Military in Politics: A Review', *The Journal of Conflict Resolution*, vol. ix, 1 (March 1965), pp. 139-46.

9. See Edward Shils, 'The Military in the Political Development of New States' in John J. Johnson (ed.), *The Role of the Military in Underdeveloped Countries* (Princeton, 1962), pp. 7-68. See also his *Political Development in the New States* (The Hague, 1962).

10. For general discussions, see Alfred Vagts, *The History of Militarism* (New York, 1937), Katherine Chorley, *Armies and the Art of Revolution* (London, 1934), Johnson, William Gutteridge, *The Armed Forces in New States* (London, 1962), S.E. Finer, *The Man on Horseback* (London, 1962), Samuel P. Huntington (ed.), *Changing Patterns of Military Politics* (New York, 1961), Morris Janowitz, *The Military in the Political Development of New Nations* (Chicago, 1964). For the Middle East, see Morroe Berger, *Military Elites and Social Change: Egypt since Napoleon* (Center for International Studies, Princeton: Research Monograph, no. 6), Majid Khadduri, 'The Role of the Military in Middle East Politics', *American Political Science Review*, vol. xlvii, 2 (June 1953), pp. 511-24, Dankwart A. Rustow, 'The Army and the Founding of the Turkish Republic', *World Politics*, vol. xi, 4 (July 1959), pp. 513-52, Daniel Lerner and Richard D. Robinson, 'Swords and Plowshares: The Turkish Army as a Modernising Force', *World Politics*, vol. xiii, 1 (October 1960), pp. 19-44, Sydney N. Fisher (ed.), *The Military in Middle Eastern Society and Politics* (Columbus, Ohio, 1963), Gordon H. Torrey, *Syrian Politics and the Military* (Columbus, Ohio, 1964).

11. *Al-Fakhri* (Cairo, 1899), pp. 45-6.

12. Two such descriptions by Egyptians in English are Rashed al-Barawy, *The Military Coup in Egypt* (Cairo, 1952), and Anwar El Sadat, *Revolt on the Nile* (London, 1957). See also Keith Wheelock, *Nasser's New Egypt* (New York, 1960), and my book cited above, Chapters 3-5.

13. I have used the term *stratiotocracy*, the rule of soldiers, in preference to others in order to express a more inclusive use of the military institution. It is borrowed from the Greek word for soldier, *stratiotes*. The term *strategós* commonly used for *general*, also denotes *commander*.

14. The term 'modernising leader' as it is used here comes closest in connotation to the Roman *princeps*. But it is also akin to the Machiavellian concept of *il principe* in the sense of a dynamic leader who seeks to rescusitate and strengthen his nation and state. The modernising leader in this context is the supreme patriot. Moreover, he possesses a vision of a national future. His leadership is both demanding of his followers and protective of them. He plays the role of both an *eghétis* and *prostátes*.

15. Even the activities of the Sufi *tariqas* with a reported membership at one time of 3,000,000, have, since 1960, come under strict state control. Thus, one of the traditional checks on power in any Islamic society has been effectively removed, or at least neutralised. The bureaucratic control of the state is now complete over the religious teachers, upholders of tradition, and the Sacred Law. Their mobilisation in the service of the socialist revolution became complete with the promulgation of the Law for the Reorganisation of al-Azhar in June 1961. See my 'Islam and the Foreign Policy of Egypt', J. Harris Proctor (ed.), *Islam and Inter-*

national Relations (New York and London, 1965), pp. 120-57.
   16. This is when, as William Kornhauser has argued, a mass becomes available for mobilisation by an élite. See his *The Politics of Mass Society* (Glencoe, Illinois, 1959).
   17. A feature of radical revolution in both Egypt and Algeria has been the rejection of 'intellectualism' as an alien Western conception and activity. As such, it is associated with the previous rather moderate — in many instances superficially — liberal nationalist leadership in these states. It is, therefore, considered anti-populist (anti-*sha'bi*) and pro-imperialist. Not only are men of action and popular ruler-leaders (*zu'ama'*) preferred in these circumstances, but intellectuals are reduced to purveyors of the policies, pronouncements and programmes initiated and decreed by the leader. The terminology and dialectic of the revolutionary ideology, including such movements as Arabism (*al-qawmiyya al-'arabiyya*), is most interesting and deserves separate study. See the interesting discussion 'The Language of Politics' in Hisham B. Sharabi, *Nationalism and Revolution in the Arab World* (Princeton, NJ, 1966). Generally, on the role of the intellectuals in the Arab radical revolution as illustrated by the case of Egypt, see Majdi Wahba, 'Fi qalaq al-muthaqqaf al-'arab', *Hiwar* (Beirut), vol. i, 4 (May 1963), pp. 29-40, and P.J. Vatikiotis, 'Al-muthaqqaf al-'arabi wa'l-mujtama' al-hadith', ibid., pp. 41-51. See a discussion and rebuttal of the latter article in *al-Jumhuriyya* (Cairo), 13 and 19 June 1963.
   18. *Al-ittihad al-'arabi al-ishtirakt.*
   19. See *al-Tali'a* (Cairo), vol. i, 2 (February 1965), pp. 9-26.
   20. On the foreign and Arab policy of Egypt see my 'The Foreign Policy of Egypt', Roy C. Macridis (ed.), *Foreign Policy in World Politics*, 2nd rev. edn. (Englewood Cliffs, NJ, 1962), pp. 335-50, and 'Islam and the Foreign Policy of Egypt'. See also Charles Cremeans and Leonard Binder, 'Nasserism: The Protest Movement in the Middle East' in Morton A. Kaplan (ed.), *The Revolution in World Politics* (New York, 1962), pp. 152-74, and 'Egypt's Positive Neutrality', pp. 175-91.
   21. See a most recent assessment by Patrick Seale, *The Struggle for Syria* (London, 1965); also Malcolm H. Kerr, *The Arab Cold War*, Chatham House Essays (London, 1965).
   22. See Riyad Taha, *Mahadir muhadathat al-wihda* (Cairo, 1963), for the proceedings of the Summit Conferences in March-April 1963 between Iraq, Syria and the UAR.
   23. See a recent assessment by Jean-Claude Froelich, 'L'Egypte et les peuples noirs', *Orient*, vol. ix, 32-3 (1964-5), pp. 13-28.
   24. It should be noted that in his speeches, President 'Abd al-Nasir often encourages and sustains this public image of himself as a protector. For example, in his address to the opening of the second session of the National Assembly in Cairo on 12 November 1964, he made it clear that Egypt considered the continued presence of British bases in Cyprus, south Arabia and Libya a threat to Egyptian security and to the Arab nationalist cause. In his annual victory speech at Port Said on 23 December 1964, he reiterated his leadership of the Arab nationalist struggle against imperialism.
   25. See my essay, 'Egypt 1966: the Assessment of a Revolution', *The World Today* (June 1966), pp. 241-52.

10 THE MODERN HISTORY OF EGYPT ALLA FRANCA

The writing of great history began when Herodotus set out 'to preserve the memory of the past by putting on record the astonishing achievements both of . . . the Greeks and of the Asiatic peoples', and 'to show how the two races came into conflict'. But great critical history was born with Thucydides, whose outlook upon, and approach to, historical study is revealed in his sharp remarks on the writing of history and his own method: 'The historian must not be misled by the exaggerated fancies of the poets, or by the tales of chroniclers who seek to please the ear rather than speak the truth . . .' Such scepticism is, however, not held as a prelude to cynicism. Nor is the realism associated with such an outlook an excuse or justification for an immoralist view of man's history; it is only an antidote to wishful thinking, some of which derives from man's attraction to magic, his wish for revelation, his search for certitude. Or, to borrow Pascal's definition, it is the use of reason in order to indicate reason's limitation.

It has been said that if all history could be explained by man's symbols and recourse to symbolism, mankind would have been a collection either of bland saints or incorrigible rascals. Man would bow to a historical inevitability whose force and impact could be explained in turn only by magician-saints or con-artist rascals. After all, one of the earliest social experiences and needs of man has been religion in one form or another. For a while, after the scientific revolutions of the seventeenth and eighteenth centuries, European man at least was inclined to think that science dispensed with the need for religious belief; in its place a new faith could be devised without the mystery or mumbo-jumbo of traditional religion. Since the nineteenth century, the rise of a modern gnosticism, with its belief in the inevitability of the historical process moving along in a pattern of determinist causation towards an envisioned telos, seized man. All human phenomena were to be explained within its tyrannical context. The old distinction between sacred and profane history was triumphantly abolished.

Source: A review article of Jacques Berque, *Egypt, Imperialism and Revolution*, translated from the French by Jean Stewart, foreword by Albert Hourani (Faber and Faber, London, 1972), first published in *Middle Eastern Studies*, vol. 10, no. 1 (January 1974), pp. 80-92.

History came to be seen as the unfolding of man's will in a grand design and march towards liberation from restrictions, natural and human: from necessity, from the burden of history itself and, in its metastatic worst, as a substitute for reality. It may not be difficult to accept the Heraclitean-Bergsonian (that is, in part, Hegelian and Marxist) proposition that the world, the universe, in its present form is the outcome of movement: man's consciousness unfolding, as Teilhard de Chardin would put it. But is man's consciousness synonymous with his will? How does this relentless forward movement account for or deal with, chance, inadvertence, accident and all the other scourges of the forward movement of progress?

Could some of these scourges be psychological and not economic, sociological or collective? That is, might they be, to a lesser or greater degree, the consequences of transmitted or learned behaviour? The ancients, incidentally, emphasised with a persistent instinct the role of *passion* in the vagaries of human affairs: fear, desire, envy, hatred, etc. The moderns seem to have rediscovered it. The rediscovery however has been somewhat traumatic, for it occurred at a time when the conjunction of fantastic scientific advance and elaborately designed professionalism in the planning (a new and forceful myth) of social organisation and life seemed to spell salvation.

For some twenty years now, many students have tended to examine the modern history and politics of so-called developing societies within the context of the dynamic of a grand historical design which entails a salvationist eschatology; 'development', 'modernity', 'liberation of consciousness', 'socialist bliss', 'recapture of true identity', 'authenticity'. Without going into a detailed critique of the paradoxes and intellectual convolutions of this type of study, recent events have exposed the weakness and inadequacy of this approach. An analytically more rigorous examination and evaluation of post-colonial national rule, which is relatively free of rigid ideological commitments, has been found necessary.

Objectively, students accept the proposition that Egypt in 1952 was ripe for political upheaval. This came by way of a military conspiracy which succeeded in overthrowing the old regime of the monarchy, and generation of politicians who emerged from the social and political conditions, forces and events in the first two decades of this century. Today, twenty years later, it is realised that the Free Officer movement did not introduce a new political form of rulership, even though it abolished the institution of the monarchy, as well as that of parliamentarianism and its paraphernalia. It did not, that is, constitute a revolutionary beginning in an architectonic sense, because no new political principle governing the relation between ruler and subjects was introduced. If the objective conditions were right for a new political beginning, what prevented it from occurring? What is needed in any attempt to deal with this question is straightforward historical analysis based on evidence, not exercises in futuristic prescription; that is, diagnosis, not prognosis.

Until some thirty or forty years ago, writing about the history of modern Egypt was — and this is an arbitrary categorisation — of three kinds, in three languages. British officials, connected with the administration of the country after 1882, published accounts of the record of that administration, as well as reminiscences of their own personal experiences. Cromer, Lloyd, Milner, Colvin, Russell, Storrs and several others come to mind. There is still a vast backlog of private papers, memoranda, diaries and notes by many of these witnesses of the British presence in Egypt which have yet to be consulted and published. Before them, in the eighteenth and earlier part of the nineteenth centuries, travellers and sojourners of longer duration recorded and published their impressions of Egypt.[1]

In addition to such famous traveller-chroniclers as Volney and Savary, Frenchmen who had accompanied the Napoleonic expedition in Egypt (1798-1801), or who had subsequently joined the service of that great oriental despot Muhammad Ali (1805-49) or his successors also recorded their experiences. A. Clot Bey, F. Mengin and P.N. Hamont are three. Frenchmen injected the first serum of modern European education and culture into Egyptian veins, from archaeology, science and technology, to the modern arts of war and exhilarating promises provided by the ideas of the Enlightenment and the French Revolution. In the real world of politics, government and administration, however, the French after 1876 lost their prominent role and position in Egyptian affairs. They were displaced by the British. Nevertheless, under British political hegemony, they were able, and allowed, to retain and extend their educational-cultural sway in the country over other Europeans.

Judging from the number of works published in the nineteenth and twentieth centuries, the French had a sustained interest in the record of the Muhammad Ali dynasty and the history of Egypt since the Napoleonic conquest. Even subsequently, Gabriel Hanotaux's supervision of a multi-volume history of Egypt (*Histoire de la Nation Egyptienne*) under the auspices of King Fuad re-affirmed the interest of French historians in Egypt. G. Guémard, E. Driault and G. Douin are some of the scholars associated with such endeavour, not to mention the independent works of F. Charles-Roux, R. Maunier and several others.

The French were, formally at least, not directly involved in the vicissitudes of Anglo-Egyptian relations from 1882 to 1945. From 1882 until the signing of the Entente Cordiale in 1904, French policy makers, publicists, writers and historians were on the whole opponents and critics of Britain's role in Egypt. At times they were plain mischief-makers, if one considers the incident of the *Bosphore* newspaper. This coincided with the rise and growth of native Egyptian opposition to Britain within the relatively free political atmosphere and improved material condition of the country provided by British administration, fiscal and other reforms. France, however, retained a certain kind of political influence through the French-operated Ecole de Droit in Cairo and the first Egyptian graduates of the Sorbonne, Dijon, Lyons, Montpellier and other French universities.

Throughout the nineteenth century, Egyptian historians retained their chronicler approach in the writing of their country's history, Jabarti, the most famous among them, was in the tradition of Maqrizi and Ibn Iyas. Lesser historians like Mikhail Zakhura and Ilias Ayyubi carried on with this tradition. Our knowledge of Egypt, the Egyptians and their rulers was enhanced by the encyclopedic works of Ali Pasha Mubarak, Amin Sami and Ahmad Chafiq Pasha. Equally comprehensive in its coverage, regardless of its quality, has been the lifelong endeavour in this century of 'Abd al-Rahman al-Rafi'i to record the story of his country's historical evolution from the time of Muhammad Ali until the military revolt of 1952.

While Milner, Cromer, Lloyd and others recorded the history of Egypt's economic, political and administrative history since the occupation, W.S. Blunt took up the banner of Egyptian opposition to that occupation. In doing so, he also publicised and, to some extent, inflated, the image and magnitude of a nascent Egyptian nationalism. Much historical writing about Egypt until then was confined to recording the achievements, strengths and weaknesses of dynasts, their governments, their relations with their suzerain, the Sultan in Istanbul, and related matters. Muhammad Ali and Khedive Ismail received wide attention in these respects. Nevertheless, authors were content, by and large, to write history in the commonly understood sense of the term. In 1927, however, G. Young published his book on Egypt. Its departure from straightforward history was 'justified' by its aim to further convey the spirit of modern Egyptian nationalism.

In 1835, the Library of Useful Knowledge published in two volumes E.W. Lane's *The Manners and Customs of the Modern Egyptians*, which was described as 'the most remarkable description of a people ever written'. It was not a history, but a *description* of the country and its people. Lane had spent a total of five years (1825-8, 1833-5) in Egypt, where he assumed native dress and style of life. His was a daring experiment of relatively long duration in field research about another and different society. There has not been a European — or at least Englishman — like him since.

In contrast, the *Description de l'Egypte*, a massive reference work on Egypt's geography, topography, climatology, flora and fauna, the Nile, mineral and other resources, was the product of the collective efforts of French scientists and scholars who had accompanied the Napoleonic expedition. The French in this century continued to write about Egyptian rulers, until Marcel Colombe in 1951 published a general historical survey of independent Egypt. It was no more than an illuminating outline.[2] In the same year, a young Egyptian, Subhi Wahida, published an original and controversial economic interpretation of Egyptian history.[3]

Until Jacques Berque's massive tome, books about Egypt emanating from France in the last twenty-five years have been of two kinds: those penned by Egyptian exiles in Paris which tried to interpret modern history according to Marxist conceptions or theories on one hand, and those written by journalists about recent developments on the other.[4]

Professor Berque's previous work on Egypt, *Histoire sociale d'un village Egyptien au xxème siècle* (1957), was a serious social anthropological study of village and provincial life. In 1960, however, he published *Les Arabes d'hier à demain* (English translation, *The Arabs: their history and future*, 1964). Insightful in parts, turgid and lyrically mystifying in others, this was, on the whole, an obscurantist, obfuscating study of 'national character'. The author's preferred approach here was what he described as a random discovery of a few significant movements. Contrary to the book's sub-title, it was not a history. At first glance, it appeared to be a sociological interpretation of what was happening to the 'Arab personality'. The difficulty lay in the dubious existence of this 'personality'. There was no attempt to determine if such in fact existed as a datum, or whether one is confronted with a diversity of Arab personalities. In any event, the author did not even try to describe so-called Arab social attitudes.[5] He simply theorised about them in the manner of Grand Sociological Theory.

There was a blithe assumption in Professor Berque's *The Arabs* that the history of a people — even in the face of the reality that they do not constitute one homogeneous society — can be recorded and its salient features accurately conveyed by a description of sentiments and preferences. The actual conditions of their society, indeed, their several societies, constitute an irrelevant, irritating riddle which can be lightly overlooked. In this way, 'popular enthusiasm' and 'instinctive decisions' are better guides to historical 'truth' and to historical study. Feeling and fantasy are supreme. The question arises though, whose feeling and whose fantasy: that of the Arab, or the student or historian of the Arab?

In *The Arabs*, Professor Berque left his readers with the enigmatic message that the traditional Arab is still a Hellene — a curious description to say the least.[6] In his more recent *Egypt, imperialism and revolution*, he sets out to restore the Egyptian's Islamic, or native, authenticity in the face of the disastrous consequences of his confrontation with Western civilisation. This exercise consumes over 700 pages of print, within the chronological framework of Egypt's history from the British occupation in 1882 to the military *coup d'état* in 1952. It is essentially an immanentist, eschatological treatment of the 'process of decolonisation', which parallels the author's other work.[7] It does not merely describe the process, but also prescribes and forecasts its entelechy; and that is done by a combination of Eleusinian mystery and the sonorous, solemn pronouncements of a Delphic oracle:

> The social whole that is the object of this sort of research is really more immediate, more active, and easier to observe than the action of its particular parts. (p. 24)
> Thus the close scrutiny of a particular case with all its individual characteristics, its figures and its colours, would contribute to a sociological study of world problems that is at present dominated by (or should be dominated by) the analysis of decolonization: that is to say the analysis of the movement of the world towards a juster sharing-out of collective roles, or in other words towards a re-founding of history. (p. 25)
> Can it be that the new being now struggling to emerge from the ordeal amidst violence and misunderstandings is really recreating the synthesis of which Western man had lost all hope? . . . that is what he must needs do. The alternative is his downfall. He must reconcile his specific personality and his universal humanity . . . While deeply rooted in the soil, he must aspire towards a supremely rational future. He must ensure that this crisis of his personality and that of society as a whole correspond to one another in purpose and in significance, and join in commitment to a single end.
> He knows that he must belong to the world, or cease to be. That is his form of socialism. (p. 30)

There is implied here the need for a kind of gnosticism in the study of history, the *logos* of which only the properly initiated can possess. The gnostic is not interested in the concrete reality of human action, the good and the bad. Rather he is interested in the movement from bad to good, on a sort of moral spectrum of history. To this extent, the author's mystical ticket for entry into the esoteric truth of modern Egyptian history also derives part of its validity from the anti-historical — and historicist — approach to the study of the past which is rooted to a great extent in Positivism and Romantic Idealism.

Whereas history for some of us by definition has no future, only a beginning and an end which, incidentally, is the present, in both *The Arabs* and *Egypt* the author gives it a definite future which he envisages by the invocation of some latent, mysterious potential inherent in the society under consideration. Unlike the historian's, his picture of the society whose history he is studying does not stand in strict relation to the evidence. It does not have to, because history is considered to be synonymous with change, with progress, with the very re-making of the world.

One discerns in the author's approach the combination of an eminent French intellectual tradition (at least one which has characterised French historiography), consisting of Positivism and Bergsonian evolutionism on the one hand, and on the other a Hegelian essentialism inherent in the notion that large-scale historical changes are due to a dialectic which operates objectively, by necessity shaping historical process. Positivism lay in the author's search for general laws which govern the course of history, as for instance in his entertaining a 'science of decolonisation'. The Hegelianism consists of finding a slot for modern Egyptian history in a necessary, universal dialectic of historical design. Bergsonian evolutionism is partly expressed in the author's readiness to immerse himself (through a mystical relationship of love for his object of study) into the movement of the history he is investigating to the point where this movement begins to occur within himself. Sympathy for his subject often becomes the basis for a sparkling, though quaint and esoteric, interpretation of its history.

While such a combination of intellectual tradition and approach may, on one level, reflect an author's desire for popularity, on another, it manages to convey a vivid characterisation of a particular historical period. But the danger inherent in all of this remains: history and nature are fused; mind and nature are indistinguishable from one another. Facts become fused too; they are all one. History and its factual data tend to become subjective constructs of the historian's mind. Knowledge tends to derive comfortably from feeling, sentiment and mystical fusion. Positivism, Creative evolutionism and Hegelianism are combined in the task of the historian, which is to recount events of a particular period as they fit general laws of history and a grand universal design of historical necessity with love and sympathy, regardless of the evidence.

Professor Berque then is not writing history in the ordinary, or even accepted, sense of the term. His is not an historical inquiry in the sense of finding things out, or raising questions about the actions of men in the past, or critically evaluating and interpreting available evidence about a period, or even finding out what Egyptians have done in the recent past which might help one understand what kind of people they were and are. After all, the period covered, 1882-1952, is a well-documented one, as indeed Professor Berque's work itself shows. The experience of that epoch, then, can be reasonably recalled and reported. The author, however, is not primarily interested in doing that. Rather he is concerned with a more general question which goes beyond historical inquiry. It is one that brings to mind medieval historiography which saw its task as the discovery and exposition of a divine plan in history.

'Under what circumstances, according to what correlations, does liberation result dialectically from dependence?' is the general question to which Professor Berque addresses himself in his interpretation of Egyptian history from 1882 to 1952. The history of Egypt during that period, that is, serves as the case study for an analysis of a world process of decolonisation, and as a heuristic model which illuminates the movement 'towards a re-founding of history'. But the author himself comes to this interpretive historical study with his own vision of a world to come, and a grand design for its history which is basically a study of man's will unfolding and the obstacles to it. He invokes 'Promethean lyricism' in his unilinear historical design, because the Egyptian has deliberately willed and determined to travel its course. Nothing in this ineluctable process is left to chance or inadvertence; it is all part of an inevitable, relentless re-making of the world.

Stripped to its barest essentials, the main argument the author puts forward in his *Egypt, imperialism and revolution* is that the British occupation caused the 'denaturation' of the Egyptian, especially the peasant. It concealed and arrested his 'authenticity' by a hypocritical veil of inadequate modernity. It obstructed his vitality. There is a deliciously contrived partial thesis here that whatever material and cultural advance Egypt had achieved until 1882 was largely due to the efforts of the fellah. An end was put to all of this vitality and creativeness by the British. The liberation after 1952 will permit the Egyptian to re-discover his true identity, recapture his vitality and go on heroically to 're-make' his society, country and the world. He will revert, that is, to his true nature. Writing in 1934, Lord Lloyd concluded the two volumes of his *Egypt since Cromer* by taking up some of these matters. He observed that[8]

> More and more clearly the conclusion seems to emerge that the real danger to those countries which have come under our control arises when the claims of good administration are subordinated to the claims of political theory.

Then he raises the question of the consequences of the association between Egypt and Britain, and remarks:[9]

> They will say that association with Western races destroys the organic natural growth, and puts nothing of value in its place: that we break off short and kill a tradition that has at least the mellow charm of age and continuity, and try to substitute for it a jerry-built product which has no foundations in the soil upon which it is placed.

But can it be proved conclusively, he asks,[10]

> that the conditions which they describe are the direct consequence of alien domination? We have always been careful not to interfere with indigenous customs and traditions.

In fact, he asserts:[11]

> It was French culture which Egyptians so keenly sought and of which they obtained so strong a graft . . .

There is, one feels, a mixed religious-sexual allegorical resonance to the titles of the main parts of Professor Berque's text: 'Part I, the Interrupted Country' (Chapter and Section headings: 'Rhythm and Symbol', 'A Contest between Signs' or, in Part II, 'Katabasis'); 'Part III: The Hopes of 1919' (Sub-headings: 'The dialectics of native quantity', 'The advent of *wijdan*'); 'Part IV: Aspirations Cheated'; 'Part V: Phantoms in Power'. Some may feel there is a theatrical, operatic sound to them. Upon closer examination of the contents, one soon discovers the need for such cryptic titular descriptions and esoteric allusions.

In Part I of the book, there is an attempt to romanticise Egypt of the pre-1882 nineteenth century. It was, one is told, a country doing its own thing, so to speak, with the help of the odd Frenchman or Italian. The peasants ('Rural Bases') and villagers went on undisturbed with their authentic, native practices, their sense of community and feeling of solidarity intact. The 'local reality', one is informed, was maintained. The author wonders if any of these rural practices survive today. He is inclined to suggest that the local reality has been undermined, essentially and primarily, by the perfidious British with their newfangled efficient administration, fiscal, agricultural and judicial reforms.

As for the rural practices, one gathers from other competent sources that many of them survive today. Père Henri Ayrout, W.S. Blackman, J.W. McPherson and Hamed Ammar at least report to that effect.[12] Their gradual or rapid abandonment is not the consequence of the perfidious actions of a particular ruler, native or foreign. It is rather the result of cumulative changes in modes of production, the pressures of government policy, and plain individual choice. In Egypt, as in most other countries, it also occurs with the widespread migration of people from the countryside to the town, or city.

The 'local reality' the author writes about is a vague emotive construct. Which 'local reality' one might ask? That under the Pharaohs, the Greeks or Romans, the Byzantines or Arabs, the Mamluks or Turks, or their satrap diadochs such as Muhammad Ali the Great and his progeny? Did all of these in turn 'interrupt the country?' Under all of them, the ruler, the government, was the Chief Landlord of Egypt. It was he or they, if anyone, who tampered with the so-called local reality of village, town, craft, guild and religious shrine. It was the oriental despot, Muhammad Ali, who imported 'the confusion of production', with the assistance, one might add, of the Frenchman. It was his son, Said Pasha and his grandson, Khedive Ismail, who welcomed the construction of the French-sponsored, designed and financed Suez Canal.

Muhammad Ali's imperial ambitions had already been thwarted by the European powers as far back as 1840. By the time his grandson Ismail nurtured parallel ambitions in Egypt and Africa, Britain was already firmly established in India and the Persian Gulf; France was entrenching herself in North Africa; the Ottoman Padishah was a declining power in the East. In short, what kind of development is one to assume was interrupted by the British incursion in Egypt, an incursion originally clamoured for by European states, chief among them France?

An answer to this question is provided in Part II of the book, 'Colonial Egypt'. There, one is given to understand, a revolt of what the author calls 'village-born intellectuals' who were about to revive the native idiom and lead the country into an era of national revival was arrested and quashed by force of British arms. One is further regaled with a picture of masses of peasants taking part in this sacred national rebellion. That there was a rebellion of army officers motivated by specific, military bureaucratic grievances against the ruler there is no doubt. But whether there was a national revolution that failed is a different matter. Who were Orabi's allies or cohorts in this revolt? What motivated them, and to what extent can they be considered 'national cadres' (an anachronistic and therefore misleading appellation), are questions the author does not deal with. In fact, he ignores any work which has unearthed fresh evidence about such matters.[13] What seems important is that the Orabi affair constitutes a romantic episode in Egypt's history, whatever its precise or detailed aims may have been. It is doubtful whether 'the people sought immediate self-government'; in fact, there is no evidence to warrant such an inference. What is historically more certain, in the sense that it stands in strict relation to the evidence, is the fact that a group of army officers, in alliance with disparate groups of politicians, landowning notables, high officials (any of these indeed were hopelessly involved in intricate oriental cobwebs of intrigue as clients of one or other Ottoman Turco-Egyptian potentate or patron) sought to wrest power from the appointed khedive in order to govern the people.

During the 'colonial period' (Egypt, incidentally, was never a British colony), the author complains disarmingly, 'the possibility of development from within occurred to nobody'. Theoretically, there was no reason, of course, for such development not to have taken place. In fact, it had been occurring for over sixty years before the British occupation. It could not, however, have taken place without outside, i.e. European, help. But, alas, it ran aground in the complex and, in some respects, anomalous, relations of Egypt with its suzerain, as well as in the latter's arrangements with the European powers. By 1879, Ismail's Egypt was bankrupt, hopelessly in debt to European creditors. These demanded action from their governments to safeguard their investments. It was agreed that it should be concerted, collective action. Yet in the end Britain was left to act alone.

The thrust of the author's presentation of 'Colonial Egypt' consists of an attack on British policy and a denigration of its administrative and other achievements. 'Egypt à l'Indienne' (alluding to the importation of British civil servants from India, and to Cromer himself) achieved 'nothing definitive'. '. . . thus the maturation of a failure was disguised under apparent progress'. '. . . Baring lagged far behind Dufferin! His acknowledged ambitions were confined to re-establishing finance, security and administration.'

The author deplores 'the establishment of the colonial economy' for its economic, social and political consequences:

> The gradual ruin of Egypt's craftsmen, the demoralisation of traders, the interruption of traditional circuits, the abdication of the corporative honour. (p. 186)
> Every advance in perennial irrigation was an advance of the central bureaucracy, and consequently of the new authorities. (p. 188)

'Work', he goes on to lament, 'became a saleable commodity'. 'Colonialism imposed its quantitative values on the remotest villages . . .' The old community broke up. He takes Englishmen (Milner, Cromer and others), who have written about the tangible achievements of their administration, severely to task:

> These documents, which have been published, describe the people and things of Egypt with apparent objectivity; as Milner's book has done and as Cromer's own book was to do, while professing a sincerity which is merely a blend of camouflage and exhibitionism, they administer a subtly insolent rebuke to Egyptian opinion. (p. 330)

After all, he argues, 'They ruled by might rather than by right. And they were checked only by the impenetrable character of Eastern society, the resistance of certain groups.' Their colonial regime, he asserts, 'had been set up for, and to some extent by means of, cotton; . . .' Worst of all, 'The propaganda of the regime doubtless tended to obliterate the memories of the efforts that had preceded it: the technical contributions of the French, the work of the Egyptians themselves.'

In the context of this diatribe against the British record in Egypt, the author introduces the rise of Egyptian nationalist opposition to British tutelage, and the native religious reaction to it in the form of Islamic reformism. His discussion here consists mainly of simple biographical sketches of some of the personalities involved, without reference to the complexities of political intrigue, conspiracy and external involvements. Thus the journalist and political agitator Sheikh Ali Yusuf, the Nationalist leader Mustafa Kamil and the young Khedive Abbas Hilmi appear as straightforward, uncomplicated standard-bearers of the Egyptian movement for self-determination and a popular nationalist regime.

Remarks such as Milner's, 'The native ruling class was vicious and incapable . . .',[14] and the chapter in his book on French opposition to British policy[15] (despite his tribute to French services in Egypt) might conceivably exercise any Frenchman. Perhaps, also, administrative and other practical reforms in a country long used to the ways of oriental despots do not appeal to the resounding, often phantasmagoric, promises of the French revolutionary tradition. For it was not the British who introduced a colonial economy in Egypt. That – if the work of Charles Issawi and others is to be accepted – had already been introduced by Muhammad Ali and Ismail. The British did not rule by might alone, nor were they 'checked only by the impenetrable character of Eastern society, the resistance of certain groups'. Rather it was their own self-restraint, and doubts over their indeterminate, undefined position in Egypt which checked them. 'Is it necessary', Milner asked in 1892:[16]

> in view of these facts, to explain any further how the indefiniteness of British authority, and the irregular methods by which it is exercised, inevitably increases the friction which must in any case arise between two Governments standing to one another in the relations of guardian and ward?

In the final analysis, the author discerns in his own interpretation of the history of that period

> . . . a line leading gradually to liberation, through and despite accumulated obstacles, through and despite self-imposed formulations or those attached to it by others. (p. 262)

To what extent however this development was a consequence of British 'misrule' is not made clear. Nor is the perfectly legitimate and sensible question asked: To what extent might it have been the consequence of British rule?

Britain was not in Egypt, initially, for economic reasons; her imperialism there was not an economic one. It was for political and strategic considerations related to India that Britain sojourned in Egypt for over seventy years. Similarly, it was Britain's reduced power in the inter-war period and after 1945, more than any other single factor, quickly followed by her exit from India, which heralded Egyptian liberation.

According to the evidence, Britain did not introduce a colonial economy based on cotton. That was already a marked development under Ismail. The alacrity with which Egyptian landowners turned much of their cultivable land over to that great cash export crop, cotton, was only human – and was some time before the British came on the scene. Nor did British economic policy destroy the craftsmen of Egypt, or the traditional circuits of trade. These were already in decline nearly a century earlier. Muhammad Ali's industrialisation policies and programmes sealed their fate, and made labour a saleable commodity.[17] Equally, public works connected with irrigation had long been the crucial sinew of central bureaucratic power before the British came to Egypt. Muhammad Ali's record in this respect is impressive. In short, the erosion of a partly romanticised, idealised past in which rural Egypt enjoyed local autonomy had already occurred with Muhammad Ali's first cadastral survey in the early period of his rule.

The difference after 1882 was that these officials, whom the author finds unpleasant and unacceptable, sought to infuse a degree of order amidst widespread chaos and a measure of probity in that venal, hydraulic master of the Egyptians — the government. By French standards, of course, they were not versed in, or inclined towards, formulating the paradisical images or promises of a political ideology. What is certain, however, is that without their 'dubious' achievements ('nothing definitive') the author's heroes — Muhammad Abduh, Mustafa Kamil, Saad Zaghlul and many others — might have remained prey to the head-chopping whims of a native potentate. Nor were these Indian-type civil servants, alas, versed in, or aware of, 'that sort of spontaneous and implicit democracy, which had its parallels in village administration'.

Professor Berque's treatment of Egyptian history from 1918 to 1952 is engaging. It too moves with the firmness and certainty of pace which characterise the inexorable historical movement towards liberation. Individuals and their motives, we are told, are unimportant; 'movements and structures are what make history'. Thus King Fuad's 'psychology and personality are relatively unimportant . . .' Great ideas are embodied in crowds, especially with the advent of youth into the political life of the country. Peasants instinctively realise the incompatibility between the twentieth century on the one hand and their country's political and economic dependence on the other.

Under this ideological rubric, the intricate political behaviour of individuals, groups, parties and governments lends itself to a necessary, dialectic interpretation. Exclusively government-sponsored trade unionism becomes a political force, not an instrument; the student 'movement' of the thirties becomes a credible independent political arbiter. The younger generation's 'Gersch (Piastre) Appeal' becomes an unfettered expression of the nationalist struggle. Nowhere in this treatment are the murky squabbles among politicians, political agitators, parties and foreign-power agents over the financing, control and direction of student groups, the scandalous corruption and collapse of the 'Gersch Project' and the trade unions, referred to. Muhammad Bilal, Ahmad Hussein, Nur al-Din Tarraf, Fathi Radwan, Halawani and others are portrayed as disinterested national idealists. Mahmud Azmi was not simply 'that excellent journalist'. He was also a complex inter-Arab intriguer, at times a paid foreign agent. Detailed information on all these matters is available in both Egyptian and British archives. The muddled political history of the inter-war period cannot be examined simply on some ideological spectrum. It also needs to be de-loused.

Professor Berque seems to dismiss with deliberate scorn British sources dealing with the inter-war period, especially the 1930s, when the Egyptian attack upon the brief experiment in secular politics gathered momentum. A perusal of these indicates the British were not concerned with, or confined to, superficial observations in Egypt as the author would have one believe. Nor were their speculations based on surface happenings. In these situations the historian's duty of discovering who was doing what, when, in what context and to whose advantage or disadvantage, is just as great as that of relating what was happening. Exercising one's fantasy in unwarranted *ex post facto* attributions to individual actions and movements is no substitute, even when this comes up with its endearing inventions, as for example, 'the underground station in Heliopolis', which never existed.

Still, Professor Berque could well be justified in his conclusions. By 1952, the Egyptian opted against efficiency and for authenticity. He wished to rediscover his identity. He sought to restore justice through violence. Green Shirts, Blue Shirts, Muslim Brothers, army officer conspirators, all shared that objective. The question is, though, which authenticity, what personality? That of an idealised Arab-Islamic model of the past, that of the Pharaohs, or that of the Mamluks; or again, simply that of an oriental despotism? For, by the 1930s, the Abdel Hamid Saids, Saleh Harbs, Ali Mahers, Hasan Bannas, Ahmad Husseins, Aziz Ali Masris of Egypt were already hard at work at the restoration of the native idiom in politics. They were assisted in their work by the behaviour of the appointed and elected political leaders of the country, as well as that of their monarch, which undermined the chosen, partly imported, political order. The maintenance of the latter depended in part on the relationship of the new hegemonies to a foreign power. Once the latter was removed (or removed itself) from the scene, the whole edifice collapsed; the return to the native idiom became inevitable — in fact, it soon followed. Yet it did not do away with political and economic dependence, nor did it provide a packaged formula for the Egyptian's restoration of his true identity, or his authenticity.

It is not so much some of Professor Berque's conclusions one disagrees with, but rather his explanations and his historical method, encumbered as it is with ideological baggage. The Egyptian, alas, failed to attain his declared inevitable *telos* in his history of decolonisation. No amount of epic heroism and nostalgic mush can convince the Egyptian of the post-1952 generation that 'an apocalypse postulates new birth'. Black Saturday (26 January 1952) was, as Professor Berque rightly asserts, an event of anthropological significance, one which 'no discoveries in the field of secret history can reduce' in significance. Yet it landed Egyptians in the lap of a Mamluk-style autocracy, unchecked even by the resistance of the inscrutable Easterners. The future (1952-72) turned out to be a bitterly humiliating and agonising one in which, as Tawfiq al-Hakim forcefully put it, Egyptians 'lost their consciousness' and self-respect.

One sympathises with Professor Berque in seeking to evoke the true flavour of Egyptianity. To that end he copiously cites Mubarak's *Khitat* and more recent Egyptian literature. In an absolute sense, one may even agree with him that it might have been better for the Egyptian not to have been exposed to Europe. The fact remains that his own masters sought out Europe for what it could offer them by way of new techniques which they considered useful in the pursuit of greater power. Egypt, in particular, has always been exposed to outside influences, encroachments and incursions, from both East and West. Had the 'denaturation' not happened then, or under British occupation, it would have occurred at some other time.

What the historian discovers about Egypt's recent past is that the retreat, removal or ejection of European influence and/or domination has enabled Egyptians to revert to a more native way of doing things. Yet, with or without Europe, the contemporary historian also observes that the Egyptian's search for so called modernity, however defined, continues, despite the pull of, or clash with, authenticity. So does the Egyptian's political and economic dependence; and for that matter the dependence of many other peoples and nations.

If by authenticity and true identity the author means a return to some pristine, heroic Arab-Islamic past (but for Egypt, which past?), it is difficult to see how such total detachment and transportation will occur. It smacks of a Sorelian condemnation of history as it happened, in favour of a nostalgic, heroic 'brave old world' to be restored by an act of apocalyptic violence which generates its own ethic. It pleads, one feels, for a sort of medieval millenarianism.

The purpose of historical study is to discover, not invent, something about the past. What the historian discovers must be related to evidence about a particular people, country, or society, in a specific place over a specified period of time. Alas, no historian can hope to visualise, reconstruct or uncover evidence about the whole of that history. Nor can such history be synonymous with the processes of natural evolution, or with progress. There is no law of nature which guarantees human progress, or one which postulates that the history of a subsequent period is, by definition, a *better* one. The fact that British administrators in Egypt devoted their attention to administrative and fiscal reform, whereas Egyptian rulers after 1923 or 1952 preferred to exert their efforts in suppressing political opposition at home, mobilising the masses, or leading a pan-Arab movement, is not a question of progress or the lack of it. As far as history is concerned, the two instances as recorded indicate a difference between situations. They may constitute progress or its opposite only in the conception of one or the other group. Thus the author's attack on the fifty odd years of British hegemony in Egypt and his encomium of what followed it is not a historical distinction. If anything the distinction tells us, with respect, more about the author than his subject.

There was, the author tells us, a 'revolutionary synthesis' in Egyptian society from which the Egyptian will find himself again. Such is the struggle between his authenticity and drive towards modernity. Orabi in 1882, Zaghlul in 1919, Nasser in 1952 are all part of this process, whose end is liberation, and in the observation of which one can discover generic causes of failure and success. The author seems to feel that this kind of dialectic affords his historical study a scientific quality. But single-theory, universal conceptions of science, or of the science of society, tend to explain everything and nothing. They have a dogmatic quality about them. It is not the way either of natural or historical science.

Egypt, Imperialism and Revolution is too ideological to qualify as a successor to E.W. Lane's *Manners and Customs of the Modern Egyptians*, or a sequel to Ali Mubarak's *Khitat*.

Notes

1. See Bernard Lewis, 'Some English Travellers in the East', *Islam in History* (London, 1973), pp. 33-50, reprinted from *Middle Eastern Studies* (London, 1968), vol. 4, no. 3, pp. 296-315.
2. *L'evolution de l'Egypte, 1924-50* (Paris, 1951).
3. *Fi usul al-mas'ala al-misriyya* (*The Origins of the Egyptian Question*) (Cairo, 1951).
4. For example, Anouar Abdel-Malek, *Egypte: société militaire* (Paris, 1962; in English, New York, 1968); *Idéologie et renaissance nationale: L'Egypte moderne*

(Paris, 1969), Jean et Simonne Lacouture, *L'Egypte en mouvement* (Paris, 1956; in English, London, 1958).

5. Among such serious works, see Hamed Ammar, *Growing up in an Egyptian Village* (London and New York, 1954), Ali al-Wardi, *Dirasa fi tabi'at al-mujtama' al-'iraqi* (*A Study in the Nature of Iraqi Society*) (Baghdad, 1965).

6. See this writer's review in the *Bulletin of the School of Oriental and African Studies*, vol. 28 (1965), pp. 629-32.

7. See his *French North Africa: the Maghreb between two World Wars* (London, 1967), and his *Depossession du monde* (Paris, 1964).

8. London, 1934, vol. 2, p. 358.

9. Ibid., pp. 358-9.

10. Ibid., p. 359.

11. Ibid.

12. See H. Ayrout, *The Egyptian Peasant*, translated by John Alden Williams (Boston, 1963), W.S. Blackman, *The Fellahin of Upper Egypt* (London, 1927), J.W. McPherson, *The Moulids of Egypt* (Cairo, 1941) and Hamed Ammar.

13. See, for example, Elie Kedourie, *Afghani and Abduh* (London, 1966).

14. *England in Egypt* (London, 1904), p. 19.

15. Ibid., Chapter XIII, 'The Difficulty with France', pp. 334-48.

16. Ibid., pp. 31-2.

17. Cf. Charles Issawi, *Egypt in Revolution* (London, 1963), 'Egypt since 1800: a Study in Lopsided Development', *Journal of Economic History*, vol. 21 (March 1961), no. 1, pp. 1-25, Gabriel Baer, *Studies in the Social History of Modern Egypt* (Chicago, 1969) and *Egyptian Guilds* (Jerusalem, 1964).

11 RELATIONS BETWEEN EGYPT AND ISRAEL, 1977-82

A series of events which began six years ago culminated in the establishment of formal diplomatic relations between Egypt and Israel. The two countries had been technically at war with one another from the proclamation of the state of Israel on 15 May 1948 to the signing of the peace treaty between them in March 1979, a period of just over thirty years. To be sure, Egypt was the first country to sign an armistice agreement with Israel in Rhodes, in 1949, under the auspices of the United Nations; this ended the hostilities of the first Arab-Israel, or Palestine, War. After that, Egypt and Israel fought three successive wars, in 1956, 1967 and 1973. 1956 and 1967 for the Egyptians were not simply wars between them and Israel, but between the Arabs and Israel, since under Nasser's rule they considered themselves leaders of the Arab world, its champions and protectors against imperialism and Zionism.

Although the first direct contacts between Egypt and Israel were inaugurated and established by President Anwar Sadat when he went to Jerusalem in November 1977 to address the Knesset, there were, as the world subsequently learned, secret private meetings, through a variety of venues and intermediaries, between Egyptian and Israeli emissaries. Such were the series of secret meetings held in Romania, Morocco and elsewhere between 1975 and 1977, which paved the way for Sadat's dramatic flight to Jerusalem. One can also point to the direct meetings between Egyptian and Israeli senior military officers in the period 1974-5, during which the series of disengagement of forces agreements after the October, or Yom Kippur, War were negotiated. At first, the USA acted as a mediator — an honest or acceptable broker — in bringing about these early agreements between the belligerents. Later, however, in the negotiations of the Camp David Accords in 1978, the United States became a fully-fledged party to the peace settlement between Egypt and Israel. But even as far back as 1954, and periodically thereafter, there were indirect contacts between the two countries, either by correspondence or messages via third parties. This was particularly the case in the indirect contacts between Nasser and Ben Gurion in the early

Source: *Annual of Jewish Affairs* (1982).

and mid-1950s, before Nasser had settled on his radical Arab nationalist, and Third World neutralist, policies.

Clearly though, the initiative for peace, entailing the recognition of Israel and the establishment of diplomatic relations with her, came from Egypt, and in particular President Sadat. One must therefore ask not only about the latter's motives, which are not always easy to fathom, but also about the more objective reasons, the need for peace, which propelled Sadat to his dramatic gesture in November 1977, with all its many consequences. These are especially significant and poignant in the case of a man who, in his rather chequered career had become known as one of the most articulate, vociferous and consistent opponents of the West in general and Israel in particular. Moreover, in his past opposition, Sadat had appealed for, and evoked, a strident Islamic tone and ambience.[1]

Needless to say, the defeat of Egyptian arms in 1956 and especially in 1967, left an indelible mark not only on Sadat, but on all Egyptians. The weaknesses of the Nasser regime, or of the 1952 revolution, as it is referred to by Egyptians, were, after June 1967, in full view. The October War in 1973 regained for them and their arms a measure of honour and self-assurance and for the Egyptians themselves a measure of respect. More important, it attracted serious American efforts to find an accommodation between the chief belligerents in the Middle East conflict, Egypt and Israel. That is, it made effective diplomacy possible. This, however, would have been more difficult without the long process of Egypt's gradual disengagement from her involvement in inter-Arab, or Arab regional, politics, dating back to Nasser's policies in 1969-70. At the same time, a gradual reorientation of Egypt's external policy towards the West was of the essence.

More pressing was the domestic situation. The decline of the economy in the period 1965-70, its attendant social consequences, and the latent dissatisfaction and disillusionment with the regime of the Free Officers converged upon a new president, himself identified with the original 'makers of the revolution', in 1971. This required a dangerous purge of the Nasserite establishment, and was followed by an equally dangerous disengagement from the Soviet embrace, a violent shift to the Right of the Arab political spectrum in order to attract oil money, urgent measures being taken to meet the economic impasse and placate the social-political discontent which threatened to subvert domestic security. But perhaps the greatest realisation propelling Egypt under Sadat towards a peaceful settlement with Israel was that of the inconclusive nature of repeated war, even its futility, either for the restoration of the

Sinai to Egyptian sovereignty, or for the resolution of the wider Arab-Israel conflict. A population of over 40 million, half of them under twenty, and the problem of feeding them, apart from anything else, presented almost insurmountable problems. War, which in 1973 cost Egypt $10 million an hour, was an activity she could ill afford to indulge in every ten to fifteen years.

Elsewhere I have considered at length the reaction of the various strata and groups of Egyptian society to Sadat's peace initiative. I concluded that without the assent and desire for peace, or at least an end to war, of the vast majority of the Egyptian people, Sadat would not and could not have taken the step he took in 1977. More important was the assent of his major constituency, the armed forces. The argument that the mass of Egyptians believed or expected that peace with Israel would deliver them from their economic difficulties and other daily miseries has been overworked. It was war they no longer wanted, in the hope that the country's resources would somehow and, in time, be diverted to the satisfaction of their immediate economic and social needs. Whether or not this will be done, and how effectively, will depend on their own political leaders, and no-one else. But there was also a more subtle psychological undercurrent, a new attitude and perception, among Egyptians that had possessed them ever since the October War, and even before. This was the realisation that only as Egyptians would they be able to face their adversary and restore their sovereignty over Sinai. The tedium of wider adventures, leading the Arabs in a crusade of liberation, surfaced after the October War, when they once again recognised the importance and relevance of their pre-1952 national history. Galvanised with old-fashioned patriotism, they admitted Muhammad Ali the Great and his son Ibrahim Pasha, the founders of a virtually independent Egypt and the carvers of a sizeable empire in Arabia and the Levant in the nineteenth century, into their pantheon of national heroes.[2]

It was this psychological undercurrent which Sadat spotted, capitalised upon, and manipulated, in order to make the break, firstly, from the cycle of expensive and indeterminate wars, and secondly, from the seamless web of Arab politics. He reminded his people that they should be proud to be plain Egyptians again: pragmatic, secular, flexible survivors, and the masters of national longevity. On a more practical level, the senseless civil war in the Lebanon (1975-6), with its protracted chaos, the intransigence of the so-called 'rejectionist' and Arab front-line states, and the never-ending conflict between them, convinced Sadat and many Egyptians that his country's interest demanded an end to war and a peaceful accommodation with Israel. Looming large in his calculation was the belief — not wholly justified, of course, as subsequent events were to show — that the USA was the only power that could influence events in the direction of a settlement, because of its close relation with Israel.[3]

The dramatically abrupt inauguration of relations between Egypt and Israel was probably due to all the above reasons. But it was due also to the then unknown attitude of Israel to peace. A new conservative and rather extreme, militant Zionist coalition government, under Mr Begin, had come to power. Many of its members were known for their maximalist position regarding 'Eretz Israel'. Moreover, in view of continued hostility from, and rejection by, other Arab states, not to mention the PLO, few Israelis, especially among the military, were willing to give up the strategic advantage which Sinai offered them. Rather, they were prepared to sit out the interminable inter-Arab squabbles while they hoped to win by default.

Although Egypt was ready to reach a peaceful settlement with Israel, her geopolitical and strategic position in the region demanded that she seek the basis of a more comprehensive settlement of the Arab-Israel conflict beyond the outstanding territorial dispute with Israel. To this extent, Sadat and his successor have sought a settlement that would, firstly, end the state of war with Egypt; secondly, devise a scheme for real autonomy for Palestinian Arabs on the West Bank and Gaza; and thirdly, provide the basis for widening bilateral peace negotiations and agreements between Israel and other Arab states, e.g., Jordan, Syria and Lebanon.

The assumptions of the Egyptians were unfounded on two counts. First, they assumed other Arab states would be willing to negotiate directly — as they themselves did — with Israel, for a peace settlement, and that the PLO would fall into line too. Secondly, they assumed that even in the possible face of PLO and other Arab hostility and rejection, Israel would be willing to relinquish control over the West Bank and Gaza to the Palestinians living there, in return for peace. They have been proved wrong, so far, on both counts. The intransigence of other Arab states led by Iraq, Syria, Libya, Algeria and even so-called moderate ones like Saudi Arabia, turned immediately into hostility to Egypt, after the latter had signed the peace treaty with Israel in 1979. Jordan found itself in a difficult position, hemmed in between the PLO and neighbouring Arab states. Meanwhile the turmoil in Lebanon continued, with serious repercussions for the security situation on the Lebanon-Israel frontier. Israel, for her part, hardened her West Bank policy by pressing ahead with more settlements there, and a repressive administration over its Arab inhabitants. It is in this context that one can assess the differences which arose between Egypt and Israel in their negotiations for the implementation of the Camp David Accords and the peace treaty. In fact, these differences arose from each party's interpretation of the meaning of the Accords, and the provisions of the treaty for a comprehensive peace and Palestinian autonomy.

In view of the continued uncertainty regarding the attitude of neighbouring Arab states and the PLO's behaviour, Israel has been, since 1977, content with a piecemeal peace. Its treaty with Egypt in exchange for the Sinai and Sharm el-Sheikh eliminated from the conflict with the Arabs the major credible military adversary, and at the same time rendered impotent, even immobile, the anti-Israeli policy of the other Arab states. Moreover, the interposition of a multinational peacekeeping force between Egypt in the Sinai and Israel, secures the latter's southern and western flank, allowing it greater initiative and flexibility to deal with threats from the east or north, as it indeed has in Iraq over its nuclear project, and in Lebanon over the Palestinians.

To this extent then, the initial optimism of Egyptians regarding peace and normal relations with Israel has been eroded, partly by distrust and partly because it has been overtaken by events. Outside Egypt events have ranged from the ostracism of Egypt by other Arab states and the attempt by Iraq to replace her as the leader of the Arab world, to the already noted severe policy of the Begin government towards the West Bank, its support of the Islamic regime in Iran and its move to pacify by force the immediately surrounding Levant and Fertile Crescent areas, as a way of dealing with the PLO, culminating in the invasion of Lebanon by the Israel Defence Forces last June. At home there has been the mounting militancy of Islamic movements and groups which attacked senior government personnel, challenged the regime's legitimacy and the structures of the state, and precipitated the serious and bloody communal clashes of summer 1981, which culminated in the assassination of President Sadat that October.

Even though many of these developments may not have been directly related to the treaty between Egypt and Israel, they did encourage a variety of groups within Egypt to articulate their opposition to the further normalisation of relations between the two countries, and to call for an immediate return to a closer relation between Egypt and other Arab states. They naturally placed serious constraints on the country's political leadership and its policy makers, and these became even more effective in the face of the Israeli government's position over the outstanding issue of Palestinian autonomy on the West Bank, and, in terms of local, regional and international public opinion, its damaging invasion of Lebanon and siege of West Beirut. Needless to say, formal diplomatic relations have been maintained despite these difficulties, but a measure of the new constraints on further normalisation has been, for example, the unwillingness of the new President Mubarak to visit Israel. In the meantime, even relations between Egypt and the USA carried their own abrasive quality, partly because the USA after 1979 found itself the patron superpower of two erstwhile antagonists who, in a treaty relationship, still had outstanding differences, over which they tended to lobby the patron on arms supplies, financial assistance and negotiating positions regarding the West Bank. At the same time, they competed over the strategic control of the same core area in the Middle East.

The attitude of the intelligentsia in Egypt to the normalisation of relations with Israel became one of extreme caution and hesitation. The Leftists and Nasserites in particular have been vociferous against normalisation. They argue the need to rejoin the Arab family of nations on cultural, national and state interest grounds. In connection with the last, they point to Israel's aggressive policy in the Lebanon which threatens not only the Palestinians, but also the Arab states in the immediate vicinity. There are those among them, of course, whose opposition to the normalisation of relations with Israel is motivated by personal reasons, such as their professional and employment connections, or opportunities in the richer parts of the Arab world, as for example Saudi Arabia and the Gulf states, where the journalists and writers among them enjoy a wider audience, and all of them higher financial remuneration. Moreover they point to the very practical matter of Egyptian migrant labour for these oil-rich countries, about 1½ million people who, in turn, support some 3 million dependants in Egypt and remit over $2 billion annually. But there are those among them, including the Muslim militants, who genuinely believe, for economic, cultural and political reasons, that opening Egypt up to Israeli economic and cultural penetration − in their view synonymous with Western penetration − would be seriously detrimental to the country. A leading Egyptian political economist, for example, argued very cogently in this vein on the basis of an analysis of the Israeli economy since 1948, its present difficulties and its urgent need for new markets. Not only would further economic ties with Israel be disastrous for young Egyptian industries, but also detrimental to Egyptian national education and culture, reducing the relationship to one of a dominant (Israel) and dependent (Egyptian) economy of consumers.[4] He also emphasised the real danger of closer ties for relations between Egypt and the other Arab countries. 'Economic complementarity between Egypt and Israel will preclude a similar economic relationship with the Arab economies', he asserts.[5] As for the cultural danger, the writer avers:[6]

> The cultural opening of Egypt to Israel will, with the passage of time, create difficulties in the face of Arab cooperation. It will reduce the Arab orientation of education in Egypt, the neglect of the teaching of the Arabic language and Arab history, even the basic tenets of the faith under the general slogan of an opening to the civilized world and the requirements of the modern age. The example of a parallel older development in the Maghreb that was subjugated to economic and cultural integration with metropolitical France is not irrelevant, when one considers the difficulties facing the Maghreb's return to a similar integration with the rest of the Arab states.

One cannot ignore the constraints on the further normalisation of relations between Egypt and Israel created by the general trend of Islamic militancy — even of the plain reassertion of an Islamic ethos and morality — in the face of the alien onslaught accompanying the Open Door Economic Policy inaugurated by Sadat, and the difficulties experienced in negotiations with Israel over the more comprehensive aspects of the Camp David Accords and the peace treaty between them. Nor can many Egyptians square Israel's peaceful intentions, in fact, its desire for peace in the region, with recent events in Lebanon, and the Israeli government's proclaimed objective of never allowing an autonomous Palestinian Arab authority or entity on the West Bank and Gaza.

On the basis of Appendix III of the Egypt-Israel treaty, several bilateral agreements have been negotiated between the two countries covering different economic aspects of the relations between them, ranging from air transport and communications, to agriculture, trade and commerce, customs, tourism and agriculture. Memoranda concerning civil aviation, air traffic services, communications, broadcasting and tourism have been signed in the last two years. Joint committees on agriculture and trade were established and agreements about transportation and culture were negotiated covering a youth exchange programme, the establishment of an Israeli academic centre in Cairo, and the movement of people and goods across the frontier.

Figures for trade between the two countries are available only for Israeli exports to Egypt. For 1981, the figure was $16 million, and in the first eight months of 1982 $13½ million. These represent mainly agricultural and other consumer goods. There are no figures available for Egyptian exports to Israel. As for human traffic through the international border between the two countries, the figures are weighted heavily one way, from Israel to Egypt. Thus in 1980, 12,354 Israelis visited Egypt with a figure of only 2,121 Egyptians visiting Israel. In 1981, 26,486 Israelis, double the figure of the previous year, visited Egypt but only 2,623 Egyptians visited Israel.

One of the tangible benefits to Israel from the peace treaty with Egypt is the sale of oil from the Sinai fields to it. This came at a critical time, when Israeli oil supplies from Iran had stopped. Israel is also keen on obtaining possible supplies of natural gas from the fields now being explored and developed in the Delta. As for the hopes regarding other kinds of joint economic projects, such as desert reclamation and agricultural development, these remain only hopes. Even if they were to be seriously acted upon, they would come at a time when the Egyptian village itself as a productive agricultural unit, is being undermined by the untoward effects of massive internal migration to the towns, inflation, unemployment and rampant consumerism.

It would appear then, that the major movement of goods and people has been one-sided, suggesting a reluctance on the part of Egypt to reciprocate. Whatever the reasons for this imbalance, the fact remains that, so far, the process has been overwhelmingly one-sided. The alacrity and enthusiasm with which Israeli academics have responded to the establishment of an Israeli Academic Centre in Cairo, for instance, have found no parallel on the Egyptian side. On the contrary, as already noted, Egyptian academics are constantly warning against the adverse effects not only of closer economic ties with Israel, but also of cultural and educational ones. In this connection, there are those who point to the very ancient cultural-historical links between Egypt and the people of Israel — the Jews. What they have in mind is the Mosaic episode, and the influence of Pharaonic Egypt on Jewish religious development. On the other hand, there are others who emphasise the more recent, persistent and deeper link between Egypt and Arab Islam.

The fact remains that the movement of people and goods remains rather sluggish, a reflection of a resistance to a brisker economic and human exchange between the two countries on the part of the Egyptians. Delaying further normalisation of relations is, in the view of those Egyptians who are either opposed to, or unhappy with, the Begin government's policies, the only sanction available to Egypt for pressing Israel into more accommodating positions over the resolution of the wider, so-called comprehensive, aspects of the Middle East conflict. Egyptians, moreover, fear that Israeli intransigence over Palestinian autonomy and the current occupation of parts of Lebanon, will stiffen Syrian and other Arab rejection of a negotiated settlement. Some Egyptians are wary of this in so far as it may allow Syria and even Jordan a greater control over developments in the West Bank, via the PLO or the Palestinians in general. They are also concerned about the unproductive, senseless if you wish, refusal by them ever to accept, or even recognise, Israel's right to exist.

Nor should one underestimate or minimise the complications of the Arab-Islamic factor in Egypt. Coupled with the desperate economic situation in the country, the trial of Islamic militants by the state, as well as the trial by a revolutionary tribunal of the late President Sadat's brother, Ismat Sadat, for corruption; the dissatisfaction of army officers, arising directly from inflation and related economic difficulties; the ugly giganticism of urban centres as a result of massive migration from the rural areas, could all subvert domestic security and political stability. A condition could develop which is parallel, if not similar, to an earlier unhappy and politically pregnant period, from 1949 to 1952. The success of a radical restorative, conservative movement in a temporary and convenient alliance with a radical leftist opposition could conceivably have serious consequences for the country's relations with Israel. At the same time, this kind of militancy in Egypt is mutually reinforced by a parallel type of militancy in Israel, especially over the disposition of the West Bank; this seems to join secular power with spiritual injunction and religious expectation, for which the old Jewish traditional distinction between prophethood and kingship seems irrelevant.

For the moment, relations between Egypt and Israel remain formal and diplomatic, although the Egyptian ambassador has been indefinitely recalled from Tel-Aviv as a protest against Israel's action in the Lebanon, possibly so long as the crisis there continues. The process of normalising relations is otherwise slow, reluctant and deliberately cautious. Some would contend that the whole process is actually in abeyance. Many Egyptians oppose what they consider to be the Begin government's intention to de-Arabise the West Bank and annex it as part of Israel. Others among them fear that the more extreme members of the Begin government and extremist groups among the Israeli electorate also desire the annexation of south Lebanon up to the Litani River.

There is a further argument put forward by many Egyptian, as well as Arab, critics of Israel's actions. It suggests that with its invasion of Lebanon, Israel did not simply intend to disperse the PLO by crushing its military power and dismantling its military-political structure of a state within the Lebanese state, but also to humiliate and disgrace all other Arabs. Neither Egypt, now it has a treaty of peace with Israel, nor Saudi Arabia, Syria, Jordan or Iraq can do much about it. In short, it is argued, Israel intended to assert and parade its military strategic predominance over the region. But the argument also alludes to a more sinister Israeli political intention, namely, to obstruct, undermine and negate new trends in American policy which recognise a strictly American interest in responding to certain Arab perceptions emanating in particular from Saudi Arabia. Israel, according to this argument, wishes to forestall the beginnings of Arab moderation, away from the old maximalist position regarding the Palestine question, and towards a more practical, reasonable handling of it. This new Arab moderation was presumably seen as being heralded by the various recent Arab summit meetings, in the so-called Fahad Peace Plan, in the cautious — reluctant? — acceptance of the Reagan Peace Plan, and in Egypt's admonition of the Palestinians and other Arabs to settle for a negotiated peace over the West Bank on the basis of mutual recognition between them and Israel. The Israeli maximalists, including the Begin government, even Begin himself and his Defence Minister Sharon, this argument continues, are anxious to pre-empt the possibility of peace negotiations between other Arabs and Palestinians over the disposition of the West Bank, since they intend to annex it.

The same Egyptian and Arab critics also contend that American policy still favours Israel's obdurate position over both the West Bank and Lebanon. This policy together with the actions of Israel, threaten the very existence of the Arab regimes which, since 1973, have led the region in a pattern of inter-state politics marked by conservative state interest, and the avoidance, if not rejection, of radical Pan-Arabism with its subversive, disturbing tendencies. They could be challenged, perhaps successfully this time, by an explosion of a disbelieving and frustrated generation.

Arab and European critics of what in effect is a separate treaty between Egypt and Israel now argue that the only way forward in the settlement of the Arab-Israeli conflict is for Egypt to rejoin the Arab states and return to the Arab nation. With Egypt, Arab unity becomes a more credible prospect and therefore a factor of stability in the area. An 'Arab solution', they argue, will be more acceptable and durable than a strictly Egyptian one. One may label this as the 'Pan-Arab' approach to peace in the Middle East. Its advocates, however, are also those who lay claim to an 'international' approach, by demanding the involvement of the Soviet Union, as well as of the European (i.e. the EEC) states in the peacemaking process. This way, they feel, the USA will not monopolise either the evolution of relations between Egypt and Israel or the further process of peace. In other words, it should not be the sole peacemaking power in the area. To this extent, these critics also welcome such European initiatives as the Venice Declaration of 1980 which supports the participation of the PLO in further peace negotiations, and recognises the right of Palestinians to self-determination. But it also recognises, by implication, the role of Arab unity in such a process. The more recent Egyptian-French peace initiative of 1982 is just as attractive to some of these critics.

The difficulty with all these positions derives from several assumptions. Thus the process of Arab unity was arrested or obstructed long before the Venice Declaration and other similar initiatives. The Soviet Union as a credible peacemaker in the area is opposed by most of the Arab regimes themselves. An 'Arab solution', moreover, must be promoted in the concrete negotiating positions of actual state regimes, not by some abstract notion of Arab unity. As for the more recent French idea, promoted by President Mitterand, of mobilising Arab, Israeli and world public opinion for peace, it can make sense only if the assumption that all Arabs can and do accept Israel as an independent state in the Middle East is proved. Similarly, those who argue that if the USA cannot press Israel to make concessions on the West Bank, then Europe could, by imposing trade sanctions damaging to the Israeli economy. But they cannot guarantee that the Arabs will, under these conditions, be more amenable. On the contrary, some of them may well decide that the Europeans can, with such a policy of trade sanctions against Israel, harm and weaken their enemy, so they need make no concessions, not even one of recognition.

Leaving all these considerations aside for the moment, under what conditions should Egypt return to the Arab fold or the Arab nation? Egyptians themselves are interested in these conditions. Must they, for example, entail the abrogation of their treaty with Israel? This, for the moment, the Egyptians are not prepared to contemplate. Nor are they impressed by what Egypt, together with the Arabs, can accomplish, for they tried this for over thirty years, to Egypt's detriment. The return of Egypt to the Arab nation remains a slogan, since Egypt remains part of the Arab nation already, culturally, historically and even economically.

However one considers the matter, regional parameters influence relations between Egypt and Israel. More significant, though, is the impact of Israel's relations with the USA, especially today, over the Lebanon. Without exploring the intricacies of the American political system, it is clear that Israel's favoured position in the American Congress is countered by the executive branches of the government, which are more critical of its policies in Lebanon and the West Bank. Thus Egypt welcomed the Reagan Peace Plan; Israel rejected it. Egypt has called for the withdrawal of all occupying forces in Lebanon; Israel intends such withdrawal in the future on condition all Syrian and PLO forces are withdrawn too. Egypt insists on further progress in the negotiations over Palestinian autonomy on the West Bank; Israel links such movement to the resolution of the crisis in Lebanon. Egypt is pressing other Arabs, including the Palestinians, to proceed, without delay, to direct negotiations with Israel over Palestinian autonomy, based on mutual recognition; Israel precludes any development that might include the PLO, or aim at the establishment of an independent Palestinian state on the West Bank. In all of this, and especially over Lebanon, there lurks the danger of a serious confrontation between the American government and Israel, which could have repercussions for Egyptian-Israeli relations.

Yet the wariness or caution exhibited by Israel, regardless of government or regime, in readily accepting proferred formulae of negotiation with the PLO, or some combination of Arab states with the PLO, over the fate of the West Bank and Gaza is not without foundation. First, there is the reality of no appreciable movement on the part of the PLO to renounce its objective of displacing Israel in the land that was Palestine by force. Secondly, there is the continued rejection by the Arab states of Israel's right to exist as a sovereign state in peace and security. Arguments and convoluted interpretations of 'implicit or tacit recognition' do not seem, so far, to satisfy the Israelis. Thirdly, there is the real dilemma, the conundrum perhaps, over whether Egypt will soon re-engage in the Arab arena, and what this would mean for her relations with Israel. The latter therefore, for the moment, refuses any guarantees offered, say, by outside powers, not to mention the United Nations, preferring to rely for its security on its own military might. But this choice in turn makes its regional policy of pacification by force inevitable. No such policy can really be either popular or permanent, for it is unlikely that the neighbouring Arab states, despite what they think of the Palestinians, can easily completely abandon the Palestinian cause for an autonomous national home of sorts. Nor can Egypt, whatever its practical, formal relationship with Israel, be completely insulated from its fall-out effects.

Such a regional policy, moreover, prolongs the painful shock experienced by Arab and Western perceptions of the Jews and things Jewish over the last thirty years. For centuries, the stereotype Jew in their minds was of a wandering, stateless, meek member of a small exclusive community, wholly taken up with the preservation of his religious tradition, and occupied, as a matter of plain survival, in particular trades and professions. By sheer application and diligence, this Jew occasionally surfaced as a prize-winning scientist or as a prodigy in the performing arts, but he was always expected to be politically impotent, even when tolerated. Now the modern Jew, the Israeli, is not simply preserving a religious and cultural tradition but, as a citizen of an independent state, is using effective military force to ensure the acceptance of his statehood by others.

The more worrying aspect of this stalemate, if one can describe it as such, relates to more fundamental and long-term issues in, and perceptions of, the Egyptian-Israeli relationship. Are Egypt and Israel, the two most powerful military powers and the ones with the most skilled and competent human resources in the region, bound to be rivals in competition for the strategic control of the area? Will they also contest the control of regional politics in the core area of the Middle East? Can, in other words, the relationship between them ever be a complementary one? More specifically, can Egypt or Israel allow one another to dominate the Levant and/or the Fertile Crescent at the expense of the other? After all, they fought three wars over the strategic control of the Sinai, the Suez Canal and the Straits in the Red-Arabian seas. Even the dispute over a small patch of land on the border, known as Taba, which, since 1906, has been a recognised part of Egyptian territory, is ominous.

A further complication arises from America's strategic interest in the Middle East. The overriding consideration here is the perceived Soviet threat to the region. The loss of Iran has forced the USA back into the complexities of Arab politics. Similarly, the crisis in Iran and the Gulf has propelled America's European allies into the same cockpit. At the end of 1982, that is, the further evolution of the treaty relationship between Egypt and Israel is bedevilled by the intricacies and complexities of a series of regional conflicts, ranging from the Gulf to Lebanon, as well as by the rivalries of the superpowers. Yet the hard reality remains that whatever the complexities, and however wary or cautious relations between them today may be, Egypt and Israel are fated, for the foreseeable future, to be the first partners of peace on the rocky road to the resolution of the Arab-Israeli conflict. Egypt may require a generation of peace, or at least the absence of war, if it is to treat, let alone overcome, some of her economic and social ills. Israel may soon discover that it shares this need. In the meantime, each will try to check the other over the exclusive strategic control of the Fertile Crescent and the Levant.

Domestic politics are debatable, manipulable and, to a great extent, controllable. External or international politics are less so, for the vagaries of relations between states are unpredictable. In fact, they constitute a thicket, if not a jungle, through which the policy maker must hack his way, often having no idea what to expect. His objectives are often denied by the relentless force of events not easily controllable or beyond his control.[7] There is no reason why relations between Egypt and Israel since the 1979 Treaty should not be viewed with hope and optimism. Equally though, there is no reason why they should not be subject to the ambiguity and uncertainty that strongly characterise relations between states.

Notes

1. On Sadat's career and writings, see P.J. Vatikiotis, *Nasser and his Generation* (London and New York, 1978).
2. See 'Egypt' in *The Political Economy of the Middle East: 1973-8*, a Compendium of Papers submitted to the Joint Economic Committee of the Congress of the United States, 21 April 1980, (US Government Printing Office, Washington, DC, 1980), pp. 105-30. See also, 'Regional Politics' in G. Wise and C. Issawi (eds.), *Middle East Perspectives: the Next Twenty Years* (Princeton, NJ, 1981), pp. 35-54.
3. See Anwar Sadat, *In Search of Identity* (London, 1979).
4. Galal A. Amin, *Mihnat al-iqtisad wa al-thaqafa fi Misr* (Cairo, 1982).
5. Ibid., p. 80.
6. Ibid., p. 81.
7. Paraphrased from a paper, 'The Agony of Decision' by E.H. Buehrig.

12 THE NATIONAL QUESTION IN EGYPT

Ever since Lords Dufferin, Cromer, Milner and others questioned the existence of an Egyptian national community, Egyptians have been busy trying to prove the opposite. Some of them even refer to the early nineteenth-century chronicler, Abd al-Rahman al-Jabarti as having effectively reported on an Egyptian national community,[1] even though Egyptians opposed and rebelled against the French occupation in 1798, largely because it was the enemy of their religion, not strictly of their national community, but rather because it had trespassed on the land of their sovereign Sultan-Caliph and Commander of the Faithful, in Istanbul. Regarding the rallying of the Cairenes for the defence of the city against the French, Hussein Fawzi remarks that, in contrast with their long-suffering acquiescence in Mamluk and Ottoman oppression and tyranny, this was a foreign invasion

> by the army of a country that did not profess Islam . . . The mark of confusion and panic was the report that the rabble threatened to kill the Christians and Jews in the city . . . It was not a national move-ment in the modern sense of the term; it was an uprising (*hoga*) of the Muslim population of Cairo. The latter understood only one meaning to the French invasion: the return of the Crusades, since the French, as Christians, were raiding the lands of Islam.[2]

The overwhelming Islamic atmosphere is further evoked and emphasised by Fawzi. He remembers that when he was very young, in the early part of this century, when Egypt was still officially an Ottoman province, the imams (leaders of prayer) prayed for the Ottoman Sultan Muhammad Rashad, and physical training classes in elementary school were con-ducted in a language he did not understand; they told him it was Turkish. He also asserts that in reading about the various historical experiences of Egypt he has felt that behind all the successive conquests, cultures and civilizations, lay a strong national unity. Yet as a native of Cairo he confesses that of all the periods of Egyptian history, only the Mamluk one makes him feel that he is truly among his clan and fellow natives.

Source: This chapter is an adapted version of the Georges A. Kaller Annual Lec-ture delivered at Tel Aviv University in March 1983.

'The atmosphere of Cairo which overwhelmed me in my infancy and youth I felt when I was reading the history of the Mamluks.'[3] He goes on to characterise the history of Egypt under the Mamluks and Ottomans as follows:[4]

> The Egyptians were of learning, science, civilization, industry, agriculture and commerce. The foreigners were highway robbers. Egyptians concerned themselves with building and creating and innovating in art, industry, thought and science, and their conquerors were solely occupied with the collection of riches and pursuing what was beneficial to the rulers and princes. All rebellion was about power and influence and the acquisition of land.

Unlike other states in the Middle East, the Nile helped create a particular culture and civilization, even a particular political culture, one that is characterised by dense human habitation in very close proximity to the river, constituting a fairly homogenous nation, and promoting a powerful centralised state. If that is the case, then why should there be a national problem, or any difficulty with the construction of a national political community? It seems that a political formula for the organisation of the national community and a public order in Egypt has never quite been found or agreed upon. To this extent the matter remains unresolved.[5] Given the recrudescence today of religious militancy, with its corollary of sectarian-minority problems, some of these also militant, and Egypt's partial disengagement from the Arab-Islamic political arena as a result of its peace treaty with Israel, the question of where Egypt belongs culturally and politically (*intima' misr*) is once again being widely discussed. To this extent also the issue of Egypt's cultural and political identity has been revived.[6] Most important is the fact that Egyptians themselves have revived these issues. It is important at this stage and as a first step to the consideration of the problem of national community in Egypt to examine what some Egyptians themselves have been saying about this matter over the last thirty to forty years, before proceeding any further. This will allow an outline in part of the scope and seriousness of the problem.

In spite of Egypt's historical longevity and cultural-civilizational personality, a number of Egyptian writers have, in this century, laboured to deal with the problem of national community, or to use another term, not in the strict Aristotelian sense, the polity. Needless to say, the vagaries of a seven thousand year long history which has included conquests, foreign occupations and economic and natural disasters, suggest changes not only in the country's demographic composition, its relations with the outside world and its fortunes, but also in its language, religion, economic and social organisation and its political arrangements. The writers have felt the need to define Egyptian identity anew, to explore and establish its historical and cultural personality and, on the basis of these, to posit and describe the main features of Egyptian national community.

Leaving aside the massive seven-volume *Histoire de la Nation Egyptienne*, sponsored by King Fuad and edited by Gabriel Hanoteaux (1936-9), epochal events, to Egyptian eyes, have occurred in 1907, 1919, 1936, 1952, 1967 and 1973. Among Egyptians prompted to deal with the questions already cited, have been Ahmad Lutfi al-Sayid, Shafiq Ghorbal, Salama Musa, Taha Hussein, Hussein Fawzi, Subhi Wahida, Husein Mu'nis, Louis Awad, Mirrit Butrus Ghali, Gamal Hamdan and Tariq al-Bishri.[7] It is significant that this list includes both Muslims and Copts.

The questions that preoccupied the earliest of these writers were those of historical continuity and the definition of the cultural and national identity of the community. They felt these were essential to the revival of an Egyptian national consciousness that had atrophied, or been overwhelmed by, wider identities, such as those of Islam with its emphasis on religious belief, and on the Arab-Asiatic dimension of its political manifestation, or the eroding effect of a massive, separate European presence in the country for a century. Thus as early as 1913 Ahmad Lutfi al-Sayid made a statement which seemed to resolve the problem of identity and national community in Egypt for ever. He said:[8]

> We Egyptians love our country and do not accept to be part of any country other than Egypt [alluding incidentally to the Islamic Community, *umma*, and the Arab nation, *al-watan al-'arabi*] whatever our origins may be, Hijazi, Berber, Circassian, Syrian, or European.

This is the only clear statement of its kind, that is, of a strictly secular, territorial national identity, by an Arabic-speaking Muslim, and Lutfi was no non-believer. But his vision was not to be, because, in addition to the impact of radical youth and religious movements in the 1930s and 1940s, such as Young Egypt and the Muslim Brethren after 1952, lent an especially 'state output' cast to the designation, though not necessarily determination, of identity, national community and polity, overwhelming all else.

Some writers, such as Taha Hussein, Husein Mu'nis and Mirrit Butrus

Ghali argued for the special position of Egypt, with its multi-dimensional historical, civilizational and cultural personality, as regards its role in the Mediterranean, Asia and Africa. That is, unlike her Asiatic co-religionists and long-time political masters, Egypt had been part of a wider evolving culture that began in the eastern Mediterranean and moved to Europe. They pleaded that to break with one of these dimensions, as happened from the fourteenth to the nineteenth centuries, is to deny the country's history, its strategic and cultural role and development, to isolate Egypt and thus relegate it to infirmity. In fact, they openly deplored Egypt's isolation as a result of the Arab-Islamic connection and its impact on the country's cosmopolitanism.

Between, say, 1907 and 1939, Egyptian writers on these matters were clearly influenced by the British occupation, and attracted to European ideas and institutions for the secular organisation of society and government, that is, for a public order. They desired, too, to link their country once again to modern civilization. To this extent, the establishment and definition of an Egyptian cultural personality and a secular concept of national identity were an essential pre-condition for developing and legitimating a secular political community. It was, if you wish, a way, perhaps the only one, of escaping the disabilities of an ideologically, that is, religiously, defined nation. More significantly, their concerns with these matters followed and did not precede the evolution of the modern state structure created by the powerful traditional despot, Muhammad Ali. They were themselves the products of this state machine, but their forefathers had practically no say in how they were governed, for what purposes or to what ends. The gradual emergence, however, from Ottoman, Turkish or Asiatic-Islamic personal and despotic rule, and the likelihood of independence, prompted writers to reconsider questions of national identity and political community. In fact, even the attainment of a fettered independence, in 1922 and 1936, influenced the emphasis placed by some of these writers on the essential preconditions of an Egyptian national community. Hafez 'Afifi,[9] Mirrit Butrus Ghali and subsequently Subhi Wahida were all less concerned with cultural-historical considerations than they were with the economic and social conditions for the creation of a strong and cohesive secular national community. They well understood that modernity, in the sense of Westernisation, is based on a sound bourgeois industrial economy and society; that the production and distribution of wealth are important factors in shaping social conditions; and that the rejection of the link between economic activity and the destiny of the state remained a strange illusion.

Underlying the work of all these writers, however, was the awareness of a contradiction between national identity and political community, based on the predominant faith of their country's population, Islam, on the one hand, and on a longer historical tradition antedating it on the other. It was based as well on experimentation and toleration enshrined in man-made secular laws and institutions. This set the tone of all later debate on the national community issue.

It is important therefore to explore the progress of this debate, and to discover why it has been one peculiar to Egypt, almost to the exclusion of other Arab countries, with the exception, briefly, of Algeria. It is necessary to explore its strengths and weaknesses, and its implications. This will be done here by a consideration of the issues as these have been dealt with by three fairly important Egyptian writers whose works have appeared in the last thirty years. The publication of these attracted wide attention in Egypt and elsewhere.

I believe that the strongest case for national unity and an Egyptian identity to date has been made by the geographer Gamal Hamdan in his massive two-volume work, *Shakhsiyyat Misr: dirasa fi 'abqariyyat al-makan* (*The Personality of Egypt: a study in the genius of place*, Cairo, 1980-1). The most convincing case for the economic and social foundations of a purely secular Egyptian national community was made by the economist, the late Subhi Wahida, in his *Fi usul al-mas'ala al-misriyya* (*The Origins or Sources of the Egyptian Question*, first published in 1950, new edition 1977). It caused enough of a stir to attract as its most prominent reviewer in the *Ahram* no less a political figure than Ismail Sidqi Pasha. The most controversial case for a mixed secular-religious Egyptian national political community to date has been made by the historian Tariq al-Bishri in his *Al-muslimun wa'l-aqbat fi itar al-jama'a al-wataniyya* (*Muslims and Copts in the Framework of the National Community*, published in Cairo in 1980 and Beirut in 1982). It incorporates earlier shorter essays and articles on the subject which the author had published in the 1970s.

Hamdan asserts the geographical uniqueness of Egypt in so far as no other country is so much the creation of a single geographical condition as Egypt. 'The Nile', he writes,[10] 'regulates the forms of

all habitation, the distribution of life around it, and controls its location . . . Everything that is far from the river is reduced in value.

Egypt, that is, is Nilocentric; all her power and life are crowded and densely centred on one defined lifeline, the Nile.[11] Some change in the

pattern of habitation and movement did occur as a result of the introduction of perennial irrigation in the nineteenth century, but not very
much. Moreover, as an island in a desert, proximity of life to the river is
even more important. Herodotus, for Hamdan, was correct in his aphor-
ism that Egypt is the gift of the Nile, but only in natural terms, the Nile
being the raw material and environment for life. Civilizationally though,
Egypt is the gift of the Egyptian, the craftsman and worker, the *homo
faber* Husein Fawzi described so sensitively in his *Sindbad Masri*. There
is also the ideological component – Pharaonic paganism, Christian and
Muslim monotheism – that permitted innovation and cultural change.

Control of the Nile dictated the structure of Egypt's agricultural society and state because Nilotic Egypt is simply the totality of the river's
hydrological basin.[12] It permitted an artificial environment created by
man, namely, intensive agriculture and a dense population. The harmony
between river and man also implies propinquity between them, because
the river provides everything – water, habitation, fertility. Since time
immemorial, therefore, Egyptians have been one people; in fact, they
comprised the oldest nation and the first state in geographical terms,
because of the crystallisation and unity of the physical and functional
environment, and the complementarity between man and nature, land
and people. As a nation or even a nation-state, Hamdan asserts, Egypt
was never a 'geographical expression', but always a political one. Despite
the separation between Lower and Upper Egypt, after the unification
of the two regions by Menes in 3200 BC the country was never again
split up, whether as a result of internal conflict or foreign occupation.

It was, of course, this imposing, massive unity dictated by geography,
this natural concentration, which decreed, in part, the centralisation and
monopolisation of political power in its tyrannical form, buttressed by
an elaborate bureaucratic structure. It has been nurtured ever since by
Pharaonic, Arab-Islamic, Asiatic, European and native rule. 'Tyranny',
writes Hamdan,[13]

is alas a fact in Egyptian history, from its beginning to this day however forms and appearances may have changed or been modernized.
Dictatorship is the black spot in the personality of Egypt without
exception . . . until today, not only on the social (i.e., public political) but also on the personal level . . . Everything may have changed
except absolute rule and political pharaonism . . . even if what we
have today is 'democtatorship'.

Natural and political unity are closely linked. If Nilotic Egypt begins at Aswan or Shallal and ends in the Mediterranean, so does political Egypt, whose frontiers have been the same for millennia. The common recognition since the dawn of history of the threat from the desert, with its marauding herders and nomadic tribes, strengthened the social cohesion and national unity created by the river which has served as a geographic womb for the Egyptians. Moreover, the country's irrigation-based agricultural economy imposed a functional unity which in itself was a political factor, since there can be no planning for the use of water that is local or partial. 'Egypt', Hamdan asserts, 'is one hydrological unit essential to the maintenance of her ecological balance.'[14] Irrigated Egypt equally imposes close co-operation between its inhabitants, and makes compromise rather than conflict the main feature of such coexistence. This demanding natural, functional unity and the near-perfect response between man and nature enabled the germ of political unity to be early implanted. It is also manifested in the valley by the inhabited area along its banks and the Delta, comprising barely 4 per cent of the total area of the country. As such, Egypt has always been the cradle of a single big state, unlike classical Greece, Indonesia or the Philippines, with their archipelagoes giving rise to several separate statelets. Unity has been its supreme characteristic, and fragmentation or division a near-impossibility. 'As a civilization', Hamdan asserts,[15]

> Egypt is the offspring of the happy marriage between the father of rivers and the mother of the world, or of the marriage between the Nile and the Mediterranean, or of the place with the location.

One cannot find much to disagree with so far in Hamdan's geographical thesis. It is when, in his enthusiasm, he proceeds to put forward the case for Egypt as the first nation-state[16] in the sense of modern nationalism (*qawmiyya*), and to infer from the close link between natural, national and political unity the existence of a national political community, that problems arise. True, Egypt has had from the earliest times a central government whose subjects occupied a large undivided region along the river. Even when separation between Upper and Lower Egypt occurred they were still conscious of belonging to a larger unity. It is also true that Egyptians are aware that their personal security is linked to the security of the country, and that the almost total harmony and uniformity of language, religion, customs and traditions goes far back into history. All Egyptians, without exception, are exposed to the river banks, or are close to the Nile, within easy reach of central government.

One can also accept the proposition that the state of Egypt, encompassing or controlling the same territory, has never disappeared, at least since 3200 BC. (Sinai, of course, did briefly from 1967 to 1982.) The state, that is, governs the old nation formed by geography and history. Egypt may also be the classic example of a state deriving from a natural-national-political unity. But does this render it automatically a *political* nation, or a *nation state* by nature? Hamdan thinks it does, because despite conquests, the political nation (*al-watan al-siyasi*) remained fixed within the same boundaries. To this extent Egypt has a geo-political personality; it is a natural political territory. Such unsuccessful separatist uprisings as that of the Arabs in the Sa'id under Sheikh Humam in the eighteenth century are attributable to the tribal notion of the state as a separate, non-territorial entity. But one cannot have two states in Egypt, because unity is the rule, division or fragmentation the exception, since any division would lead to conflict over water. Egypt, in its old and present size, that is, is a permanent state. Or, as Husein Mu'nis vividly described this relentless characteristic of unity: 'Egypt is exempted from separatist, anti-central government rebellions.'[17]

What is interesting about Hamdan is that the logical conclusion of his geographical argument suggests the nature of the polity; not so much whether there is national/political unity, but what kind of political community this might be. Egypt's Nilotic social ecology is straightforward: a flood environment depending on irrigation (*al-rayy al-sina'i*) affects social life in so far as it requires great collaborative human effort which, in turn, calls for not only the control of the river and the organisation of its irrigation functions, but also the control and organisation of people, without which irrigation would become a bloody affair. The Egyptian must exchange his political and individual freedom for life which comes from higher authority that allocates and distributes water. Both nature and ruler are masters. Authority is the middleman between man and nature, and the guardian over relations between them. Government, in these conditions, is not an institution that approximates or conforms to the ideological and value preferences of man as articulated in mature political thought, but a structure, an apparatus, a machine necessary to maintain this delicate ecological, social and political balance. To this extent, Egypt is a model hydrological society, resulting from the interaction and co-operation of river, cultivator and governor.[18]

The kind of 'social contract' in the Egyptian polity that can be inferred from Hamdan's thesis and argument hardly goes beyond the formula, 'Give me your freedom and collective human effort and I will give you life from water.' Society in these circumstances has had to be massive, co-operative and gregarious, whereas government by necessity has had to be highly centralised, distant, powerful and autocratic. The river imposes collective social work and discourages aggressive individualism to the point of conscripted labour (*corvée*). Egypt becomes a huge administrative farm. The price of national unity, as defined by Hamdan, has been individual and political freedom. The very structure of the state, with its bureaucracy, theocracy and military caste (or today, the army, bureaucracy and the Azhar) presiding over this long strip full of teeming, toiling humanity, prevented, for a long time, any elaborate class divisions in Egypt except an elementary one, that of rulers and ruled. Dense nuclear habitation within the limited confines of a closed valley crushed individuality and the Egyptian became a receptacle for the acceptance or emulation of any innovation decreed by ruler or state. He was basically a *koinonikon on* (a social being) and not a *politikon zoon* (political animal). Islam did not make a fundamental difference to this social-political profile with its aristocracy of soldiers, bureaucracy of officials and theocracy of religious teachers and interpreters of the sacred law.

It is clear that Hamdan's thesis and his postulates are very much based on the geopolitical profile of a densely populated agrarian society. They beg the question of radical economic and social change. How many of them would remain valid if and when Egypt were to be transformed into a mainly urban industrial society? This may be an unfair question since Hamdan is mainly interested in establishing Egypt's national and political unity on geographical-historical grounds, in illustrating her important strategic position in the Arab world, and in how she is to be defended. He is not, however, particularly concerned with the problems of a national political community, or how it accommodates its members, constitutionally, legally or otherwise under the complex conditions and requirements of modernity. Regarding the Coptic community for instance, he refers to its permanence, without its massive recent extensions outside Egypt,[19] calling it the largest 'Christian island' in any Arab country. Since the racial formation of Egypt preceded its religious formation, Hamdan argues, all are Egyptians before being Christian or Muslim, especially when one notes the similarity of their social conditions and patterns of habitation. Despite sporadic, infrequent persecutions of this minority in the Middle Ages and the modern period, the strength of national unity, according to Hamdan, has held. Yet the problem of the Copts remains an unresolved one in terms of a modern national or political community. Zahir Riad, in a work entitled *Christians and Egyptian Nationalism*, argued that the only evidence of Egyptian nationality are those Copts who supported Ali Bey el Kebir (1763-1833), Muhammad Ali the Great (1805-49) and the Wafd.[20] Recently, in 1977 and 1980 respectively, Gamal Badawi and Milad Hanna set out and provided a gloss on those events which have exacerbated the communal problem in Egypt since the late 1940s, and particularly during the 1970s.[21] Both books, deliberately or inadvertently, highlight the radicalisation of the new Coptic communal organisations, as well as the growing polarisation between them and the more militant Islamic groups in the country.[22]

Hamdan's massive, rather repetitive work (two volumes, totalling 2,000 pages) on the physical, social and political personality of Egypt as this can be constructed from geography of the place and the geopolitics of the country's position, suggests that, until the nineteenth century, when there was a massive encroachment of modern European culture and technology alongside the local experience of a modernising despot, the question of national community presented no serious difficulties. Before and after Islam, the regulator of life in the Nile Valley, whether Pharaoh, Arab Muslim governor, Turkish satrap, slave warrior, Mamluk dynast or Ottoman governor, presided over a political system in which power or rule was personal and autocratic. The masses of Egyptians were not involved either in its choice or conduct, while their social order was regulated by the religious law, its teachers and interpreters. They belonged to the wider ideological community, or nation, of Islam. They served the ruler as producers of wealth, and the ruler defended their territory and the wider nation of Islam against its enemies.

Hamdan's proposition that despite Islamisation and Arabisation, Egyptians, because of their location and history, did not wholly lose their Egyptian identity as inhabitants of the Nile Valley, is valid. What did occur, of course, is that they were subsumed into a more Asiatic, loco Mediterranean land oriented *imporium* and thus isolated from the mainstream of modern, or European, cultural evolution. Their country became, in fact, especially between the twelfth and fifteenth centuries, the fulcrum of political/military gravity in Islam's contest with Christian Europe, as well as the cultural-intellectual citadel of the Community of the Faithful — the *umma*. It fought the battles of Islam against the Crusades as well as against the hostile invasions of the Mongol and Turk hordes from the steppes of Central Asia. It was the main maritime and naval base of Islam, and the strategic crossroads of its trade and commerce. The European explosion overseas via the oceans, and the Ottoman Turkish conquest, simply pushed Egypt back into desolate isolation. She was only to be yanked back into the mainstream of world history three hundred years later.

Subhi Wahida makes much of the separation of Egypt from the Mediterranean after the Arab Islamic conquest, and even more of the Turkish-Mongol incursion. The warring princes among the latter and their devastation was a factor in the decline of commercial life in Egypt and the total separation between state and society. The Arabisation of the country, into a social order based on religious faith and law, and with rule in the hands of others, without native involvement, inevitably weakened the Egyptian's consciousness of a separate national identity. Long Turkish-Mamluk rule also changed the country and its society materially and morally: it undermined its national unity and eroded its national consciousness. For seven centuries (from the ninth to the fifteenth), a new military state rose in Egypt, with war as its main occupation. Only those who bore arms had a place in the political order of things. The separation between what Maqrizi called *hukm shar'* (rule of the revealed religious law) and *hukm siyasa* (rule of politics or the state) was complete.[23] Any native élite that may have existed was displaced by soldiers, and government was the exclusive concern of rulers. 'We hardly find', Wahida writes[24]

> any trace or influence of civilian Egyptian elements in the public life of the country from the end of the Burji Mamluks, nor on the surface of society till the coming of the French except Mamluk beys, Ottoman state officials, Azhar sheikhs and a small group of merchants.

But the religious teachers were not interested in a national role, and the merchants were cosmopolitan in outlook, collaborating with the rulers. The Moallem Yaqub, Elfi Bey and even Ali Bey el-Kebir attempts at autonomy did not contain a modern conception of national independence. Nevertheless, Wahida observes,[25]

> Egypt was never divided into statelets or principalities, not even into independent municipalities with a civil urban society in them distinct from rural society that could serve as alternative *loci* of power. Authority never slipped from the capital into the hands of any corporate entity . . .

And since nationalism is very much a bourgeois concept and a national political community very much its product, Wahida is arguing, contrary to Hamdan, that one cannot approach or view Egyptian history from the Pharaohs to the nineteenth century on the basis of nationalism (*qawmiyya*). There were, to be sure, national, that is, peculiarly Egyptian, conditions. But the nation, *al-watan*, at least from the mid-seventh to the nineteenth century, was based on the ideological, non-territorial unity, or commonality, of religious belief. That is why, during this period, in identifying their *watan*, or nationhood and nationality, Egyptians reverted to being Cairenes, Manfalutis, Assiutis, Sohagis or what have you, just as Syrians became Damascenes and Halabis.

Wahida believes the weakness of the national community is due to the lack of national consensus and social cohesion. 'We saw', he writes,[26]

> how the weakness of our resistance in the political arena and the paucity of our economic productivity and intellectual output before anything else are due to the fact that our resistance and economic activity did not emanate or derive from a healthy, prosperous social life that unites all classes of society in a common endeavour.

In considering the effects of the experience between the fifteenth and nineteenth century, Wahida underlines, among other factors such as economic decline and weakness, limited economic activity, decline of social life and stagnation in Azharite thought as being of importance. By the twentieth century, the Egyptian, he asserts, was trying to accommodate himself to a new life of modernity without, however, the advantage or benefit of a relevant tradition and other proper economic and social requisites. He was buffetted between the spectre of the weighty past and the tribulations of the present, without really wishing to examine his special conditions with any objectivity.[27] Yet the fundamental problem, Wahida concludes, has been the nature of rule[28]

> promoting the mentality of dependence and the precedence of the afterlife over this life; the expectation of miracles . . . followed by the religious designation of society as part of the great *umma*. Therefore the fault in the past and since is without doubt that of those who govern.

The question, what kind of national or political community, therefore, simply did not arise under Islamic rule, in whatever form. The writers agree that it only became an issue with the acquisition of a modern state and the emergence of a national élite, a native official class, educated professionals, wealthy landowners and later entrepreneurs, all of whom aspired to become the ruling class that would replace an alien dynasty and a European occupying power.

Nor did the question arise so long as a modernising autocrat like

Muhammad Ali the Great monopolised power, economic activity and all other aspects of public endeavour. It was only when the new élite had acquired wealth and status that they were able to challenge the autocrat's authority and seek both to curb and share in his power. Their aspiration to power converged with the coalescence of common interests. But until the Second World War at least, foreigners virtually controlled their economy. It was difficult to achieve a minimum of consensus and social cohesion in a national or political community beyond the goal of political independence. This was the main task of the Wafd, and the significance of its role in between 1919 and 1923. It was equally difficult to shift from an agricultural economy to profitable economic pursuits in industry and commerce.

For a variety of reasons already alluded to, the new national élite in this century pursued its political objectives on the bandwagon of a modern territorial nationalism, and from the premises of a secular polity. This was inevitable, since they were themselves products of the close link between the construction of a modern state and the beginnings of a national Egyptian community. Although, like Hamdan, Bishri ventures a general formulation of the origins and basis of the Egyptian national political community by saying,[29]

. . . Islam from one side and the Christianity of the Copts from the other, together with the civilizational-cultural interaction of Muslims and Copts in Egypt . . . generated the historical, intellectual, social and psychological climate for the crystallization of the national idea of the Egyptian political community,

he is more interested in the historical evolution of this political community, not as an abstract idea but as a dynamic living organism. And this evolution can only be traced through a study of the efforts to develop constitutional and parliamentary government, with its institutions ranging from the crown, political parties, legislative, judicial and administrative structures to religious institutions, populist, religio-political and other radical movements. Yet in the first instance it was not in political parties or movements, but in the institutions of the state, such as the army and the administration, that 'Egyptianity' (*al-misriyya*) and modernity grew − a contrast with Hamdan's view to say the least. An Egyptian state structure and organisation therefore preceded a consciousness of Egyptianity. It was Muhammad Ali the Great who created the modern state in Egypt as its foremost national institution, and on its shoulders the Egyptian national community grew. To this extent,

Muhammad Ali is the founder of the modern Egyptian national political community. He revived Egyptian society, but as a means to a personal empire. No wonder then that Bishri bluntly states in the first chapter of his book, 'In the beginning was the state.'[30] Even though the Muhammad Ali experiment produced great material advance and an elaborate state structure, it was not accompanied by any political thought regarding the nature of the national political community. Egyptianisation, that is, preceded nationalist thought, since the latter was still part of the traditional perception of a religious community. The Copts, for example, were out of it at first. The transformation and expansion of governmental functions; the advance of secular legislation uniformly applicable to the whole national community at the expense of the *sharia* (the religious law); the establishment of national courts with Copts in their hierarchy; the abolition of the *jizya* (the poll or head-tax on non-Muslims), allowing Christians to be conscripted into the army; the legislative assemblies with Coptic members; state schools educating the children of both religious communities; and the nationalist stand of the Coptic Church against foreign, especially Protestant, missionaries were all, according to Bishri, indications of a coalescing secular national community.

The Egyptianisation of the state apparatus leading to the new slogan, 'Egypt for the Egyptians' during the Orabi revolt and after, followed by the 1881 constitution and the 1913 Legislative Society, culminated in the 1919 affair, when Egyptianity, or Egyptian national identity, became the symbol of the community. Tahtawi's work, in the meantime, had highlighted the widespread perception of the national community in religious terms and the contradiction between it and a secular one.[31] Although Islam tolerated other religions, the problem remained one of how to translate this into a secular political formula.

This century began rather inauspiciously as far as a harmonious national community goes. The intensity of sectarian conflict in its first decade was partly the reflection of the growing struggle between a rising new secular national élite and a more popular traditional one that favoured the *umma*, or Islamic political community. The contest was further complicated by British control of the country and its protection of a diverse collection of resident foreign minorities. Bishri, for example, believes that British policy deliberately promoted sectarian division in an effort to fragment the national community, and in order to justify the British presence in the country.[32] Although both Coptic and Muslim Congresses in 1911 rejected the principle of confessional representation in representative councils, Law 29 of 1913, setting up the Legislative Society (*al-jam'iyya al-tashri'iyya*) introduced it.

It is idle to deny the Wafd's leadership in its determination, during the period from 1919 to 1923, to create a secular national community. This was the essence of the Egyptianity of that particular national independence movement: *al-din lillah wa 'l-watan liljami'* (religion belongs to God and the nation to all); *al-wataniyya dinuna* (nationalism is our religion). The Wafd was organised on the basis of the principle of nationality and citizenship (*muwatana*) alone, irrespective of religious belief. The fierce debates in the 1922-3 Constitutional Commission led finally to the rejection of special proportional representation for minorities in parliament. However, some damage was done to the development of a secular national political community by the formal recognition in the 1923 constitution of Islam as the official religion of the state. Similarly, the Royal Succession Law enshrined the rule that the head of state must be Muslim.

The monarch, for his own political purposes, together with a variety of Islamic groups and the whole panoply of the Azhar, representing the official religious establishment, undermined this potential secular evolution for the next two decades at least. So did his caliphal ambitions, that would have strengthened further his autocracy. Equally, the new administrative structure, despite its secular constitutional-legislative basis, afforded politicians a vast discriminatory patronage. Both state secular and religious education became areas of control to be contested by secularists and religious traditionalists. Bishri is right in arguing that the lingering duality and coexistence of traditional and modern secular institutions of state, such as education and the judiciary, undermined the formation of a more effective secular polity.

The convergence of aggressive foreign missionary activity with the appearance of radical religio-political movements and organisations such as the Society of Muslim Brothers and the Young Men's Muslim Association (YMMA), as well as radical youth, anti-foreign, pro-Egyptianisation groups in the 1930s, overwhelmed the promoters of a secular national community; so much so that they were themselves forced to retreat to the more native idiom, largely that of the Islamic Community, for political survival. Thus the preaching about the economic and social foundations of a secular polity by Mirrit Butros Ghali, Subhi Wahida and Hafez Afifi, or even Muhammad Alluba (Pasha), with its Arab nationalist overtones were no more than voices in the desert.[33] The effect on Egyptian identity which the purveyors of the wider Islamic ideological nation had was confusing and disorienting, to say the least. They presented secular modernity, which they equated with Europeanisation, as a deadly threat to Islam. Soon they espoused the Palestine Question as a cause for all Muslims in Egypt. The impact of these forces and trends on a barely nascent secular national élite and governing class was devastating. 'Me too' for them meant not only political, but in certain cases also physical, survival.

Religion was now being put forward as the basis of two things: the political community, and Egypt's regional leadership. Regarding the first, Islam was not viewed as presenting any problems for minorities. Yet it was not so much secularism that was under attack as the Wafd as a political party, for it had briefly achieved a consensus on a secular national identity and political community at the expense of its rivals. By 1945, the lines of battle had been sharply drawn between it as the representative of a secular national community, and the Muslim Brethren as that of a religious political community. The Palace, smaller parties and a diverse constellation of populist, radical groups contributed to the contest. The battle was fought not so much over domestic issues as over external matters, especially the role of Egypt in the wider movement of Arab nationalism, and the more specific issue of Palestine. Yet the rivalry for the allegiance of the Egyptian public was fierce, and the experiment of a secular national community, based on consensus, was, as a result, shortlived. The Wafd finally succumbed.[34]

The military regime which came to power in 1952 ended the debate over the nature of the national community by suppressing both secularists and Islamic nationalists. Instead, it decreed a new identity, the Arab one, and enshrined it in the 1956 constitution. It had no need to take any practical steps towards greater national unity since it reverted to traditional despotism. When in the late 1970s it became necessary to curtail the activities of the remnants of liberal and leftist elements, Islam was used by the ruler as the instrument for that purpose, and this inevitably revived and emboldened religious militants. Unfortunately, it also rekindled the sectarian or minority issue, since the Copts became terrified and, for nearly a decade (1972-81), sectarian conflict erupted periodically and violently on the surface.[35]

The new wave of religio-political militancy is not the only, or most important, factor in the confusion over the problem of a national community, or the right kind of polity. Practical constitutional, legislative and judicial arrangements for the firm establishment of a legal-political formula for citizenship, one that accommodates non-Muslims, are involved. Despite the abolition of religious courts for both Muslims and Christians nearly thirty years ago, problems remain. Thus the very principle that only a Muslim can rule, or hold power, over the community, or the concessions made to the *sharia* as the basis of legislation are in themselves serious limiting factors. As Gamal Badawi, borrowing from Yusuf al-Qardawi, put it, 'the first principle in the treatment of *dhimmis* (non-Muslims) is that they have rights like those of the Muslims, except in certain well-defined exceptional cases . . .'[36]

Bishri does a masterful job of presenting the evolution of the perception of the national political community in the context of the juxtaposition between a wider religious ideological and secular national trend. He surveys in great detail the political forces with an interest in sectarian division, such as autocratic rule, an earlier imperialism, and the various populist radical religious movements. Unlike others, however, he yields to what he describes as historical necessity when considering the new religio-political trend as being genuinely popular, not artificial, as it was under the Palace in the 1920s and 1930s. It is, he pleads, wrong to combat it, because after all, it is opposed to a much greater threat, that of intellectual and cultural penetration from the West. Nor should it be linked, according to him, with conservative economic interests, since it purports a popular, distributive social and economic programme.[37] Above all, he insists, it is part of the historical-intellectual formation of the Egyptian people. 'It is not Islamic thought that causes stagnation but domestic and external conditions,' and Bishri is not for replacing it with derivative or imported thought (*al-fikr al-wafid*). Yet these statements remain assertions, influenced as Bishri is by the massive outpouring of Islamic writing and extensive proliferation of religious groups over the last decade in Egypt and throughout the Middle East. His recent emotional attack on American-funded joint research projects in Egypt suggests that he is keen to defend the irreconcilable cultural (and political?) hostility between a basically Muslim Egypt and the non-Muslim world.[38]

In effect, then, two political groups, representing diametrically opposed conceptions of the national community have existed and exist today alongside one another in Egypt. One emphasises the secular constitutional, legal and administrative arrangements for the social, economic and political dimensions of the polity; its intellectual orientation is largely imported. The other superimposes a traditionally inherited ideological view on these matters. Both these groups must wrestle with the problem of citizenship (*muwatana*). Who of those living in Egypt have the rights and duties of citizenship? Do they constitute one national political community? The proponents of the religious political community insist on the application of the *sharia*, thus begging the question of the rights and duties of non-Muslims in this Islamic polity. Can there be equality before the constitution and the law between Muslim and non-Muslim citizens? The Islamic protagonists assert there can, in everything except the forbidding of a ruling role to non-Muslims and, after all, why should they be rulers when they are a minority?[39] Moreover, for many of them, Egyptian national identity cannot be separated from Islam. Others argue that through *ijtihad*, an accommodation between the religious and secular national law of the land will be found, especially if one makes a clear distinction between *fiqh* (jurisprudence) and *sharia*, or between Islam as *din wa dawla* (religion and state) on the one hand, and religious government as such, on the other. In other words, they are not demanding Islamic government, but a government the legal, moral, historical and cultural basis of which is Islam.[40]

It is in this respect that Bishri's optimism regarding an accommodation between an Islamic political community and a secular legal state is controversial and interesting. Since the secularist intellectual trend of the last century produced a dreadful dichotomy and impasse, and since the *sharia* is an element of unity for the majority of Muslims, especially Arabs and Egyptians, it is preferable as the basis and principle for the organisation of the national political community to an alien, borrowed one. Since the Coptic church as a Christian church has no juridical code for the regulation of human affairs, then a judicious and broadly interpreted use of the *sharia*, alongside secular legislation deriving from tradition and the actual conditions of society, would lead to the Egyptianisation of *fiqh*, and therefore be acceptable.[41] It can also be used against the alien intellectual and cultural onslaught.

Bishri, however, is honest enough to admit the obvious: applying the *sharia* to non-Muslims would be problematic. The ways and means of constructing such a state, system of government and national community may be found, but the difficulty would be in making them effectively workable, with all the attendant problems of implementation, practice, patterns of behaviour and attitudes.

All these writers correctly assert that, compared with other Arab and Islamic countries, conflict between the Muslim majority and the Christian minority in the national community has been rare, infrequent and minor. They further assert that the Copts are an integral part of the historically very old Egyptian nation as this is defined by Hamdan, Wahida, Mirrit Butros Ghali and others. Such assertion, however, must be qualified by the references made already to both Coptic and Muslim writers regarding the political and other grievances and anxieties of the Christian minority, as well as the uneasy relationship between the two communities.

What is clear is that despite the relentless secularisation of the state administration, of education and the judiciary, as well as of economic and social life over the last 150 years, the oscillation between the ideological basis of national identity and the political community, including the basis of its constitutional-legal framework, from religious to secular, persists.

More recent writers, like Hamdan and Bishri, while recognising a distinct Egyptian identity deriving from geography, history and political evolution, are loath to accept the strictly territorial limits of the national community and polity as set by the traditional boundaries of Egypt, which were accepted by an earlier generation of secular nationalists, at least until the Second World War. Hamdan, for clearly stated reasons of national security, strategy and economy, insists on a leadership role for Egypt in the Arab region. Bishri goes much further: he is prepared to risk a polity governed by a mixed secular-religious state, and an Egyptian identity as a component part of the wider national community of Arab Islam.

In reality, though, a powerful executive type of government, allowing limited public political participation, forcefully imposes the rule of a secular state on the Egyptian public, and so far shows no inclination to consider publicly the question, what kind of polity? In fact, it suppresses those who raise such a question, to challenge the modern secular state first created by Muhammad Ali with its two greatest institutional mainstays, the army and the administration.

Yet there is, as Hamdan contends, an old nation in the Nile Valley that is Egypt — a very old state indeed. Despite the division of its population since the tenth century into an overwhelming Muslim majority and a small Christian minority, the latter, for historical and other reasons, has never been separatist (except perhaps for the developments that occurred in the last forty years); it has become, however, in recent years, migratory.[42] Both groups may be basically loyal to the nation. What they have not as yet agreed upon is the nature of the political community; that is, of the political order and system of government which can offer them equal rights regulated by clear uniform rules, under a law of the land, affording them security.

A very serious difficulty in this connection is the central concept of the body politic in Islam, the *umma*. Without elaborating on its pre-Islamic tribal antecedents, members of this community must be believers, that is, Muslims, since they must all participate in the same religious rites. As such, the emphasis is on the commonality and solidarity of its members. After all, the term *din*, usually rendered as religion, does not merely refer to faith or belief, but the total conduct of man under its precepts. To this extent, non-believers, or non-Muslims must exist as separate groups; in short, isolated from the main community and, by extension, the body politic. The element of religious homogeneity emphasised in the case of both the *umma* and the non-Muslim communities only serves to underline the separation between them. An individual has no rights whatsoever except as either a member of the *umma* or one of the several religious communities. What is even more complicated is the assumption that the *umma* is divinely ordained. Over the centuries, Muslim religious teachers and jurists elaborated a vast intellectual-cultural superstructure for the community, regulated by a clear system of law and morals. As such the *umma* is the embodiment of all Muslim values. It is only in it that a Muslim can realise his potentialities as a believer, render his life meaningful and attain salvation. To be sure, in the first century of Islam, Arabs tried to claim an exclusive right to this earthly paradise; imperial expansion, however, integrated within it millions of non-Arab Muslims. Bishri at least seems to think that it may be possible today to encompass within it Arabic-speaking Christians and, in the case of Egypt, the Copts.[43]

Man in Egypt is still not the measure of all things; nor is he the sole determinant and arbiter of a finite, mundane political order. Nor has he as yet found and accepted a transcendent referent for his public earthly behaviour, other than the divine one provided for by a religious faith which enjoins him to implement and realise the divine pattern of the world revealed by God in His message to His apostle and the believers. But a sizeable community of another faith is not so enjoined, and the two faiths, one both transcendentalist and immanentist, the other solely transcendentalist, must coexist as one national community within the boundaries of a territorially-defined state. The problem, that is, is how to accommodate religious, not to speak of ethnic, diversity under an agreed political principle, for an integrated national community and public order.

I am not suggesting that the problem can be easily resolved, or that it ought to be resolved. Nor am I arguing for a secularist resolution of it. Apart from the extreme difficulties and near-insurmountable obstacles involved in this, it may not be the right solution to the problem. It is interesting, nonetheless, that Egyptians themselves continue to be seriously concerned with the problem and consider its resolution absolutely crucial to the well-being of their country and society. What I have done in this chapter is no more than examine the writings of some Egyptians about this national problem, through them highlighting certain aspects of it. A proper study, needless to say, would require a detailed examination of the various groups involved and their interests, and a consideration of state legislation and adjudication over the last century.

Notes

1. *'Aja'ib al-athar fi'l-tarajim wa'l-akhbar*, 4 vols. (Cairo, 1870-1, 1882 and 1904-5).
2. *Sindbad Masri* (Cairo, 1961, 1969), pp. 51, 53.
3. Ibid., p. 71.
4. Ibid., p. 83.
5. See Nadav Safran, *Egypt in Search of Political Community* (Cambridge, Mass., 1962).
6. A strict Western view would be that the matter of a national political community is more of a political, not a cultural or religious, problem.
7. See Ahmad Lutfi al-Sayid, *Al-muntakhabat* (Cairo, 1937-45), and *Safahat matwiyya* (Cairo, 1946), Shafiq Ghorbal, *Takwin Misr* (Cairo, 1957), Salama Musa, *Tarbiyat Salama Musa* (Cairo, 1947, in English as *The Education of Salama Musa*, translated by L.O. Schuman, Washington, DC, 1961), Taha Hussein, *Mustaqbal al-thaqafa fi Misr* (Cairo, 1938), Subhi Wahida, *Fi usul al-mas'ala al-misriyya* (Cairo, 1950, 1977), Husein Mu'nis, *Misr wa risalatuha* (1st edn Cairo, 1956, 4th edn. Cairo, 1973), Louis Awad, *Plutoland* (Cairo, 1947), Mirrit Butros Ghali, *Siyasat al-ghad* (Cairo, 1938) and 'The Egyptian National Consciousness', *Middle Eastern Journal*, 32 (1978), pp. 59-77, Gamal Hamdan, *Shakhsiyyat Misr: dirasa fi 'abqariyyat al-makan*, 2 vols. (Cairo, 1980, 1981), Tariq al-Bishri, *Al-muslimun wa'l-aqbat fi itar al-jama'a al-wataniyya* (Cairo, 1980, Beirut, 1982).
8. *Al-Jarida*, 9 January 1913.
9. *'Ala hamish al-siyasa* (Cairo, 1938).
10. Vol. ii, pp. 209-10.
11. Ibid., p. 211.
12. Vol. i, Chapter 1. See also the interesting study, John Waterbury, *Hydropolitics of the Nile Valley* (Syracuse, NY, 1979).
13. Ibid., p. 41.
14. Ibid., p. 42.
15. Vol. i, p. 43.
16. See especially the discussion in Vol. ii.
17. *Misr baldaton mu'afat min al-fitan*, p. 131.
18. This is reminiscent of Karl Wittfogel's thesis in *Oriental Despotism* (New Haven, Conn., 1957).
19. After 1965 there has been massive emigration of Copts to North America, especially Canada and Australia. Estimated figures for this emigration vary between 75 and 100,000.
20. *Al-masihiyyun wa'l-qawmiyya al-misriyya fi'l-'asr al-hadith* (Cairo, 1979). See also, P.J. Vatikiotis, *Egypt from Muhammad Ali to Sadat* (London, 1980, 1983) for a historical survey of these instances.
21. See Gamal Badawi, *Al-fitna al-ta'ifiyya fi Misr, judhuruha wa asbabuha* (Cairo, 1977), and Milad Hanna, *Na'am aqbat wa lakinna misriyyun* (Cairo, 1980).
22. See also, Raghib Mikha'il, *Farriq . . . tasud, al-wihda al-wataniyya wa'l-akhlaq al-qawmiyya*, Samira Bahr, *Al-aqbat fi'l-hayat al-siyasiyya al-misriyya* (Cairo, 1979), William Suleiman, *Al-hiwar bayn al-adyan* (Cairo, 1976).
23. *Kitab al-khitat al-maqriziyya* (3 vols., Beirut, 1959), vol. ii. Other editions:

2 vols., Bulaq, 1853, and 4 vols., Cairo, 1906-8.

24. *Fi usul al-mas'ala al-misriyya*, p. 108. Cf. Carl F. Petry, *The Civilian Elite of Cairo in the Later Middle Ages* (Princeton, 1981).

25. Wahida, pp. 114-15.

26. Ibid., p. 206.

27. Ibid., p. 224.

28. Ibid., pp. 212-13, 227.

29. *Al-muslimun wa'l-aqbat fi itar al-jama'a al-wataniyya*, p. 44.

30. Ibid., p. 9.

31. Tahtawi's major works are: *Takhlis al-ibriz fi talkhis bariz*, a record of his sojourn in France from 1826 to 1831 and known as the *Rihla* (1st edn. Bulaq, 1834, 2nd edn. Bulaq, 1849, 3rd edn. Cairo, 1935, new edn. Cairo, 1958), *Manahij al-albab al-misriyya fi manhij al-adab al-'asriyya* (1st edn. Bulaq, 1869, 2nd edn. Cairo, 1912), and *Al-murshid al-amin lil-banat wa'l-banin* (Bulaq, 1873).

32. Bishri, pp. 107-30.

33. For the last, see *Mabadi' fi al-siyasa al-misriyya* (Cairo, 1942).

34. Bishri is very good on the narrative of these events and the exposition of the developing trends. See pp. 471-542.

35. See note 21, above.

36. Badawi, *Al-fitna al-ta'ifiyya fi Misr*, p. 107. See Yusuf al-Qardawi, *Ghayr al-muslimin fi'l-mujtama' al-islami* (Cairo, 1977).

37. Here Bishri depends heavily on the writings of conservative Muslims and Muslim Brothers, as for example, Yusuf al-Qardawi, Hasan el-Banna, Sayyid Qutb, Sheikh Muhammad al-Ghazali, and others.

38. See *Al-Ahram al-iqtisadi* (Cairo, April and May 1983).

39. See my forthcoming *Islam and the Nation-State*, where some of these matters are discussed.

40. See Muhammad Sa'id al-'Ashmawi, *Usul al-shari'a* (Cairo, 1979), who denies any connection between religion and state in Islam. This is reminiscent of the position taken by Sheikh Ali Abd al-Raziq nearly fifty years ago in his *Al-islam wa usul al-hukm* (Cairo, 1925). The position stated here, however, is argued by 'Abd al-Hamid Mitwalli, *Azamat al-fikr al-siyasi fi'l-'asr al-hadith* (2nd edn Cairo, 1970). See also his *Buhuth islamiyya* (Alexandria, 1979), and *Mabadi' al-hukm fi'l-islam ma' al-muqarana bi'l-mabadi' al-dusturiyya al-haditha* (4th edn. Alexandria, 1978).

41. Bishri notes, of course, the wide use of the *Mejelle* (1869) as a legal code applicable to all the subjects of the Ottoman Empire.

42. See note 19, above.

43. On the Muslim Community (*umma*) generally, see, W. Montgomery Watt, *Islam and the Integration of Society* (London, 1961), H.A.R. Gibb, *Studies on the Civilization of Islam* (London, 1962), J. Wellhausen, *The Arab Kingdom and Its Fall* (Calcutta, 1927 and London, 1973), G.E. von Grunebaum (ed.), *Unity and Variety in Muslim Civilization* (Chicago, 1955), Louis Gardet, *La Cite Musulmane* (Paris, 1954), H.A.R. Gibb, *Modern Trends in Islam* (Chicago, 1947), W.C. Smith, *Islam in Modern History* (Princeton, 1957), Gibb and Bowen, *Islamic Society and the West*, vol. I, parts 1 and 2 (OUP, 1950, 1951 and 1957).

INDEX